The M & E Business S[illegible]

The purpose of this series is t[illegible] needs of students following business studies courses whether for the Business and Technician Education Council (BTEC) or for the examinations of the major professional institutes. The books have been written to conform with syllabus specifications and are constructed around a series of objectives stated at the beginning of each chapter, with assignments and self-assessment questions where appropriate.

Other M&E books of interest:

HANDBOOKS

Business Organisation
Modern Commercial Knowledge
Office Administration

Other

Computers in Management and Business Studies
Office Management
Senior Secretarial Duties and Office Organisation

The M&E Business Studies Series

Administration in Business

JOSEPHINE SHAW
MInstAM, FBIM, FBSC, FInstD
Training Consultant for Management and Support Services

SECOND EDITION

Macdonald and Evans

Macdonald & Evans Ltd
Estover, Plymouth PL6 7PZ

First published 1982
Reprinted (with amendments) 1982
Reprinted 1983
Second edition 1984

British Library Cataloguing in Publication Data

Shaw, Josephine
Administration in business.——2nd ed.——
(The M&E Business Studies series, ISSN 0266–4917)
1. Management 2. Business
I. Title
658 HD31

ISBN 0–7121–0186–1

Phototypeset in Linotron 202 Times by
Western Printing Services Ltd, Bristol
Printed in Great Britain by
J. W. Arrowsmith Ltd,
Bristol

Preface

I kept six honest serving men
They taught me all I knew,
Their names are what and why and when,
And where and how and who.
Rudyard Kipling

Administration is the foundation upon which any organisation, any event, any series of activities is built. If the foundation is weak the entire structure above it is in danger of, at best, cracking and, at worst, collapsing. Whether we consider the government of a country, the international activities of the United Nations' many agencies, the management of national and multi-national business organisations, or the day-to-day running of the "corner" shop, the administrative function has to be carried out. Administration is not restricted to business life. It is an integral part of social life—voluntary organisations, social clubs, these too must be administered. It plays a part in the home. Applications for services have to be made; accounts have to be settled; expenditure has to be budgeted; information has to be obtained; letters have to be written, and so on.

Administration is defined as involving the receiving, processing, transmitting, storing and retrieving of information. The primary objective of administration is to provide an effective and efficient support service. In this book we shall consider the administrative support service needed by business. The main systems and procedures will be discussed.

Since information is the cornerstone of administration we shall use Kipling's verse (*see* above) as our guide and ask the questions What? Why? When? Where? How? Who? in relation to each topic.

Administrative procedures and the means of carrying them out are now so varied that it is impossible to cover them in detail. The aim of this book is primarily to enable students to recognise the importance of good administrative practice in business, its impact on the production and marketing functions and the extent to which the human factor influences administrative support.

The assignments at the end of the chapters are intended to provide a basis on which the students can work to discover for themselves the systems and procedures used in various organisations. Some of the assignments involve group work. Although difficult to grade, the ability to work as a member of a team has to be acquired. It is suggested that students be encouraged to allocate specific responsibilities to each member of the group. There might also be some merit in appointing an "observer" (or "supervisor") who would have the responsibility of overseeing the work of the group and reporting on individual efforts when assignments are worked in college.

Some of the assignments have been devised with full-time students in mind, others specifically for part-time students who are employed. The co-operation of employers in allowing students to work assignments based on the employing organisation is very valuable, and is appreciated by college staff. An example of the kind of co-operation which may be needed is allowing access to non-confidential information appropriate to a particular assignment, or studying the procedures of a system.

December 1981 J.S.

Preface to Second Edition

The advance of technology into more and more areas of administration is creating as many problems as it is solving. Although the paperless office has become a reality in some organisations the office without a computer is still with us. This means that the "old manual systems" still form an integral part of administration in general. Though many students are, or will be, employed in medium to large organisations where the use of technology is increasing, there are those who will be expected to do a good job in a small office without access to sophisticated machinery. In any case no organisation is an island unto itself and the largest organisations normally do business with the "midgets" at least to some extent. For this reason information on older systems has been retained in this edition, though in most cases it has been curtailed so that more up-to-date information can be included.

Another aspect of technological advance is the human problems which are being created. Machines cannot talk to you, sympathise with you or encourage you. Consequently social relationships within the working environment are perhaps more important than ever before. When asking delegates on training courses what they like best about their job the author almost invariably finds that near the top of the list comes "the people I work with". It is vitally important that we are constantly aware of the fact that at each end of a communication, and often at several points along the line, there is a person or group of people. In order that the "people element" is given its full value it is essential that the budding administrator not only knows his systems and procedures, but also has the ability to adapt them and himself and his attitudes to changing situations and development.

The main aim of this second edition is to bring up-to-date information to the student so that his fundamental knowledge gives him the necessary basis from which to deal with people at all levels and in all situations.

1984 J.S.

Acknowledgments

Many people have given advice and encouragement during the writing of this book. Their support is gratefully acknowledged. Thanks are due to the organisations which have provided information and photographs for reproduction. Miss Iris Broom and Miss Isabel Marshall have given time to research elusive details and John Cooper has given help with the chapters dealing with computers. I greatly appreciate their help and that of the Business Studies staff of Guernsey College of Further Education, Highlands College, Jersey, and South Downs College of Further Education, who have given advice on content, exercises and assignments. A special word of gratitude goes to my mother for her unfailing and cheerful support in the seemingly endless task of welding the material into a book.

Contents

List of Illustrations

CHAPTER ONE

The Functions of the Organisation

CHAPTER OBJECTIVES

After studying this chapter you should be able to:
* describe the main functions of an organisation;
* discuss the relationship of those functions to corporate objectives;
* describe the activities which may be carried out in fulfilling the functions.

DEFINITION AND PURPOSE

Before we can discuss the functions of an organisation we ought to determine what is meant by the words "functions" and "organisation" and terms related to them.

One dictionary definition of the word *organisation* is "an association or society of people working together to the same end, e.g. a business firm or a political party". It can be any type of profit-making organisation, from a small private company to a large group of companies. It can be a non-profit-making body such as a voluntary association, a Government department, a borough council or a professional association.

The phrase in the dictionary definition quoted above, "working to the same end", can be expressed as *corporate objectives*, i.e. the ultimate objectives of the organisation and of all the people who are involved in one way or another in the running of that organisation.

The word function, when applied to an organisation, means a broad area of activities which have to be carried out in order to achieve the corporate objectives.

Every organisation has a reason for being in existence. The ultimate objective is to make a profit. Even non-profit-making organisations have to cover their costs and finance further development. Making a profit means receiving more money from the provision of goods or services than is spent on producing or providing them. In a profit-making organisation the surplus is used partly to develop the organisation, renew plant and equipment, etc., and partly to pay for the use of money loaned by the owners or members of the public. A non-profit-making organisation makes just enough profit, or surplus, to continue in business and provide for growth.

FUNCTIONS

There are five major functions in any organisation. They are not always called by the same name but they cover the main groups of activities involved in running an organisation. They are all interrelated. Indeed, some management theorists maintain that there is no such thing as a division of functions. Nevertheless it is easier for us to identify the activities which are undertaken in an organisation if we have broad groups. The five main areas are finance, production, marketing, administration and data processing.

Finance

The provision of resources in any organisation depends on the availability of funds. The achievement of the corporate objectives depends in the end on whether or not funds are available to provide land, buildings, plant, equipment, technical/professional expertise and labour which is necessary to produce the goods or provide the services the organisation has been established to provide. The day-to-day expenditure of running an organisation must be budgeted for and controlled. Development plans must be taken into consideration when pricing policies are decided. Depreciation of existing plant and equipment, and inflation must be borne in mind when considering the development of the organisation.

Production

Whether an organisation is making aeroplanes, high-speed trains, glass bottles for medicines, clothes or pins, or providing a garden, dry-cleaning, restaurant, banking, insurance or chimney-sweeping service, the ultimate objective is to meet public demand in terms of quantity, quality, style and price. This must be done in relation both to funds available for the provision of appropriate and adequate resources and to profitability, i.e. receiving more for the goods/services than the cost of producing them.

Marketing

The term marketing is used here in its widest sense, covering any activity which is connected with the distribution of the goods/services to the people who are going to buy them. (The word is sometimes used in the narrower sense of only those activities involved in informing the public of the availability of goods/services, not of the actual sales process.)

Marketing has an extremely important role in an organisation, both before and after production. The art of marketing has been described as "the provision of goods/services at a price people will pay in the quantity which the producer wishes to provide". There is a basic truth in that over-simplified statement: production levels must be related to market demand. At the same time prices are related to production levels and market demand is related to prices. Many other factors are important too, such as quality, style, durability, after-sales service, to mention a few.

It may be argued that non-profit-making organisations such as Government departments do not market anything. In fact any service must be marketed in the sense that its availability must be made known to the public. For example social security benefits must be publicised in some way so that people know their entitlements.

Administration

Nothing can happen anywhere without administration. In your own home if a water pipe bursts you will either have to telephone the plumber or go to his house and leave a message for him to call (assuming you are unable to mend the pipe yourself). This is administration which has to be carried out before the job can be done. Without it the plumber cannot know that you need him.

Every aspect of an organisation has to be supported by administration. Every person in the organisation is involved in administration to a greater or lesser extent. A machine operator may have to clock in and clock out so that the wages department staff know the times when he arrived and left. Clocking in and out is a means of giving information.

Administration is therefore a service function providing an infrastructure on which the rest of the organisation stands. The standards of the organisation as a whole are determined to a very great extent on the standard of administration. If there is a hitch somewhere in the flow of information someone or something will eventually suffer in some way.

Data processing

In large organisations data processing has become the title of the department which houses and runs the computer. In fact data processing is, like administration, happening all the time in every part of the organisation. The secretary who types a table of figures and then checks the arithmetic is processing data. The manager who receives various items of information which he analyses before making a decision is processing data. The van driver who records his mileage on a form is processing data. The form is the means of conveying the information which is a part of the administration function. Hence the almost total integration of administration and data processing.

In the past "data" was used when referring to numerical information and "information" was used to mean textual material. It is rare for this clear distinction to exist: most information is made up of both text and figures. A fairly recent definition defines data as "raw" facts which are meaningless in themselves. When fitted together meaningfully the facts are called information. It must be remembered of course that a certain group of facts may be meaningful to one person in a given situation, but be meaningless to a different person who has different objectives.

FUNCTIONAL ACTIVITIES

So far we have been discussing broad areas. The function of finance is to ensure that all the financial aspects of the organisation are controlled so that the other functions can be fulfilled to meet corporate objectives. The functions of production and marketing are closely interlinked to ensure that market demand is met. The administrative function has to ensure that information flows smoothly into, out of and around the organisation as required by the other functions. Similarly the processing of information, data processing, is the life-blood of the organisation.

The objectives of each function are met by the performance of a wide variety of activities. These activities vary from one organisation to another in scope, form, importance and frequency. Some activities are not carried out at all in certain organisations. We shall consider a general cross-section of activities normally carried out in each function in an average organisation.

Financial activities

Budgetary control

The various departments and sections in an organisation estimate their financial revenue (income) and expenditure, usually for the next twelve months. These estimates are normally based on last year's actual revenue and expenditure with adjustments for inflation, capital expenditure, i.e. purchase of equipment, etc., and the organisation's corporate objectives for the following year. The estimates are scrutinised by the board of directors (or its equivalent) and when approved become a budget. Thereafter it is the function of budgetary control to ensure that the budget is adhered to. A control system is designed to pick up differences between budget figures and actual revenue and expenditure figures. It is generally accepted that 10 per cent variance between individual budget and actual figures is acceptable, but the total must not be exceeded.

Stock control

There are two main aspects of stock control. First it is essential that the levels of stock held are neither more than or less than requirements for a given period. Too much stock means that money has been spent and is "lying idle" when it could be used in other ways, e.g. invested in a bank account or for purchasing equipment which would be productive. The second aspect is to ensure the security of stock.

Costing

The exact cost of producing goods/services must be established to ensure that they are sold at a competitive but profitable price. Costing involves not only keeping a check on prices paid for raw materials and labour, but also on overheads, e.g. rent, rates, light, heat, office salaries, which must all be reflected in the price charged for the end product.

Purchase accounts or bills section

Every organisation has to buy items. These items are in two categories—those which are needed actually to produce the goods or services and those which are needed to run the business. Cloth is necessary to make gloves: typing paper is necessary to carry out the administrative work involved in buying the raw materials and selling the finished product. Accounts must be maintained for each supplier showing the value of the goods purchased and the payments made.

Sales accounts

The majority of organisations provide goods/services to clients/customers in return for payment in money. An account of goods supplied and money received must be kept for each individual client/customer. We also need to know the total sales of each kind of product/service we provide.

Wages and salaries

All staff must be paid for their services. Many organisations do not now differentiate between payments made to various categories of staff. Where a distinction is made it is generally on the basis of wages being paid to the people who actually make the goods which are sold, while salaries are paid to office staff and managers who are not actively engaged in the manufacture of the products.

Cash office
Payments have to be made for goods bought. Very small amounts may be paid for in cash while larger amounts are paid for by cheque. It is the responsibility of the cash office to see that accounts are paid promptly and to ensure that discounts are obtained.

Internal audit
Large companies find it necessary to carry out a continuous audit throughout the year. This ensures that all aspects of finance are monitored constantly so that anomalies can be picked up quickly. Internal auditors work closely with a company's external auditors.

Production activities

Buying (or purchasing)
The raw materials, bought-in parts, i.e. ready-made components, and supplies needed to manufacture a product or provide a service have to be obtained. Buying must be done on the basis of obtaining the best quality goods for the purpose for which they are to be used at the most economical rate. In some organisations the buying of non-production materials, e.g. office equipment, etc., is also undertaken by the buying section.

Storage
There are two types of storage needed in many organisations, viz. storage of raw materials and components and storage of the finished goods. In a dry-cleaners, for example, storage is required for clothes, etc., waiting to be cleaned, for the materials used for cleaning and for the cleaned items awaiting collection.

Design
All the products have to be designed. Once in production a design may have to be modified from time to time, perhaps to meet changing market demand, to provide improvements or to make production less costly.

Research and development
This activity is not appropriate in all organisations but any large organisation involved in manufacturing usually has an R and D section or department. R and D staff are responsible for producing the information which will enable the designers to get to work on new products and to amend and modify the design of both new and

existing products to meet standards for production, marketing, safety, etc.

They may also be involved in improving or changing methods of production, or undertaking market research in areas or fields not previously covered.

There are organisations which work exclusively on research and development, selling the knowledge thus acquired to other companies or working on a consultancy basis for other organisations.

Production planning

This activity has to be undertaken in close liaison with the marketing staff. It is at this point, the planning of production, that the accuracy of estimates of market requirements is vital.

Production capacity, i.e. the quantity that can be produced with available resources, must be used to the maximum, at the same time taking into account the need for maintenance and the possibility of breakdowns, staff illness, etc.

Production

The making of the goods or the provision of the services is, of course, the kingpin of the production function.

Quality control or inspection

All products and most services have to meet pre-determined standards. These standards may be international standards, standards set by the British Standards Institution or standards of safety set by the appropriate government department. There are also quality standards. Any article which is not perfect cannot be offered to the public as a perfect article. If this happens inadvertently the manufacturer is responsible and has to make reparation. Substandard goods may be sold but must be clearly marked "Imperfect" or "Substandard".

Work study

Any activity which involves movement of people and materials needs to be scrutinised and monitored to ensure that it is being performed in the most economical manner, i.e. it should be performed cost-effectively. It is necessary therefore to look at the way the activity is carried out so that the minimum fatigue is induced and the maximum amount of work can be done in the allotted time without loss of accuracy.

Transport

Because the production of goods and services usually involves moving goods and people around, transport is usually considered to be an activity within the production function. It may equally apply to marketing and administration. Vans, lorries, etc., are often needed in the production process from the point of collecting new materials to the point of getting the finished product into the store. In many organisations they are also needed for distribution to wholesale or retail market places. In such cases it is usually agreed that the control of transport should be centralised and it is the responsibility of the transport manager to ensure that vehicles are available in good order where they are wanted at the times they are wanted.

Transport has to be scheduled and it is important that there is close liaison between the production and transport departments, and between the sales and transport departments, so that available vehicles can be used as economically and effectively as possible. Routes have to be scheduled—in retail organisations it is usual to have specific delivery areas allocated to specific days. Maintenance of vehicles also has to be scheduled. Documents for overland foreign routes have to be obtained. The cost of transport, including running costs, labour costs and depreciation of vehicles is an important factor in the costing of goods. Hence one of the reasons why transport may be included in production costs.

Packaging

Many products are packaged; indeed the type, design and quality of packaging can be an important aspect of the organisation's corporate image. The type of packaging used depends on the type of goods, the method used for delivery and whether or not the goods are exported. Printing on the packaging may include the manufacturer's name, etc., details of the content of the product, instructions for use and the standard to which it has been manufactured. The style of printing must reflect the company's image and is a major factor in the corporate identity.

Packing for despatch

Many organisations have to pack products for despatch to customers all over the world. Packing must be carried out in such a way as to ensure the safe arrival of the goods at their destination. This may entail different methods of packing depending on whether the goods are to be despatched by road, rail, air or sea. Again, depending on the organisation, the despatch may be considered to be within the marketing function, since it is distribution of the goods to customers.

Marketing activities

Market research

It is essential to discover what the buying public wants. This has to be done before planning production (*see* above). There are many techniques used in market research including interviewing and the use of questionnaires.

Advertising

Unless the availability of products and services are made known to people they cannot be expected to buy them. The many advertising media are used to inform the public of products and services, their purposes and uses, price, etc., and also to keep the organisation's name in the public mind.

Public relations or customer relations

All organisations need to establish an image in the public mind. This is done in many ways, from the design of the letterhead and the livery of delivery vans to the way the telephone is answered. The design of packaging, mentioned above, the handling of customer complaints and the presentation of information to the media at press conferences are examples of public relations activities.

Sales

It is usually convenient to deal with sales on the basis of the sales in the home country and sales overseas. The administration involved is more complex for exports, and the financial arrangements may differ considerably. Sales involves the obtaining of orders from customers and the fulfilling of these orders in accordance with the agreed terms.

After-sales service

The successful implementation of this activity can have a major influence on the organisation's sales. After-sales service can take many forms, from regular inspection of equipment for a nominal charge to rectification of faults, etc.

Administrative activities

Administrative activities are undertaken in every part of an organisation, regardless of function. Within the administration function itself there are some major activities.

Legal

There are many aspects of business which need to be carefully controlled to ensure that they do not contravene any laws. The buying, leasing, renting and maintenance of property, the purchasing of goods, the selling of goods, the employment of staff, the insuring of goods, all have important legal implications.

Manpower planning
No organisation can function without people. Corporate objectives are normally established for several years ahead so it is possible to estimate what manpower requirements will be in terms of numbers, levels and types of skill, etc. Current staff turnover gives an indication of the number of people who will leave over the next few years, while the ages of existing staff will indicate the number of people who will retire. Manpower planning can never be exact but it can provide a useful guide for recruitment purposes.

Personnel
The descriptions of jobs and the type of people required to fill them, the advertising, the selection, testing and appointment of staff, the monitoring of performance appraisals or reviews, the welfare of staff, the handling of termination of employment are all personnel activities.

Training
There are many reasons why staff have to be trained, from preparing them to work in the organisation (induction) to preparing them to do a completely different job (re-deployment). Staff may need training to improve weaknesses in job performance or to enable them to take on more responsibility. It is the responsibility of every employer to enable the individual to develop his potential.

Organisation and methods study
Just as in the factory, work study is necessary to ensure that work is done as economically and cost effectively as possible, so organisation and method study is necessary in offices for the same purpose. O and M, as it is commonly known, looks at the structure of the organisation, or section of the organisation, and at systems and procedures followed.

Office services
Many services are necessary to keep information flowing—telephone, teleprinter/telex, mail, reprographics, secretarial. Equipment must be maintained, accommodation must be cleaned and kept in good order.

Security
In recent years security has become a major activity in many organisations. The safety of the staff is of paramount importance. They and the buildings must be protected from terrorism. Visitors must be screened so that undesirables are kept out. The security of property is also important.

Data processing activities

Systems analysis
The analysis of systems is closely related to, indeed is often a part of, O and M. It is the means by which the activities carried on in the pursuit of given objectives, e.g. the procedures involved in raising and despatching invoices, is reviewed, decided, modified or changed and validated. Systems analysis is always carried out when it is proposed to computerise a system, but the end result of the analysis should not be a foregone conclusion. It may be decided that the existing manual or machine system is still appropriate.

Programming
All large organisations now have a computer. The writing of programs to instruct computers what to do has to be done for each individual system or operation, unless it happens to be a common system such as stock control. (Programs for these common systems can be bought.)

Operation
Computers have to be operated in the same way as any other machine. In some organisations a large number of staff are needed for this important activity.

SUMMARY

1. There are two major categories of organisation—profit-making and non profit-making. Even the latter need "to make a profit" in that an excess of revenue over expenditure is needed to ensure the survival of the organisation.

2. Five major functions have to be carried out to a greater or lesser extent in all organisations. These are finance, production, marketing, administration and data processing.

3. Each function is fulfilled by a range of activities. The extent of the activities depends on the type and size of the organisation.

SELF-ASSESSMENT QUESTIONS

Answer all questions as quickly as possible. Do not turn back to the Chapter until you have completed this test.

1. (*a*) What is profit? (*b*) Why must all organisations make a profit?

2. Decide which of the following objectives you think are the *corporate objectives* of an umbrella-manufacturing company. Give reasons for your decision:

(*a*) to buy materials in bulk in order to obtain better discounts;

(b) to achieve a 50 per cent increase in turnover during the next three years;

(*c*) to cut the cost of production by installing a new type of machine;

(*d*) to reduce office staff by 10 per cent;

(*e*) to increase profit by 10 per cent per year over the next five years;

(*f*) to improve the order processing system so that the time for processing is reduced by 24 hours;

(*g*) to introduce training for senior specialist managers;

(*h*) to install a word processor to handle all repetitive typewriting and text editing done in the company;

(*i*) to produce a new range of umbrellas for the down-market customer;

(*j*) to tighten up on standards to reduce wastage to less than 5 per cent.

3. (*a*) What are functional activities? (*b*) Describe briefly three activities of each of the five main functions.

4. Do you think there should be a distinction between the words *data* and *information*? If so, give examples of how this distinction could be made. If not, give your reasons.

ASSIGNMENTS

Assignment 1

Refer to question 2 of the self-assessment questions. In groups of four or five discuss the following questions. (Be sure you know which of the objectives listed are corporate objectives, and why.)

(*a*) Which of the non-corporate objectives will directly influence the achievement of the corporate objectives?

(*b*) Which functional activities may be affected by efforts to achieve these non-corporate objectives and how might they be achieved?

(*c*) What effect or effects is the achievement of these objectives likely to have on the personnel involved in the various functional activities affected?

Assignment 2

In groups of four or five discuss the interrelationship between the main functions of an organisation. The following guidelines may be used to start the discussion.

(*a*) Decide the kind of company you wish to discuss. This may be imaginary or a company you know.

(*b*) Determine at least two corporate objectives for the company.

(*c*) For each function determine at least one objective which will have to be achieved if your corporate objectives are to be met.

(*d*) Discuss what sort of communications there would have to be between people working in the various functions, what decisions/agreements would have to be made, and what monitoring/control might be necessary to ensure that all objectives are met.

CHAPTER TWO

The Structure of an Organisation

CHAPTER OBJECTIVES

After studying this chapter you should be able to:

* relate the departmental structure of various types and sizes of organisation to the main organisational functions;
* explain the way in which a departmental job description is developed;
* state the purpose of a departmental job description;
* explain the importance of co-ordination of activities within and between the departments of an organisation;
* assess the possible results of lack of co-ordination within and between the departments of an organisation.

DEFINITION AND PURPOSE

What is an organisation structure? When a group of people work together "to the same end" it is essential that each person knows what is expected of him, what part his role plays in the achievement of corporate objectives, and how his role relates to the roles of other people in the group. The functional activities discussed in Chapter One have therefore to be analysed to determine the work involved. It will then be possible to decide how the organisation itself shall be structured.

To take the analogy of building a house, one first decides what sort of house is wanted (corporate objective), then designs it to meet the functional requirements, and then determines the structure of the house to satisfy the activities which will be taking place in it. Of course it is not always possible to have the ideal house for reasons such as lack of money or non-availability of the particular materials required to achieve the effect you want. In the same way it is not always possible to have exactly the organisation structure which would be ideal. As we saw in Chapter One, many of the functional activities are closely interrelated, so much so that the performance of an activity within one function may strongly influence the performance of an activity in another function. Consequently it is essential to have a structure to ensure that resources are provided for all activities in the right proportion, at the right time and in the most suitable way. If for example advertising produces a lot of new customers it is essential that production can produce the goods or provide the services in the quantities needed without delay. Close liaison is essential and everyone in the organisation must be very clearly aware of his responsibilities and of the authority he has to carry out his duties.

FUNCTION ANALYSIS

In Chapter One we listed the main common activities involved in fulfilling each function. The next step is to determine what work is involved in performing the various activities. For example the work involved in the training activity may include:

(*a*) assess training needs;
(*b*) determine training priorities;
(*c*) prepare a training plan;
(*d*) devise training programmes;
(*e*) conduct training courses;
(*f*) select external courses;
(*g*) keep records.

The extent of the work involved in each of these duties is then estimated on the basis of current requirements. The grouping or departmentalisation of the work can be considered.

If training activities are a major aspect of certain functions, e.g. production or a highly specialised field such as computers, consideration would be given to establishing training activities within those functions, instead of centralising under the administrative function.

GROUPING THE DUTIES

The types of work involved in fulfilling the various duties for each functional activity may cover a wide range or they may be of a similar nature. The volume requirement of any particular type of work may be small for some duties and much larger for others. It is therefore necessary to look at the duties both individually and collectively to estimate the volume of each type of work.

The work involved in the various functional activities is then considered in terms of centralisation or departmentalisation. Would it be better, i.e. more efficient or more economic, to have all secretarial services provided from a single large secretariat, from small secretariats based in certain locations or in each department, or from individual secretarial staff? Would it be better to allow each department to be responsible for its own personnel function, with a very small central personnel staff to act in an advisory capacity and to be responsible for co-ordinating information, e.g. records? There are many computations but because so many functions are now quite highly specialised centralisation is more general.

DEPARTMENTAL JOB DESCRIPTIONS

When a decision has been made as to the general division of duties, departmental job descriptions can be prepared. A job description shows a broad outline of the duties involved in fulfilling the general aim.

Let us assume that it has been decided that each location shall be provided with a secretariat. The job description for the secretariat may be on the following lines.

Aim

To provide a comprehensive secretarial service to all senior and middle managers in B Block.

Duties

(*a*) To prepare correspondence, reports, documentation for meetings, statistical returns and other records from handwriting, corrected typescript, shorthand notes and audio-dictation.

(*b*) To receive, screen and make telephone calls.

(*c*) To make appointments for managers, co-ordinate security and reception arrangements, receive visitors.

(*d*) To arrange meetings, take notes at meetings and draft minutes.

(*e*) Make travel arrangements for inland and overseas travel by road, rail, air and sea.

(*f*) Deal with incoming mail and prepare outgoing mail for despatch.

(*g*) Monitor statistical returns.

(*h*) Provide a storage and retrieval service.

(*i*) Provide a research and information service.

It is important to have a clearly defined departmental job description for a number of reasons.

(*a*) Each individual in the department should know the general aim towards which everyone in the department should be working.

(*b*) The various types of work involved can be identified: specialist work is highlighted.

(*c*) It provides a basis for devising systems and procedures.

DEVELOPING AN ORGANISATION STRUCTURE

An organisation is a living entity and as such it should have a certain fluidity. Having analysed the functions, identified the types of work and the various workloads involved in meeting corporate objectives, decisions must be made as to what type of organisation structure would be most suitable.

The structure of an organisation is influenced by many factors. These include:

(*a*) the size and nature of the organisation;
(*b*) its objectives and functions;
(*c*) the complexity of the departments;
(*d*) the length of time the organisation has been in existence;
(*e*) the flow of business throughout the year (it may be seasonal);
(*f*) the geographical location of the various units of the organisation;
(*g*) the extent to which authority is to be given to departments or other units of the organisation;
(*h*) the ratio of administrative staff to technical specialist and professional staff; and
(*i*) the extent of mechanisation/automation.

An organisation structure which operates successfully in the offices of a medium-sized business located in one building in the main street of a town is unlikely to be successful in the offices of a group of companies with individual units located in various places around the country. Indeed the same structure may not be suitable for the various units.

It should be stressed that as a business develops, expands and changes, so the structure must be reviewed and adapted to changing needs. For example, such has been the development in the training area since the mid-1960s that in many large organisations the training department is now a separate entity, with a training director who is a member of the board. This seemed a sensible development but it has led to problems in co-ordination (*see* below). In times when cutbacks are the order of the day, for economic reasons, training activities are usually dovetailed into the personnel department. This can create problems of responsibility. The person in charge of training now becomes responsible to the head of the personnel department, which may complicate liaison with the line managers—particularly vital in training. The fact that personnel staff need to liaise with line management is not always sufficiently well recognised or carried out.

TYPES OF ORGANISATION STRUCTURE

The detailed structure of any individual organisation is probably unique to that organisation. The structure that is perfect for Smith's Nuts and Bolts Company Limited, a 25-employee company working in an old garage, would hardly be right for the ICIs and Shells of this world. Organisation structures can be closely knit and strongly hierarchical, or they can be loose and flexible. It is probably true to say that the larger the organisation the tighter the structure tends to be, in order that control can be maintained "from the top". In smaller organisations control is still vital but can more easily be built into the systems and procedures. However, today even larger organisations are tending to develop a team approach, delegating control to the teams rather than maintaining it through a long line of managers.

There are three main types of organisation structure. These are line, functional and line and staff structures.

Line organisation

Line organisation is the hierarchical structure whereby one (sometimes two) people are responsible for the achievement of corporate objectives. Each of the main functions is directed by one person who has managers responsible to him for the various activities involved in the function. The managers in turn have supervisors responsible to them for ensuring that the day-to-day duties are carried out efficiently.

Functional organisation

Functional organisation is based on specialisation. The person or people who are specialists in a particular field are responsible for that type of work wherever it may occur. Thus they may be directing and controlling a number of employees in different departments/sections. This is not generally a good thing because it means that the employees have a variety of supervisors which is bad human relations practice. In any case, if there is more than one specialist in the same field there must be co-ordination by someone which means that there is an element of line organisation even within the specialisation.

Line and staff organisation

Line and staff organisation is an amalgamation of line and functional organisations. Functional activities are carried on in departments but where the specialist advice or work of another department or function is needed it may be given on an advisory basis or functional basis. When the specialist help is on an advisory basis responsibility for organising the job and carrying out the activities rests with the department concerned. When specialist help is given on a functional basis the responsibility for its effectiveness rests with the specialist department. Recruitment is a personnel activity. Therefore when a salesman is needed, for example, it is the responsibility of personnel to recruit a suitable person for the sales department, i.e. a functional responsibility.

LEVELS OF RESPONSIBILITY

A very important consideration in building up a structure is to determine the levels of responsibility. If one particular activity is subservient to another this might determine the reporting structure for individuals. Safety is an overriding factor in certain types of industry, e.g. air transport. The person in charge of safety must therefore have authority for approving the airworthiness of aeroplanes before they fly. It would be totally unsuitable, in such a case, for the safety officer to be responsible to the commercial manager, whose responsibility it might be to ensure that planes fly as much as possible in order to maximise profit. There would be a conflict of interests. However, if the safety officer is responsible to the general manager, the commercial manager must then abide by the stipulations laid down by the safety officer.

CO-ORDINATION

Imagine a household with one kitchen and five members of the family all wanting meals at different times. It is decided that each person shall be responsible for getting his or her own meal and clearing up afterwards. If chaos is not to reign supreme the first essential would be to work out a time schedule to ensure that each person had time to prepare, cook, eat and wash up after the meal. If that was not done the second person might want to start preparing a meal only ten or fifteen minutes after the first person—obviously an impossibility you would say. Yet so often in business these "obvious" factors are overlooked or dismissed as unimportant.

A fundamental prerequisite of co-ordination is effective communication. Unless each individual knows what is expected of him and how his work is related to the work of the department and of the organisation it is inevitable that work will not be done with maximum accuracy, enthusiasm, interest, understanding and co-operation.

When the departmental job descriptions are prepared the first essential is to look for gaps in and duplication of work. Each duty may involve certain elements which are similar to the elements in other duties. It is highly uneconomic to have several people doing "bits of" similar work. Hence the development of *sections* within a department, each section being responsible for certain duties.

In the example mentioned earlier in the Chapter of training activities being hived off from personnel activities, a common factor within each department is records. There is certain information that is needed for both personnel and training purposes. If the departments are completely separate it usually means that each department keeps its own records, even though each department needs the information kept by the other. Unless a system is devised whereby both departments have access to each other's records, endless time and energy is wasted in keeping two sets of records or seeking information from the other department. There is a strong case in such an instance for centralising the records and providing easy access for both personnel and training staff.

Co-ordination is also essential to ensure that the departments of the service functions (administration and data processing) provide the services required by the finance, production and marketing functions to enable them to meet corporate objectives. If legal activities in connection with the purchase of a new building are delayed it could mean that the production of a new product cannot start on schedule. This may well affect profitability. By having a carefully prepared schedule for activities (*see* Chapter Eleven) and allocation of resources (money, personnel and materials), and control procedures to ensure that plans are adhered to, problems are highlighted quickly so that action can be taken and objectives met.

SUMMARY

1. An organisation structure is related to the corporate objectives of the organisation, the work involved in meeting those objectives and the resources available.

2. The various functional activities which have to be carried out to

meet corporate objectives must be analysed to establish the duties involved. These duties are then grouped so that similar duties are brought together wherever practicable.

3. The grouping of duties provides a basis for departmental job descriptions which give a broad outline of the aims and duties which have been brought together. The relationship of the various departments to each other provides a basis on which an organisation structure can be developed.

4. The organisation structure should not remain static but should be constantly reviewed and adapted to meet changes in corporate objectives, available resources and financial requirements.

5. There are three main types of organisation structure, viz. line (hierarchical), functional (specialist) and line and staff (a combination of line and functional). Many organisations develop a unique structure combining various aspects of these main types.

6. There are many factors which influence the development of an organisation structure, including size, objectives, type of business, location.

7. Co-ordination is a vital factor in any organisation. It is based on effective communication. Without it there are likely to be duplication of tasks, lack of staff motivation, uneconomic systems and procedures, and some tasks may not be performed at all.

SELF-ASSESSMENT QUESTIONS

Answer all questions as quickly as possible. Do not turn back to the Chapter until you have completed this test.

1. How would you define the term "organisation structure"?
2. Why is it important for an organisation to have a defined structure?
3. What is meant by function analysis? Give an example.
4. What is the purpose of grouping duties of a similar nature when they are performed under different activity headings?
5. What information is given in a departmental job description?
6. Why should an organisation structure be reviewed regularly?
7. (*a*) What are the three main types of organisation structure?
   (*b*) What are the main features of each?
8. "Co-ordination is based on effective communication." List the points which you think prove this statement.
9. What are the three main factors which have to be considered in the process of co-ordination?
10. What are the advantages of careful co-ordination from the point of view of the individual worker?

ASSIGNMENT

Consider the following types of business:

a bank
a departmental store
a publisher
a printer
a fashion house
a small manufacturer of clocks
a travel agency
a supermarket
an insurance broker
a warehouse

Choose one of the above types of business. If you are employed you may use your own organisation as the basis on which to work.

1. List the administrative activities which you think will have to be carried out in the type of business chosen in order to provide a comprehensive support service to the other functions in the organisation.
2. Analyse each activity into a list of duties.
3. Group together similar duties so that sections and/or departments are evolved.
4. Write job descriptions for at least two departments.

CHAPTER THREE

Organisation Charts

CHAPTER OBJECTIVES

After studying this chapter you should be able to:
* explain the purposes of an organisation chart;
* identify on an organisation chart:
  line, staff, functional and lateral relationships;
  levels of responsibility and authority;
  lines of communication;
* prepare an organisation chart from given data.

DEFINITION AND PURPOSE

What is an organisation chart? It is a diagrammatic illustration of the structure of an organisation. In the previous chapter we said that an organisation structure evolves from the activities and duties involved in fulfilling various functions which have to be carried out to meet corporate objectives. Not only must it be clear what has to be done: it is essential to know who is responsible for doing what, what authority each person has, and to whom each person is responsible and accountable. The purposes of an organisation chart may be:

(*a*) to show the functional structure of the organisation;
(*b*) to show the line structure, i.e. who is responsible to whom;
(*c*) to indicate levels of responsibility and authority of individuals in relation to each other, within and across departmental boundaries;
(*d*) to show the span of control of each manager/supervisor;
(*e*) to show accountability;
(*f*) to indicate lines of communication.

RELATIONSHIPS

There are four types of relationship within an organisation. These are line, lateral, staff and functional relationships, which are explained below. From the point of view of responsibility, authority and accountability it is important that everyone in the organisation recognises these different types of relationship and their implications. First we should define these terms, responsibility, authority and accountability.

(*a*) *Responsibility* means that a person has had delegated to him certain duties or tasks. He must carry out those duties or tasks in accordance with objectives and conditions that are preferably mutually agreed, i.e. agreement is reached about the time the job will take, when it is to be completed, what resources may be used in performing it and what should be done in the case of difficulties arising.

(*b*) *Authority* means the extent to which a person may take on responsibility in the process of performing certain duties or tasks. A typical example is recruitment. In a large organisation it is often the personnel manager who has the authority to recruit a person to fill a vacancy. But it may be the responsibility of the line manager, i.e. the manager in the department where the vacancy exists, to choose a suitable person. The line manager does not have authority to recruit. On the other hand the personnel manager does not have the responsibility of selecting the person for the job.

(*c*) *Accountability* means that a person has to work within the policy guidelines in the execution of his duties. Thus a chairman and the board of directors of a company must account to the shareholders for the amount of profit the company makes and the way in which that profit is made. An advertising manager has to account to the managing director for the integrity of company advertising.

Line relationship

Each individual is in a direct-line relationship with his immediate superior and his immediate subordinate. He is expected to take instructions from his superior and to be responsible to that superior for the satisfactory performance of the work which has been delegated to him. He can give instructions and delegate work to his immediate subordinate and is responsible for seeing that the work is done satisfactorily. Each person should report problems to his immediate superior.

Lateral relationship

Two or more individuals who report to the same superior are said to be in a lateral relationship. They may not give instructions to one another or to any subordinates other than their own. They must, of course, consult each other and co-operate as members of a team reporting to their superior.

Staff relationship

A staff relationship is advisory. This means that a manager can call upon a manager in another, perhaps specialist, department for advice but is not obliged to take it.

Functional relationship

The situation described above of the personnel manager having authority for recruitment is a typical functional relationship. If the personnel manager has grounds for refusing to recruit a particular person, for example because of poor references, his authority for recruitment overrides the line manager's responsibility for selection.

Span of control

The number of people who are *directly* responsible to the same person constitutes the "span of control" of that person. It is generally reckoned that six is the optimum number of people for whom anyone should have responsibility. There are certain fields where the span may be greater. In technical departments where the work of specialists has to be co-ordinated the number can be up to 20. This is rare and not advisable in the normal run of management.

TYPES OF ORGANISATION CHART

Organisation charts may be drawn to show functions, grouping of departmental duties in posts (jobs), hierarchical levels, job gradings, relationships between departments.

The charts may be drawn either vertically or horizontally. In the vertical format the straight vertical lines indicate the lines of responsibility and authority; the horizontal lines indicate lateral relationships. Dotted lines may be used to indicate functional relationships.

An organisation chart showing functions is illustrated in Fig. 1. In this chart the function of each of the organisations working under the United Kingdom Atomic Energy Authority (UKAEA) is shown.

Figure 2 shows a group organisation. This shows the major subsidiary companies which form the group and major corporate shareholdings. Important locations of group activities are also shown.

Figure 3 indicates the accountability of a public corporation.

An organisation chart may show areas of duties which give no indication of number or level of posts (*see* Fig. 4). Each area of work shown in the chart could be performed by a group of people or by individuals, or a few individuals could be carrying out a variety of duties. We do know from looking at the chart what duties are carried out.

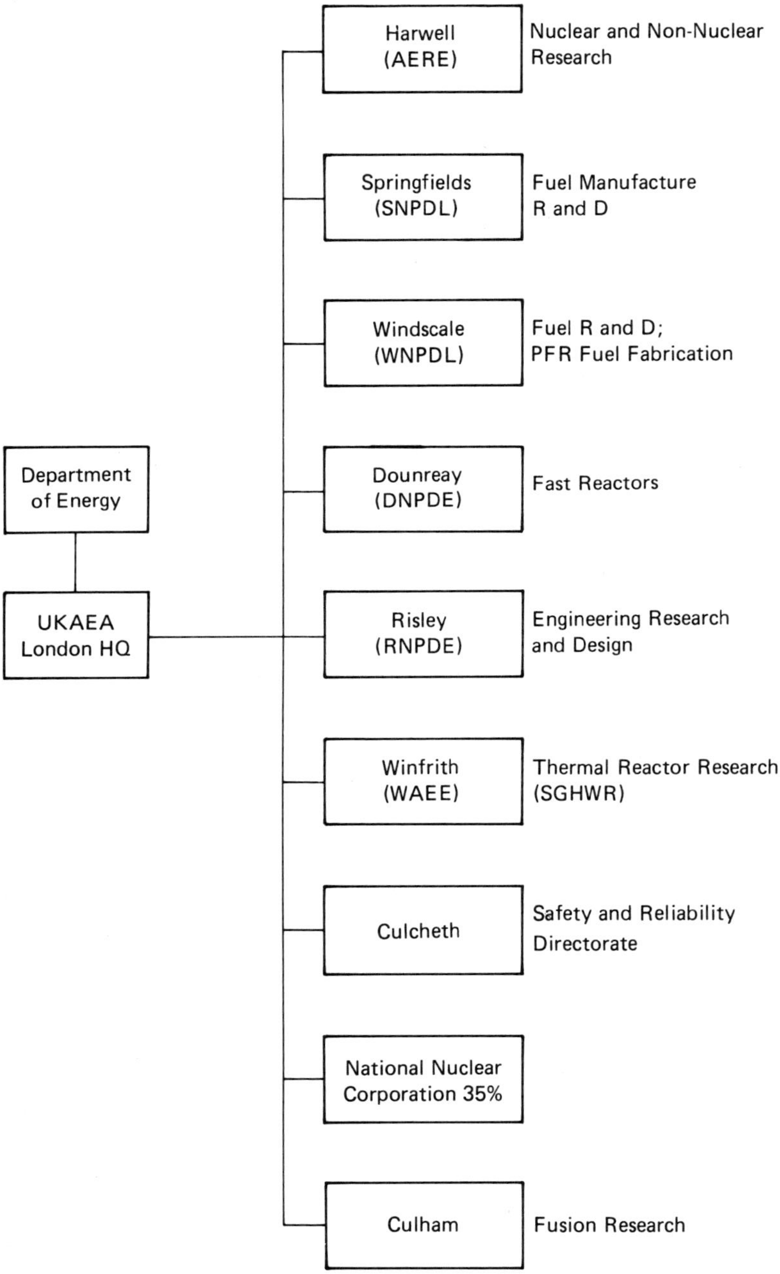

Fig. 1. *Functional structure of the UKAEA.*

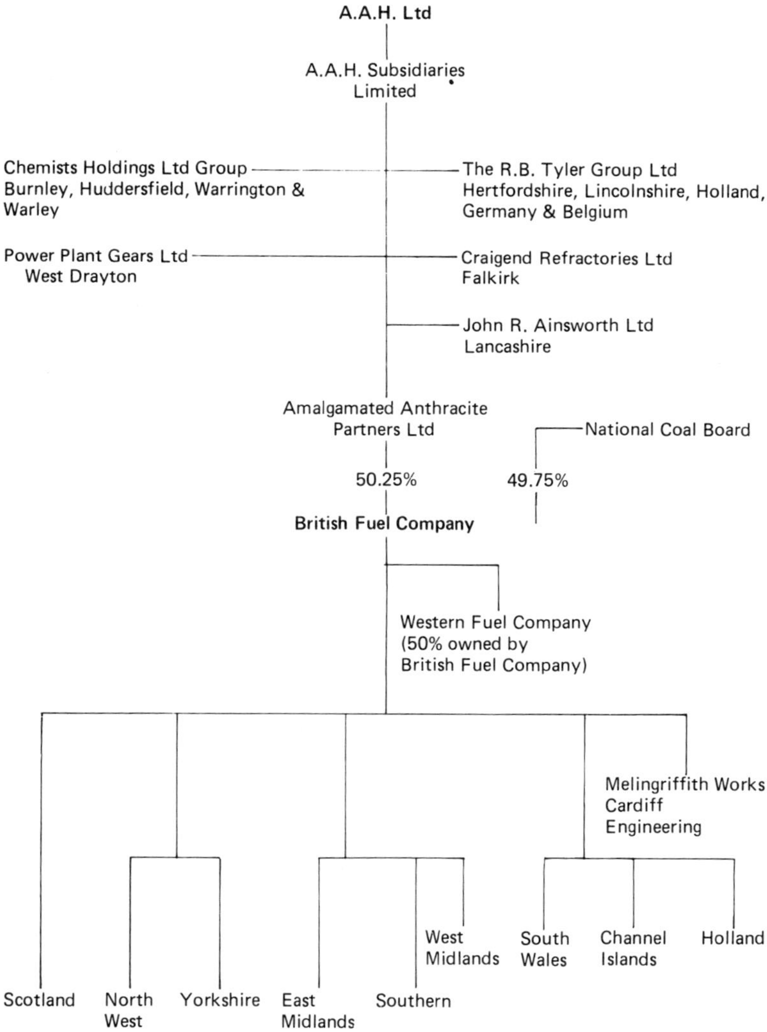

Fig. 2. *Organisation of a group of companies showing major shareholdings.*

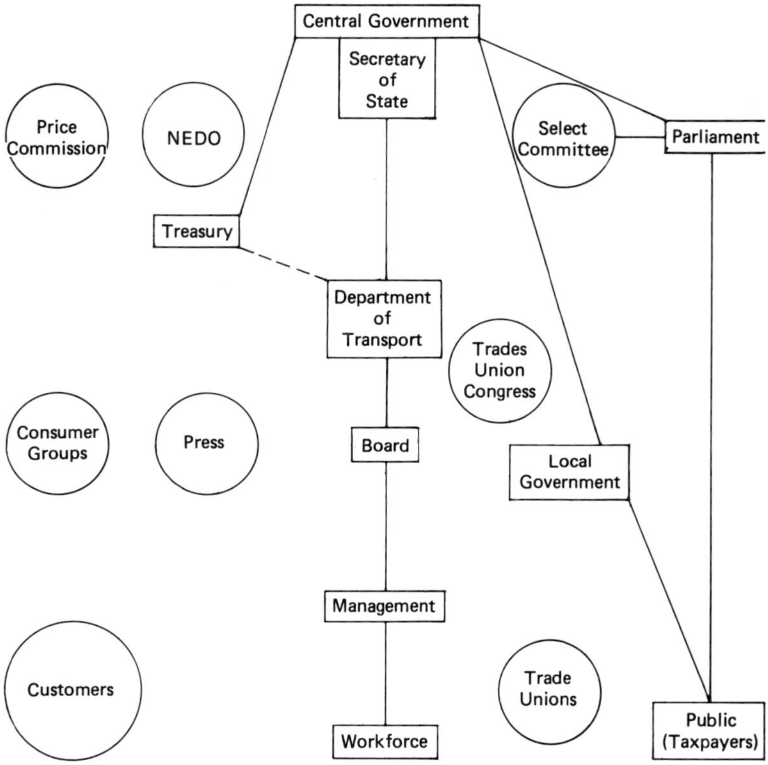

Fig. 3. *Chart showing the accountability of a public corporation.*

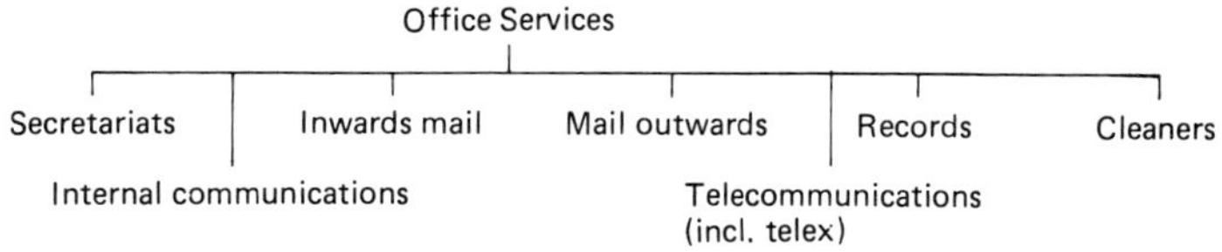

Fig. 4. *Organisation chart showing main areas of work.*

As explained in Chapter Two we should be able to assess the duties involved in each of the activities which make up office services. The volume of each type of work can then be assessed and "posts" can be identified. The organisation chart might then look as is shown in Fig. 5.

From the chart in Fig. 5 we can see who is responsible to whom,

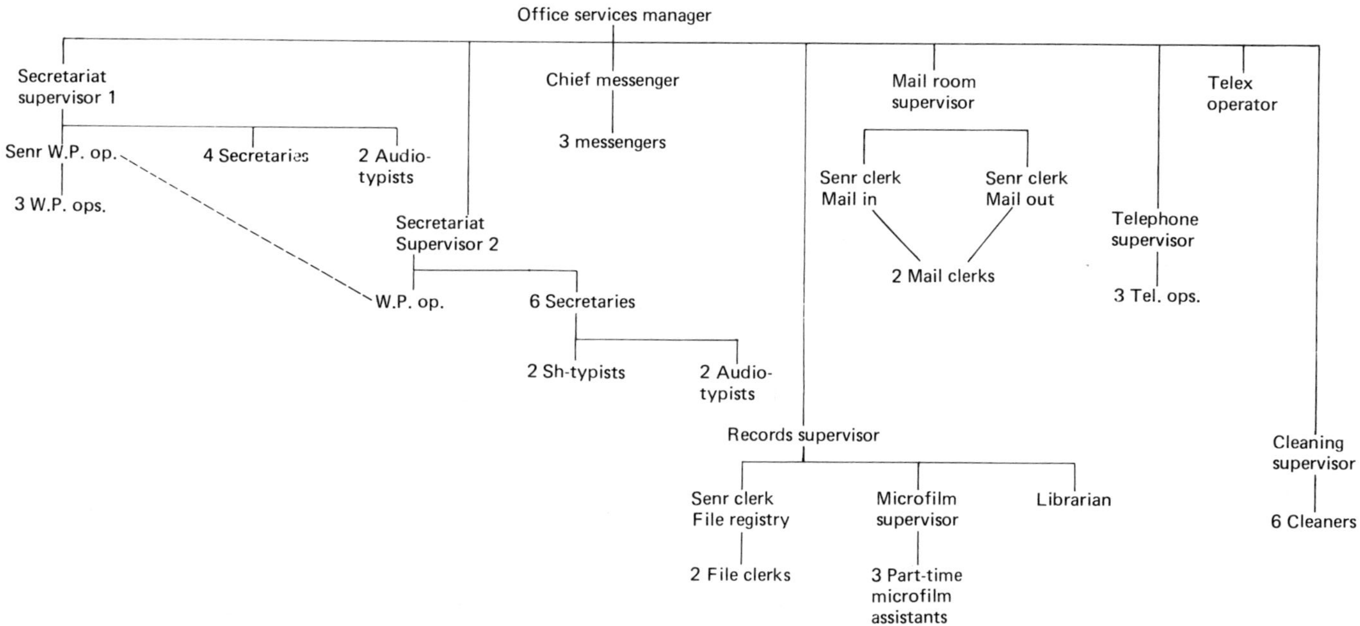

Fig. 5. *Organisation chart showing posts.*

e.g. the three messengers to the chief messenger. The lines of communication are clear. Theoretically subordinates in one section should always communicate with subordinates in another section via their own supervisor and the supervisor in the other section. In practice this would be too cumbersome and time-consuming. However *instructions* may be given only by a person to his *immediate* subordinate. The mail room supervisor delegates to his two senior clerks but may not delegate directly to the mail clerks. If he did so he would be usurping the authority of his senior clerks since they would not be in a position to know what work the mail clerk had been given. No one in a lateral relationship may give orders either to his colleague, e.g. the telephone supervisor to the telex operator, or to a subordinate of a colleague, e.g. secretariat supervisor 1 to a subordinate of secretariat supervisor 2.

In the record section the filing clerks are responsible for extracting archive material from the files, ensuring that it is in sequence and passing it to the microfilm section for processing. One of the part-time microfilm assistants is responsible for checking the material for microfilming to ensure that the quality is good enough. If any document is not suitable the assistant should pass it to the microfilm supervisor who will pass it to the senior clerk in charge of the file registry. It should not be passed back directly to the file clerks. This is because a decision has to be made as to what must be done with that document.

In the case of the mail room the two mail clerks are responsible to both the senior clerk mail inwards and the senior clerk despatch. This is because the work load fluctuates heavily between the two sections so that in the morning both are needed on mail inwards, during the day one is needed on each section, and towards the end of the day both are needed on despatch.

In the two secretariats there is a link between the word processor operators. The dotted line indicates that the operator in secretariat 2 is technically responsible to the senior operator in secretariat 1. This means that if a technical decision has to be made about the work the senior operator is responsible. This is a functional relationship.

The chart in Fig. 5 does not show levels or gradings, although they can easily be inserted. A section of the chart with gradings is shown in Fig. 6.

It would also be possible to give a summary of the duties of each post but the chart would become somewhat difficult to read unless produced on a large sheet. The advantage of including duties is that everyone can see what everyone else is responsible for doing. On the chart in question (Fig. 5) the posts are self-explanatory.

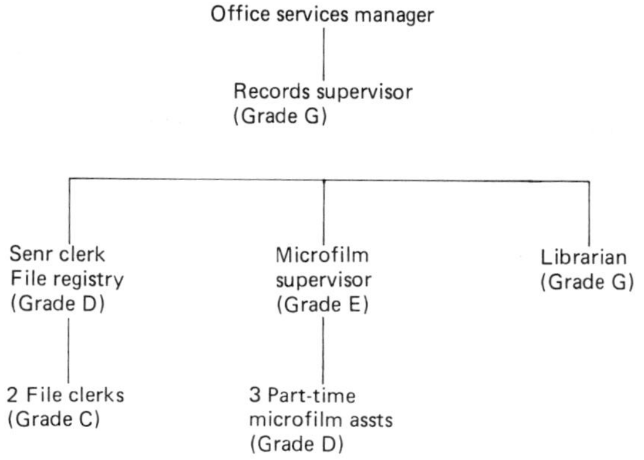

Fig. 6. *Organisation chart showing post gradings.*

Organisation charts can be shown horizontally instead of vertically with the senior position/s on the left, and subordinate positions progressing to the right of the page.

SUMMARY

1. An organisation chart is a diagrammatic illustration of the structure of an organisation.
2. An organisation chart may be drawn to show functions, activities, line structure, posts, lines of responsibility, levels of authority, accountability, lines of communication, span of control.
3. The four types of relationship in an organisation are line, lateral, staff and functional.
4. The span of control is the number of subordinates who report *directly* to the same superior.
5. Organisation charts are usually drawn vertically or horizontally.
6. Functional authority is shown by a dotted line between the technical superior and subordinate where they are in different sections or departments.
7. Where an individual is responsible to two seniors lines are drawn from the subordinate position to both senior posts.
8. Job gradings may be shown on an organisation chart.

SELF-ASSESSMENT QUESTIONS

Answer all questions as quickly as possible. Do not turn back to the Chapter until you have completed this test.

1. Why is it necessary to have an organisation chart?

2. State five possible purposes for which an organisation chart may be used.

3. What is the difference between "responsibility" and "authority"?

4. Give an example of "accountability" in a college of education.

5. The Home Sales Manager, Export Sales Manager, Advertising Manager and Public Relations Manager all report to the Marketing Manager in Grand Enterprises Limited. (*a*) What is the relationship of: (i) the Home Sales Manager to the Public Relations Manager; (ii) the Advertising Manager to the Marketing Manager; (iii) the Public Relations Manager to the Advertising Manager? (*b*) What is the Marketing Manager's span of control?

6. Study the organisation chart below.

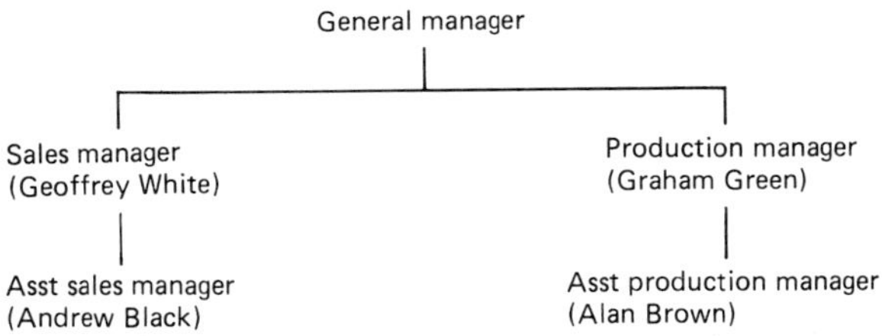

Mr Black has just obtained a large order from a customer. Mr White asks him to brief Mr Green on the production requirements for the order. When Mr Black goes to Mr Green's office and explains the purpose of his visit Mr Green says "I'm not taking orders from you." Is Mr Green justified in saying this? If so, what should have been done? If not, what can be done?

7. Draw an organisation chart of either: (*a*) your college organisation structure; or (*b*) the structure of the organisation where you work.

8. (*a*) What special facts are revealed by the organisation chart on p. 33? (*b*) If the works manager has a production problem affecting a sales order of one particular sales representative how should the representative be informed, i.e. what is the correct line of communication?

ASSIGNMENT

You have been appointed Office Services Manager at Newton Engineering Co. Ltd. It is a new appointment and you have responsibility for completely reorganising the office services which have been allowed to "run themselves" in a haphazard way.

You investigate the existing services and find the following.

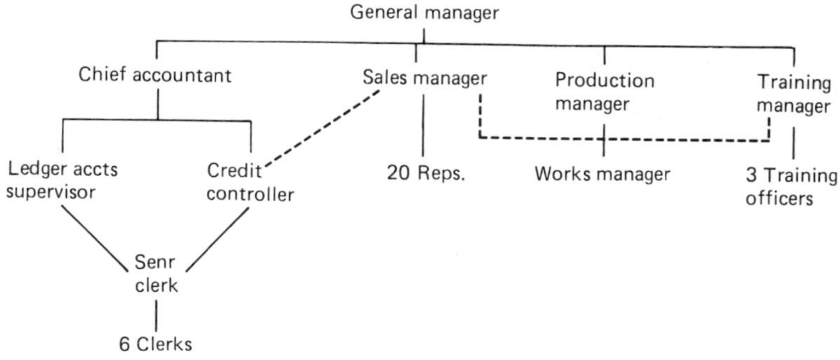

1. Mail room	1 senior clerk and 2 clerks handling all inwards and outwards mail including a large number of outgoing parcels.
2. Secretarial	6 senior secretaries each working for 2 or 3 senior managers; 8 shorthand/audio-typists working in various departments for middle managers and professional technical staff. 3 word processor operators in a room by themselves receiving work from anyone who cares to hand it in.
3. Telecommunications	2 telephone operators (1 with 8 years' experience in the company, 1 with 4 years' experience); 1 telex operator (1 year's experience); Telex machine in switchboard room.
4. Stationery and equipment	1 clerk who deals physically with stock handling and maintains manual records.
5. Maintenance	1 handyman (specialists called in when necessary).
6. Cleaners	3 office cleaners.

All staff except the secretarial staff nominally report to the Company Secretary. The secretarial staff report to their respective managers. Some secretaries are overworked, others are frequently idle.

(*a*) Bearing in mind that it is your responsibility to provide cost effective and efficient office services, draw up an organisation chart showing the structure you think would be most suitable.

(*b*) Justify your proposed structure to the Company Secretary, who has not been happy about appointing an Office Services Manager but has been overridden by the Managing Director.

(*c*) Write a job description for one of the sections in your structure.

CHAPTER FOUR

Data Systems

CHAPTER OBJECTIVES

After studying this chapter you should be able to:
* describe the types of data systems used in business;
* identify basic documentation and procedures related to various functions and activities carried on by the organisation;
* analyse and explain the use of data contained in standard business documents;
* list the sequence of activities carried out in processing the documents used in a standard business transaction;
* explain the importance of information processing in planning, co-ordinating and controlling work.

DEFINITION AND PURPOSE

What is a data system? Data or information is received from within or outside the organisation and must be processed. The activities or procedures involved in processing, the order in which they are carried out, and the documents needed to convey the information to the right people and control the activities, make up the system. The way in which the procedures are carried out is also a part of the system. Methods and equipment for processing data are discussed in the next chapter.

STAGES OF A BUSINESS TRANSACTION

A transaction normally takes place between two organisations, one of which is selling goods or services, the other buying. The two organisations may be in the same country or in different countries, in which case the documentation involved is greater in volume and detail.

The organisation wanting to buy may have a system whereby each department makes its own purchases, or it may have a central purchasing department headed by a purchasing officer or chief buyer. The need for the purchase may be a "one off" requirement for something like a piece of equipment or machinery, or it may be for a regular supply of consumable items such as stationery or a regular supply of raw materials or components for manufacturing goods or providing a service. Except in the case of "one off" requirements a system of *stock control* is normally operated so that the right amount of goods is purchased at the right time.

For the purchaser the stages in the transaction are:

(*a*) indication by stock control that goods should be ordered;
(*b*) goods are ordered;
(*c*) goods are received and stored;
(*d*) goods are paid for.

The organisation receiving the order may have the goods already in stock or may be able to provide the service on demand. If the goods are not readily available they will be placed on order so that each customer is supplied in turn as the goods are manufactured. A system of *production control* is necessary to ensure that the organisation is able to supply orders as promptly as possible but at the same time not have large stocks awaiting sales.

In business most sales take place on a credit basis, i.e. the goods are supplied or services provided and are then paid for in accordance with previously agreed terms. It is therefore important that the vendor is satisfied that the purchaser will be able to pay for the goods, and for this purpose many organisations have a system of *credit control* to ensure that no customer has more than a certain amount of debts outstanding.

For the vendor the stages in the transaction are:

(*a*) receive the order;
(*b*) check whether goods are available;
(*c*) arrange for production of goods if necessary or supply of services;
(*d*) check credit status of customer;
(*e*) supply goods;
(*f*) receive payment for goods.

STOCK CONTROL

Procedures

The purpose of stock control is to ensure that goods are available when required. Since stock represents money no organisation wants to hold more stock than necessary to meet requirements. The procedures involved in stock control are as follows:

(*a*) receive goods and record quantity and/or value—update balance;
(*b*) check goods received tally with order;
(*c*) store goods;

(*d*) issue goods and record quantity and/or value—update balance;

(*e*) check re-order level (re-order level is the quantity in stock at which an order should be placed; it is determined on the basis of delivery time and average quantity used over a period, e.g. weekly or monthly); re-order if amount in stock is down to re-order level; ensure amount ordered will not exceed maximum level (maximum level is determined on the basis of usage over a given period, e.g. a month, three months or six months);

(*f*) check minimum level (the minimum level is the "danger" level, i.e. if the order placed at re-order level has not yet been received it must be chased immediately).

It is necessary to check stock at intervals to ensure that the physical stock tallies with the records. *Stocktaking* may be carried out in various ways.

(*a*) A complete check of all stock may be carried out once or twice a year.

(*b*) Spot checks of a variety of items may be carried out at various times throughout the year.

(*c*) A perpetual inventory may be taken, i.e. a different series of items are checked at regular intervals throughout the year. The main advantage of this system is that the disruption caused by an annual stocktaking is avoided.

Documentation

The following documents or records may be completed in the process of controlling stock.

(*a*) A *goods received note* (*see* Fig. 7) is completed when goods are received. This is then checked against the order form.

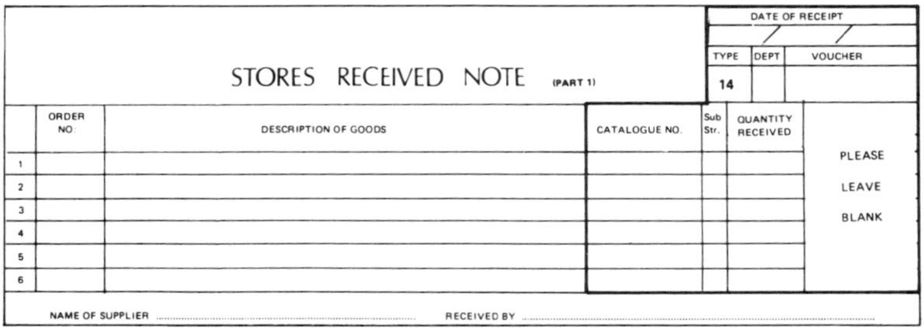
STORES RECEIVED NOTE (PART 1)

DATE OF RECEIPT / /

TYPE	DEPT	VOUCHER
14		

	ORDER NO.	DESCRIPTION OF GOODS	CATALOGUE NO.	Sub Str.	QUANTITY RECEIVED	PLEASE LEAVE BLANK
1						
2						
3						
4						
5						
6						

NAME OF SUPPLIER .... RECEIVED BY ....

Fig. 7. *Stores received note completed by the purchaser when goods are delivered.*

(*b*) A *stock record* is kept. This may be in the form of a bin card, record card, or inventory sheet. The information may include the quantity of items in hand, i.e. the balance, the quantity of items issued and received with dates, value of items, either at cost or selling price, maximum, re-order and minimum levels. A stock record card and stock record computer printout are illustrated at Figs. 8 and 9.

ITEM	Copy paper /80gsm		MAX	100
UNIT	Ream		RE-ORD	20
CODE	0672 – 41		MIN	10

DATE	RECEIPTS	ISSUES	BALANCE	RE-ORDER DATE
26.6.81	100		100	
29.6.81		10	90	
7.7.81		50	40	
16.7.81		7	33	
30.7.81		20	13	31.7.81
6.8.81		5	8	
10.8.81	90		98	

Fig. 8. *Simple record card.*

CODE NO	ITEM	SIZE	BALANCE	MAX LEVEL	RE-ORDER LEVEL	MIN LEVEL	UNIT COST	VALUE AT COST
0048651	MALT BISCUITS	8 OZ	482				00.09	43.38
0048652	CHOC BISCUITS	8 OZ	348	1000	350		00.15	52.20
0048653	WHEAT BISCUITS	12 OZ	421				00.11	46.31
0049718	ANGEL CAKE MIX	6 OZ	134			135	00.17	22.78
0049719	SULTANA CAKE MIX	6 OZ	267				00.20	53.40
0049720	CHOC CAKE MIX	6 OZ	199	500	200		00.22	43.78

Fig. 9. *Typical record on computer printout.*

(*c*) A *stock-taking inventory sheet* on which is recorded the quantity of goods counted. This is later checked against the stock record and any discrepancies are then investigated.

ORDERING GOODS

Procedures

The department requiring goods must have some form of authorisation which may be the re-order level indicated by stock control, the agreement by the head of department and/or sanction of the finance department for the expenditure involved. The procedures involved in ordering the goods may be:

(*a*) complete a departmental requisition form—which may have to carry the authorising signature—and send to buying department;

(*b*) obtain estimate, quotation or tender including delivery times—sometimes this is done by the department before completing the requisition form;

(*c*) choose supplier and negotiate price and/or delivery time, etc., if necessary.

SMITH & COMPANY
16 Old Street
LYNDHURST
SO3 2AB

Excel Decorators Limited
14 New Street
SOUTHAMPTON SO2 6PR

Dear Sirs

QUOTATION

Following our discussion yesterday will you please send me a quotation for redecorating my office as follows:

1 Strip walls and all woodwork
2 Clean ceiling
3 Paper ceiling with chipboard and paint with 2 coats cream emulsion
4 Apply vinyl to all walls
5 Paint all woodwork - 2 undercoats and top coat gloss cream

All materials to be supplied by you.

Will you please state the date on which work can begin and the expected completion date.

Yours faithfully

J D Smith
Partner

Fig. 10. *Request for a quotation.*

REDISET

PURCHASE ORDER No 005723

Macdonald & Evans Group of Companies

Estover Road, Plymouth PL6 7PZ
Telephone: Plymouth (0752) 705251
Telex: 45635

Date

To

Address Invoice to

MACDONALD & EVANS
(PUBLICATIONS) LTD

Please supply

Quantity	Description	Price
12	HB PENCILS	
3	PENCIL ERASERS	
3	ROLLS OF SELLOTAPE	

Date required	Deliver to
	These offices

We reserve the right not to accept the goods or pay invoice if our order number is not quoted on all advice notes, invoices, etc.

Signed

Fig. 11. *Order form sent by a purchaser to a supplier.*

(*d*) complete order form—this is done either by the buying department or individual department;

(*e*) send order form to finance department for authorisation of expenditure which may be necessary to ensure that the individual department is not overspending its budget.

Documentation

The following documents and records may be completed in the process of ordering goods:

(*a*) *requisition form*—contains details of goods required and may indicate the supplier;

(*b*) *request for estimate, quotation or tender* (*see* Fig. 10)—sets out the details of the goods required or specification of the job to be done;

(*c*) *order form* (*see* Fig. 11)—contains details as given in the requisition form plus delivery address, method of payment and any other special instructions.

RECEIVING GOODS

Procedures

(*a*) Check goods if possible when received to ensure that they are not damaged. This is not always possible but the packing should always be inspected. The delivery, despatch or consignment note is signed but a note should be made if the goods have not been inspected.

(*b*) Inspect the goods.

(*c*) Complete a goods received note.

(*d*) Prepare a report on damaged goods.

(*e*) Check goods received against order.

(*f*) Prepare a report of discrepancies, i.e. goods ordered but not received, goods received but not ordered, wrong items delivered.

Documentation

The following documents and records may be completed in the process of receiving goods:

(*a*) *goods received note* (*see* page 37);

(*b*) *damaged goods report* which gives date and number of order, date goods received, delivery/despatch/consignment note number, details of goods damaged;

(*c*) *discrepancies report*—similar details to damaged goods report.

STORING GOODS (STOCK-KEEPING)

Procedures

Stock is stored in different ways depending on the type and quantity of items. It is usual to ensure that new stock items are placed under or behind existing stock on the principle of "First In First Out" (F.I.F.O.). This ensures minimum deterioration of stock. All items, whether packed or not, should be placed so that they can be identified on sight, e.g. box labels should be the right way up for reading.

Easy location of stock items is vitally important. It is usual to code goods and store them in code sequence. A terminal digit system of coding may be used (*see* page 92) by which the bays of racks, shelves and shelf divisions are identified. Any coded system must be simple.

The physical storing of goods does not usually involve the completion of forms or records.

PURCHASE CONTROL

Procedures

Most purchases are made "on credit", i.e. the goods are received and then paid for at a later date. The following procedures are involved in ensuring the accuracy of documents and payment for goods purchased from suppliers in this country.

(*a*) An invoice is received and checked against the order and goods received note. Discrepancies are investigated with the suppliers. A credit note should be received for any goods reported damaged, missing or returned as not in accordance with the order.

(*b*) The invoice may be sent to the department to which the goods were supplied for signature authorising payment.

(*c*) The invoice may then be paid or it may be filed to await a statement of account. It is usual to pay an invoice if cash discount is allowed for payment within a certain period, e.g. seven days.

(*d*) A statement of account is received, usually monthly (though not necessarily at the end of the calendar month). The items on the statement are checked against invoices and credit notes. If correct, payment is authorised.

When goods are purchased from overseas it may be necessary to pay for the goods before they are received, especially if the purchaser and supplier have not dealt with each other previously. This is explained more fully on page 45.

Documentation

It is not usual to raise any documents during the process of checking documents though there may be some form of requisition for payment, e.g. a request for a cheque to be drawn. This would be passed with the relevant documents to the cash office.

PAYMENT

When making a payment to a UK supplier this is done usually either by cheque or by credit transfer. Standing orders and direct debit payments may also be used, particularly for regular payments such as rates, rent, etc. All methods are available through the joint stock banks or the National Giro.

Procedures

To pay *by cheque* the procedures are:

(*a*) prepare a payment voucher;
(*b*) draw a cheque for the amount authorised;
(*c*) send the cheque for signature—some organisations have two signatures on cheques above a certain amount to prevent embezzlement;
(*d*) send the cheque with the payment voucher (or remittance slip) and statement to the supplier—many organisations do not now send receipts if a payment is made by cheque so if a receipt is required it should be specifically requested;
(*e*) file the duplicate payment voucher and supporting documents (invoices, etc.);
(*f*) receive the receipt if it has been requested.

To pay by *credit transfer* the procedures are:

(*a*) prepare credit transfer list;
(*b*) draw a cheque for payment of the total amount due;
(*c*) send list and cheque to bank for action.

Payment by *standing order* means that the bank is instructed to pay a specific amount to the payee on a specific date or dates in the year until further notice. The amount cannot be varied without the authorisation of the payer. Procedures involved are:

(*a*) request a banker's order form from the supplying organisation;
(*b*) complete the form and send it to the supplier, who will send it to the customer's bank.

Payment by *direct debit* means that the payee informs the payer's bank of the amount to be transferred to his account. The payee normally informs the payer beforehand of the amount involved. The procedures are:

(*a*) request a direct debit authorisation form from the supplying organisation;
(*b*) complete the form and send it to own bank.

Direct debits are more commonly used now than standing orders because of rapid increases in charges for such items as rates, water charges, etc.

Documentation

The following documents are involved in making payment by cheque.

(*a*) *Payment voucher*—indicates the name of the payee, the amount to be paid and may also include the purpose of the payment.

(*b*) *Cheque*—the details include the date, the name of the payee, the amount in figures and words, signature/s.

For payment by credit transfer the documents are:

(*a*) *credit transfer voucher* (*see* Fig. 12)—states the date, the name of the paying organisation, the payees' names, the bank (or National Giro) and account number to which each payment is to be made, the amount to be credited to each account, signature;

(*b*) *cheque* for the total amount of the transfer (details as above).

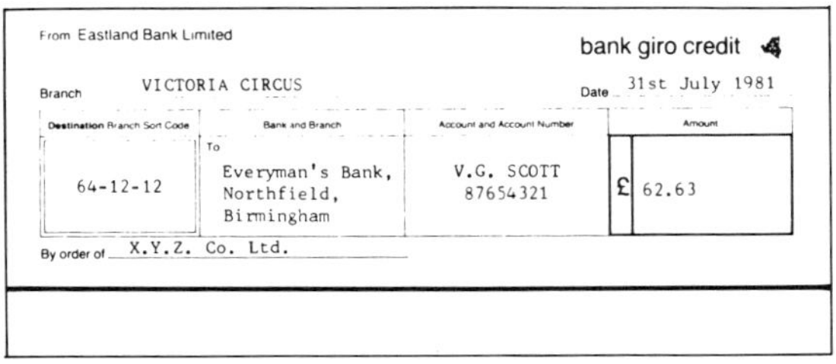

From Eastland Bank Limited

bank giro credit

Branch VICTORIA CIRCUS Date 31st July 1981

Destination Branch Sort Code	To Bank and Branch	Account and Account Number	Amount
64-12-12	Everyman's Bank, Northfield, Birmingham	V.G. SCOTT 87654321	£ 62.63

By order of X.Y.Z. Co. Ltd.

Fig. 12. *Example of a credit transfer voucher or dispersal credit, i.e. credits for wages, salaries or pensions, or payments to traders. When a number of payments are made simultaneously the drawer pays one cheque to the bank for the total amount to be transferred. The clear band at the bottom of the voucher is for MICR or OCR code line, as on cheques (see page 199), which was introduced on 1 January 1984 to enable credit transfers to be processed electronically in the same way as cheques.*

(Courtesy Banking Information Service.)

When goods are purchased from overseas, payment is usually made through a bank in one of the following ways.

(*a*) *Mail transfer.* This is simply an instruction to the bank to transfer a stated sum of money from the purchaser's account to the supplier's account overseas. It may be arranged by airmail or by telex.

(*b*) *Bill of exchange.* This is simply a cheque payable overseas but may be paid "at sight", i.e. as soon as presented to the bank, or at 30, 60, 90 or 180 days. This means that the money is not actually credited to the supplier's account until the expiry of the stated period. This serves two main purposes:

(*i*) the delay in payment may cover the delivery period so that the purchaser does not actually pay for the goods until about the time he receives them;

(ii) it is a way in which suppliers give extended credit to the purchaser. This method is commonly used by UK suppliers to developing countries, especially those which have a shortage of foreign exchange.

(*c*) *Documentary credit.* This method means that the purchaser pays for the goods at an agreed date before they are shipped. The money is transferred to the supplier's bank which holds the money until the bill of lading (*see* page 51) is produced by the supplier. The amount is then credited to his account. This provides security for both purchaser and supplier and is commonly used between organisations which have not traded together for any length of time.

Transfer of money by computer telecommunications links is explained on pages 232–3.

RECEIVING AN ORDER

Procedures

When an order is received it is usually passed to the sales department for processing. Orders may be obtained by sales representatives who complete an order form, by mail, telephone, or telex, or by customers visiting the organisation.

The procedures involved are:

(*a*) obtain from the customer all details concerning the goods required;
(*b*) negotiate if necessary price, delivery charges, delivery dates;
(*c*) agree terms of payment—cash with order, deposit with order, payment on delivery, credit terms;
(*d*) check whether goods are available ex stock; if not check when delivery is expected.

Documentation

The following documents may be received or raised depending on the method of ordering (*see* above).

(*a*) *Order form* containing:
(*i*) name and address of organisation ordering goods;
(*ii*) date of order;
(*iii*) order numbers (customer's and supplier's);
(*iv*) address for delivery;
(*v*) full details of goods (or services) to be supplied including reference number, e.g. catalogue reference, quantity, quality, colour, size, unit cost, price of each series of items;
(*vi*) date or dates for full, part or "call off" delivery (explained on page 53);

(*vii*) method of delivery, e.g. collection by customer, delivery by road, rail, air or sea;

(*viii*) terms of payment including discounts.

(*b*) *Acknowledgment of order*, which may indicate only the date and number of the order.

PRODUCTION CONTROL

The purpose of production control procedures is to ensure that:

(*a*) delivery dates can be met;
(*b*) there is a smooth production flow;
(*c*) manpower, materials and machines are used to the best advantage;
(*d*) bottlenecks in production are prevented.

The procedures and documentation involved in production control vary greatly depending on the type of goods, size of the organisation, type of production, i.e. one off, batch or flow/continuous.

Procedures

The main procedures involved in production control are:

(*a*) scheduling, i.e. planning quantities and dates of production;
(*b*) allocation of machine capacity;
(*c*) allocation of personnel;
(*d*) allocation of raw materials and/or components;
(*e*) issuing instructions;
(*f*) progressing.

Documentation

The following documents may be raised in the process of fulfilling an order:

(*a*) *job card* illustrated at Fig. 13 (or works order) which contains the sale order number, details of goods to be manufactured or supplied, delivery schedule;

(*b*) *route card* which indicates manufacturing methods and the timing and sequence of operations—this would apply if several operations and possibly various staff are involved;

(*c*) *materials list* showing the items required for the job;

(*d*) *stores requisition* showing items to be drawn from stores which may include tools as well as components and materials;

(*e*) *inspection tickets* (or dockets) completed by quality control

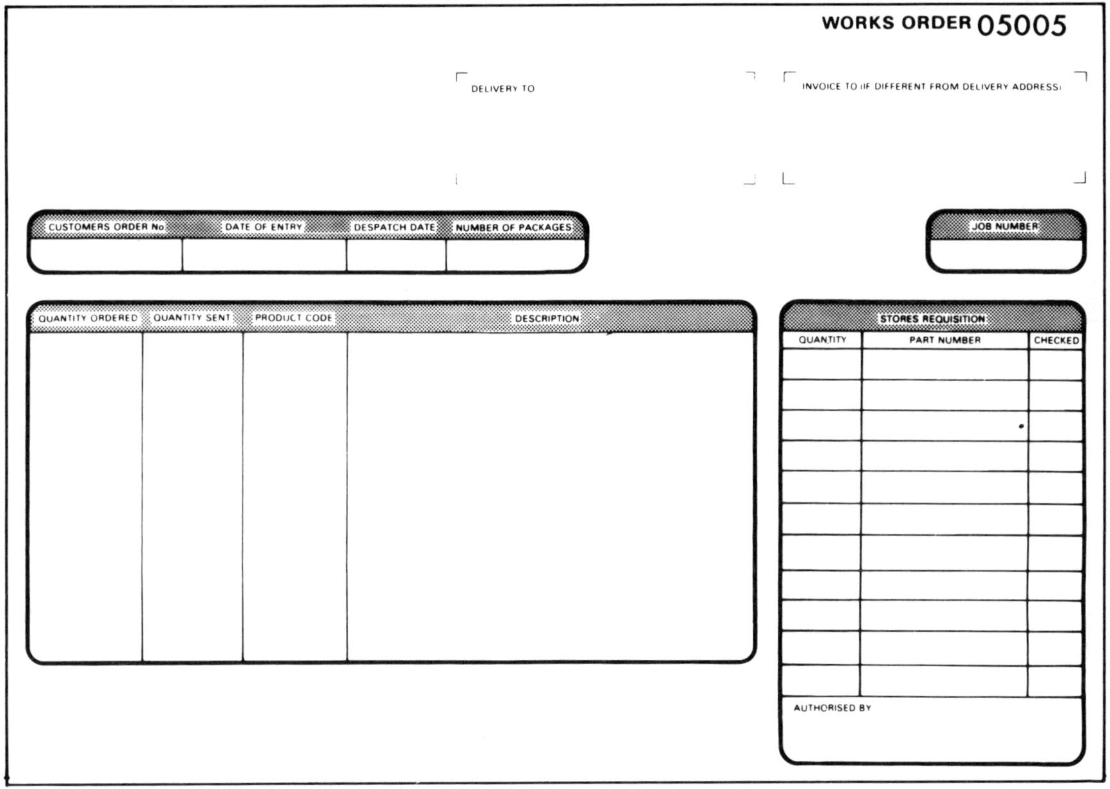

Fig. 13. *Works order (or job card) used to record materials and supplies used. (Courtesy Wiggins Teape (UK) PLC.)*

staff to indicate that the finished product has been inspected and found to meet the required standard.

CREDIT CONTROL

When goods are sold on credit it is important for the supplier to have a system of credit control to ensure that payment is not delayed by customers for long periods. It is usual when a new customer wants to open an account that the supplier obtains references from the customer's bank and one or two other traders. He may also obtain a *credit rating* from a professional organisation such as Extel. A credit limit is established which means that customers may not receive goods beyond the limit fixed until payment is made.

Procedures

(*a*) Determine the amount of credit to be allowed.
(*b*) Obtain references.
(*c*) Open account for customer.
(*d*) Inform customer of account number, credit limit and terms of payment.
(*e*) Ensure system of credit checking and authorisation is adhered to by staff.

Documentation

(*a*) *Application form* to open account to be completed by customer.
(*b*) *Request for reference* from bank and/or organisations with whom prospective customer trades.
(*c*) *Ledger card* indicating name and address of customer, account number and credit limit. (Details of future transactions will be recorded on this card.)
(*d*) *Form* notifying customer of account details.
(*e*) *Account card* which is issued to customer if personal shopping is involved.

Many customers now use *credit cards* to pay for goods/services supplied. It is usual for suppliers to check the customer's credit status with the central computer department of such credit organisations as Access, Barclaycard, etc., if the amount involved is above a certain level.

DESPATCH/DELIVERY OF GOODS (BRITISH ISLES)

When goods are available ex stock or have been manufactured to order the goods have to be despatched to the customer in accordance with the method agreed.

Procedures

(*a*) Inform customer of cost of goods.
(*b*) Arrange insurance if necessary.
(*c*) Inform customer when goods will be despatched and by what method.
(*d*) Send insurance policy to customer if appropriate.
(*e*) Prepare despatch document.
(*f*) Prepare packing list.
(*g*) Collect goods for packing and check against order.
(*h*) Pack goods depending on type of goods and method of despatch.
(*i*) Address package/s.
(*j*) Remove packages to loading bay.
(*k*) Load goods for delivery to customer or to transport terminal.
(*l*) Customer receives goods and signs receipt note.

Documentation

(*a*) *Pro-forma invoice* which indicates the unit cost of the goods, i.e. the cost of each item.

(*b*) *Advice note* which indicates when the goods will be despatched and by what method. It may also give instructions concerning notification of non-delivery of goods or damage in transit.

(*c*) *Packing note* contains details of individual items packed.

(*d*) *Despatch note* or *transport docket* which instructs the transport department to provide the necessary vehicle. (This enables the transport officer to programme deliveries cost effectively.)

(*e*) *Waybill* which the van/lorry driver presents to the security officer at the gate when leaving the manufacturers. The security officer may inspect the van before allowing it to pass through the gate/security checkpoint.

(*f*) *Delivery note* in duplicate, usually used when supplier delivers the goods—one copy is retained by the customer who signs the duplicate copy and returns it to the van driver.

(*g*) *Despatch note* or *consignment note* which states the number of packages and the contents. This is usually included with the goods, and may take the place of a packing note.

(*h*) *Receipt note* which may be a tear-off section of the consignment note or a duplicate of it. The customer signs the receipt note to indicate that the goods have been delivered. If it is not possible to check that all the goods have been received and that they are not damaged the receipt note should be signed "subject to inspection of the goods". There is usually a limited period for reporting missing or damaged items so that checking should be done within a day or two of receiving the goods.

DESPATCH/DELIVERY OF GOODS (OVERSEAS)

The procedures for sending goods overseas are more complicated. A number of additional forms have to be completed and authorised. Large organisations have an export department which is staffed by people trained to deal with the formalities involved. Smaller organisations usually use export agencies or the facilities offered by local Chambers of Commerce. The requirements vary considerably from one country to another and it is vitally important that the correct procedures are followed in every case. Failure to do so can mean that goods are delayed for many months awaiting customs clearance. The following outline of procedures and documentation is of necessity very general because of the diversity of requirements in different countries.

Procedures (additional to those for Home Sales)

(*a*) Obtain export licence if necessary.

(*b*) Check documentation required by overseas importer.

(*c*) Prepare documents for shipping.

(*d*) Prepare documents for importation in overseas country, i.e. for customs clearance.

(*e*) Have documents authorised by overseas embassy or appointed agent in the UK.

(*f*) Distribute documents as appropriate to bank/customer/freight carriers (road, rail, shipping, air).

Documentation

Specimens of the following documents are shown in "Systematic Export Documentation" published by the Simplification of International Trade Procedures Board, 11/12 Waterloo Place, London SW1Y 4AU.

(*a*) *Standard shipping note* includes name and address of exporter and forwarding agent, various references, details of contents including gross weight and cubic capacity, and some shipping details.

(*b*) *Export consignment note* gives similar details to the standard shipping note.

(*c*) *Export cargo shipping instructions* which gives additional information to the standard shipping note, including the name and address of the consignee, net weight of goods, information about payment and delivery of documents.

(*d*) *Certificate of insurance* gives details of items and total insured value.

(*e*) *Bill of lading* shows names and addresses of exporter and consignee, name of the vessel and ports of loading and discharge, details of contents with gross weight and cubic measurement. This document is vital because it is required by the purchaser or his agent, e.g. bank, to obtain assurance that the goods have been despatched before payment is made. It is also needed for customs clearance in the overseas country. Usually original documents only are accepted, i.e. photocopies are not acceptable.

(*f*) *Documentary collection form* which indicates the documents to be forwarded, the method of despatch, the method and date of payment and the amount to be paid.

(*g*) *Movement certificate* used in preferential trade between EEC (European Economic Community) and EFTA (European Free Trade Association) countries.

(*h*) *Specification for H.M. Customs and Excise* giving brief details of the consignment.

(*i*) *Certificate of origin* which is usually an invoice containing a paragraph certifying that the goods are of United Kingdom origin. It also certifies that the prices are current export market prices and accepts responsibility for inaccuracies and errors.

SALES INVOICING

All goods sold have to be billed either for cash sale, in which case the bill is a receipt for the money paid, or for credit sale.

Procedures

(*a*) Receive the order and price the items.

(*b*) Prepare invoice.

(*c*) Send invoice to customer. This is usually after the despatch of the goods though in some cases the invoice is enclosed with the goods.

(*d*) Issue credit note if any goods are returned or damaged, and for returned crates, etc.

(*e*) Record invoices and credit notes on customer ledger card.

(*f*) Issue statement of account at the end of the accounting period.

(*g*) Send follow up statements and/or letters if payment is not received by the due date. (This is important as few companies can afford to allow long credit periods to customers.)

Documentation

(*a*) *Invoice* illustrated at Fig. 14, which indicates the unit cost of each item, the price of the total quantity of each item, the total cost, discounts, value added tax (VAT) which must be shown separately, and terms of payment. Invoices may carry the abbreviation E.&O.E. which means "Errors and Omissions Excepted". This enables the supplier to send a supplementary invoice, usually called a debit note, if any item has not been charged or if there is an error in arithmetic.

INVOICE

OFFICE REQUIREMENTS LTD.
Specialists in Photo Copying. Systems and Office Landscaping
Suppliers of all leading makes of Office Equipment

VAT No.187 6002 54
602 Wimborne Road, Winton, Bournemouth BH9 2HR, Tel: Bournemouth 519315
and
12 Malvern Road, Shirley, Southampton SO16QA, Tel Southampton 782727

No. 14814

DELIVERY ADDRESS
J Brown & Co Ltd
14 High Street
ANYTOWN
AN16 7BA

INVOICE ADDRESS:
J Brown & Co Ltd
Bowen House
Green Street
NEWTOWN
NN67 8YP

QUANTITY	CODE	DESCRIPTION	UNIT	UNIT PRICE £	p	TOTAL PRICE £	p
10	067	Blue Apex Ring Binders	each	1	05	10	50
50	721	Copy paper 70 gsm	ream	1	85	92.	50
3	148	Concertina file	each	3	75	11	25

DESP DATE	INVOICE DATE	CUSTOMER'S ORDER No.	DATED	SOLD BY	TAX POINT
12.8.81	17.8.81	OE 678312	5.8.81	AES	30.9.81

	£	p
	114	25
NETT TOTAL	114	25
VAT@ %	17	14
INVOICE TOTAL	131	39

CONDITIONS OF SALE

Fig. 14. *Invoice charging for goods supplied.*

(*b*) *Credit note* contains the same details as an invoice related to items for which a credit is being allowed.

(*c*) *Ledger card* which shows debits (amounts charged), credits (amounts paid or allowed) and balance outstanding. (The customer's credit limit would also be indicated on this card.)

(*d*) *Statement of account* illustrated at Fig. 15, lists the dates and numbers of invoices and credit notes, the total of each invoice and credit note (VAT amounts may be shown separately), dates and amounts of payments, balance outstanding. There may also be an indication of how long overdue a balance or parts of the balance are.

It is usual to prepare several copies of an invoice to be distributed within the organisation to the accounts department (if the invoice is raised in the sales department), the sales department file, the sales

STATEMENT

TEACHING AIDS LTD
DEANSTEAD HOUSE
STATION ROAD
NEW MILTON
HANTS
BH25 6LD

ROYALES (STATIONERS) LTD
NEW MILTON, HANTS.

ZT07 36 28 FEB 1983

CASH RECEIVED AFTER THE END OF THE MONTH NOT INCLUDED

DATE	REF. NO.	TRANSACTION	DEBIT	CREDIT
		BALANCE B/FWD	11.48	
28 02 84	HI0892	INVOICE	26.04	

CASH RECEIVED AFTER THE END OF MONTH NOT INCLUDED

3 MONTHS & OVER	2 MONTHS OVERDUE	1 MONTH OVERDUE	CURRENT MONTH	TOTAL NOW DUE
		11.48	26.04	37.52

REMITTANCE ADVICE
PLEASE RETURN THIS SLIP
WITH YOUR REMITTANCE

TEACHING AIDS LTD

£

Fig. 15. *Statement of account summarising invoices and payments of the preceding month. The remittance advice slip is detached and sent with the cheque when payment is made.*

representative if appropriate, the stores for part or call-off deliveries. (Part delivery means that the order is to be delivered in more than one consignment. Call-off delivery means that the customer orders in bulk and then calls for delivery of part of the order as required. In this case it is advisable to agree a call-off delivery time.)

RECEIVING PAYMENT

In the section on Payment on page 43 we saw that there are various ways in which a customer can pay a supplier. The procedures involved in receiving the payment are similar whatever the method of payment.

Procedures

(*a*) Receive payment and check amount of cash or amount written on cheque/credit transfer slip, etc.
(*b*) Check payment against invoice or statement of account.
(*c*) Record payment on ledger card.
(*d*) Prepare receipt or indicate receipt of payment on invoice or statement of account.
(*e*) Send receipt to customer. (Some organisations do not send receipts when payment is made by cheque.)
(*f*) Record payment for banking.

Documentation

(*a*) *Ledger card* on which is shown the date and amount of payment and the balance still outstanding, which may be nil.
(*b*) *Receipt* should show the date of payment, name of customer, amount of payment in figures and words, initials of person receiving payment.
(*c*) *Cash list* headed by the date and showing the amounts received with the account number in each case. This list would then be used for banking the money.

Payments received through the bank would be notified by the bank at predetermined intervals.

WAGES AND SALARIES

Wages and salaries are now commonly paid monthly. Some companies differentiate between weekly paid and monthly paid staff, in some cases providing different conditions of service for each group. There are different methods of determining wages and salary payments as you have learned in the Organisation in its Environment Module. (For information on these methods refer to *The Organisation in its Environment*, John Beardshaw and David Palfreman (Macdonald and Evans).)

Procedures

(*a*) Arrange for a record to be kept of time worked.
(*b*) Prepare a payroll.
(*c*) Carry out cash analysis for wages which are paid in cash.
(*d*) Prepare pay statements and envelopes for each employee.
(*e*) Arrange payment of wages and salaries.

(*f*) Arrange for payment of national insurance and income tax deductions.

(*g*) Distribute wages/pay statements.

Documentation

(*a*) *Attendance record* which may be one of the following:

(*i*) clock card or time card which the employee completes by slotting it into an automatic time recorder;

(*ii*) time sheet or time book which is signed by the employee and certified by the foreman.

(*b*) *Work record* which is usually some form of job card.

(*c*) *National insurance and income tax deductions sheet P11* (more details are given below).

(*d*) *Payroll* on which is calculated the following:

(*i*) the amount of money earned by each employee whose name and clock number or personnel number is on the record;

(*ii*) the amount of money earned for overtime;

(*iii*) statutory deductions, i.e. national insurance and income tax;

(*iv*) voluntary deductions, e.g. union dues, social fund;

(*v*) net pay, i.e. gross pay (normal and overtime) less deductions.

In a large organisation a payroll may be prepared for each department. In this case a summary of the payroll would be prepared listing the various departments and the total amounts from each column on the departmental payroll.

(*e*) *Cash analysis sheet* showing the denominations of cash required for each employee so that the correct amounts of notes and coin can be collected from the bank.

(*f*) *Pay statement* must be given to each employee (Employment Protection (Consolidation) Act 1978) and must show how gross pay is made up, individual amounts of deductions and net pay. A typical pay statement is illustrated at Fig. 16.

(*g*) *Cheque* for cash (if wages are paid in cash), or *cheques* for individual employees, or *cheque* for total of credit transfers if this method of payment is used.

(*h*) *Cheque* for payment of national insurance contributions (employees and employer) and income tax deducted for each employee (less any refund of tax) together with the appropriate Inland Revenue Return.

(*i*) *Receipt book* or sheets to be signed by employees paid in cash. They should check the amount of cash before signing the book/sheet.

Earnings period No Date	1	10.4
1 BASIC	80	00
2 O/TIME	16	00
3		
4		
5		
6		
7		
8		
9		
Gross earnings for period	96	·00
Superan conts	4	·80
Pay for period	91	·20
Total pay to date	91	·20
Total free pay to date	38	·85
Total taxable pay to date	52	·35
Total tax due to date	15	·60
Tax refund this period		
Income tax this period	15	·60
NI basic contribution	5	·71
O		
A		
B		
C		
D		
E Total fixed deductions		
Total deductions	21	·31
Pay less deductions	69	·89
10 CAR ALLCE.	20	—
11		
Total amount due	89	·89
Total employee's and employer's NI contributions	15	·75
Name CLARK C. No. 416		

Fig. 16. *A typical pay statement.*

PAYE (Pay As You Earn)

"Pay As You Earn" is the system of tax collection whereby income tax is deducted from remuneration as the pay is earned. In the UK all employers are legally bound to deduct PAYE tax on all Schedule E payments, i.e. "wages, salaries, fees, pensions, or profits accruing by reason of office or employment", and to account for it to the Inland Revenue authority.

Employees are given code numbers, which vary according to their personal allowances, and by reference to special tables published by the Inland Revenue the employer can (*i*) ascertain the tax-free pay for that code number; (*ii*) calculate the total tax payable on the balance of taxable pay; (*iii*) deduct the tax-due figure (i.e. tax already paid) up to the last week or month; to give (*iv*) the tax payable for the current week or month. The earnings record for each employee must include the following:

Gross pay for week or month Cumulative pay to date Cumulative free pay to date Cumulative taxable pay to date Total tax due to date Tax deducted or refunded	All for each week or month of the income tax year

The office work in connection with PAYE can be summarised as follows.

(*a*) Obtaining P45 form from all new employees, or, if not supplied by them, notifying the local Collector of Taxes on form P46.

(*b*) In the meantime, deducting tax by reference to Week 1 or Month 1 tables and entering on a Deduction Card.

(*c*) Deducting tax each week or month by reference to the individual Tax Code Numbers supplied, and the Tax Tables.

(*d*) Maintaining running records of the cumulative pay, etc., and tax deducted on the appropriate P11 Tax Deduction Sheets.

(*e*) Once a month sending a cheque for tax deducted (together with National Insurance contributions) to the local H.M. Collector of Taxes, together with the P30 Remittance Card.

(*f*) When an employee leaves, preparing a P45 form of pay, tax deducted, etc., and sending Part 1 to the local Inspector of Taxes, and handing Parts 2 and 3 to the employee.

(*g*) After the end of the income tax year, issuing to all employees a P60 statement of pay and tax deducted in the year.

(*h*) Making a return to the local Collector of Taxes, not later than

19 April, of all tax deducted in the income tax year and a P35 Annual Declaration Certificate.

The most important forms used in connection with PAYE are as follows.

P2 Notice of Coding (sent to employee).
P6 Notice of Amended Coding (sent to employer).
P11 Deduction Sheet (monthly and weekly)—*see* Fig. 17.
P12 Simplified Deduction Card (where employees are paid at a fixed rate).
P30 Remittance Card.
P35 Yearly Summary and Certificate.
P45 Particulars of Employee Leaving.
P46 Notification to Tax Office of new employee without a Code Number.
P47 Employer's Application to Refund Tax in excess of £50.
P60 Employer's Certificate of Pay and Tax Deductions (given to employees at the end of the year).

By arrangement with the Inland Revenue authority, a company can use its own form of earnings record for incorporation with a

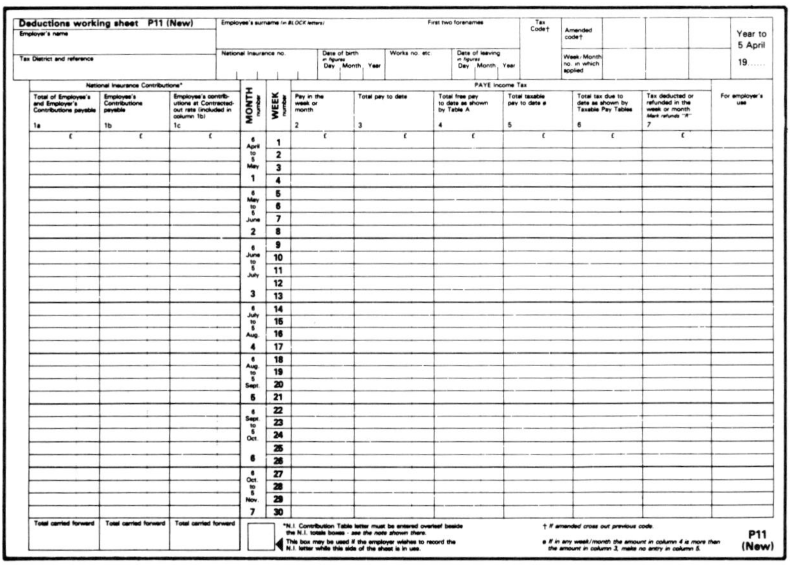
Deductions working sheet P11 (New)
Employer's name
Tax District and reference
Employee's surname (in BLOCK letters) First two forenames
National Insurance no. Date of birth in figures Day Month Year Works no. etc. Date of leaving in figures Day Month Year
Tax Code† Amended code† Week/Month no. in which applied
Year to 5 April 19......

National Insurance Contributions*					PAYE Income Tax						
Total of Employee's and Employer's Contributions payable 1a	Employee's Contributions payable 1b	Employee's contributions at Contracted-out rate (included in column 1b) 1c	MONTH number	WEEK number	Pay in the week or month 2	Total pay to date 3	Total free pay to date as shown by Table A 4	Total taxable pay to date ● 5	Total tax due to date as shown by Taxable Pay Tables 6	Tax deducted or refunded in the week or month Mark refunds "R" 7	For employer's use
£	£	£	6 April to 5 May	1	£	£	£	£	£	£	
				2							
				3							
			1	4							
			6 May to 5 June	5							
				6							
				7							
			2	8							
			6 June to 5 July	9							
				10							
				11							
				12							
			3	13							
			6 July to 5 Aug.	14							
				15							
				16							
			4	17							
			6 Aug. to 5 Sept.	18							
				19							
				20							
			5	21							
			6 Sept. to 5 Oct.	22							
				23							
				24							
				25							
			6	26							
			6 Oct. to 5 Nov.	27							
				28							
				29							
			7	30							
Total carried forward	Total carried forward	Total carried forward									

*N.I. Contribution Table letter must be entered overleaf beside the N.I. totals boxes - see the note shown there.
This box may be used if the employer wishes to record the N.I. letter while this side of the sheet is in use.
† If amended cross out previous code.
● If in any week/month the amount in column 4 is more than the amount in column 3, make no entry in column 5.
P11 (New)

Fig. 17. *P11 income tax deduction sheet used by employers to record national insurance contributions and income tax details for each employee. (Courtesy Inland Revenue.)*

mechanical or computerised payroll, but otherwise the standard P11 Tax Deduction Cards must be used.

Many ingenious devices have been introduced to lessen the work in connection with PAYE, and perhaps one of the most notable is the enlargement, on a board one or two metres square, of the free pay and of the tax equivalent to each code number in a particular week. This may be glanced at by the tax calculator, and saves a great deal of time which would otherwise be consumed in referring to separate tables.

Full information about PAYE can be obtained from the "Employer's Guide to PAYE", published by the Board of Inland Revenue. One last point is that the amount shown in the books of account as PAYE tax owing should be agreed at least quarterly with the amounts shown in different payrolls, before payment is made to the local Collector of Taxes.

National Insurance

Under the Social Security Pensions Act 1975 every employee and self-employed person must pay National Insurance contributions based on the wage/salary received or income earned. School-leavers obtain a National Insurance number from their local Careers Office. They receive a card quoting the number which is recorded at the Department of Health and Social Security at Newcastle-upon-Tyne. It should be quoted when making any enquiry or claiming any benefit, e.g. sickness or unemployment.

There are two levels of contribution, depending on whether the employer is "not contracted-out" or "contracted-out". In the former case the full contribution is payable, as follows:

Employee: 9.0 per cent of gross earning above £34.00 per week or £147.33 per month up to a maximum of £250.00 per week or £1,083.33 per month.

Employer: 11.45 per cent of the employee's gross earning within the same limits.

Contracted-out employers have pension schemes approved by the Department of Health and Social Security. The National Insurance contributions are then as follows:

Employee: 9.0 per cent up to lower earnings limit of £34.00 per week or £147.33 per month plus 6.85 per cent between lower and upper earnings limit (£250.00 per week or £1,083.33 per month).

Employer: 11.45 per cent up to lower earnings limit plus 7.35 per cent between lower and upper earnings limit.

A reduced rate of 3.85 per cent is payable by some married ladies and widows.

The percentages and figures quoted are correct at August 1983. Changes are made quite frequently and it is advisable to check details at the local office of the Department of Health and Social Security.

Statutory Sick Pay

Employers are now responsible for paying sick pay to employees. Those earning less than £34.00 per week are excluded from the scheme. Earnings of £34.00 per week and above qualify for the following amounts of sick pay

£34.00–£50.49	Sick pay £28.55
£50.50–£67.99	£35.45
£68.00 or more	£42.25

Employers can claim a rebate on sick pay paid out to employees.

FLOW OF INFORMATION

Stated individually each set of procedures and documents involved in one particular aspect of a transaction seems quite simple. When integrated to take account of the information required within the organisation to carry out the various activities involved in either buying or selling, it can be seen that the sequence and timing of the procedures is of great importance. If any link in the chain is missing or faulty the entire operation may be at risk. When the interchange of information required between the purchaser and vendor is considered the communication links become more complex. An inaccurate job card in the selling operation could jeopardise the whole order and if the wrong goods are supplied to the purchaser he may have difficulties in fulfilling his orders, and so on.

You will also realise that the payment of wages and salaries to employees is very important. Salaries are usually fixed but wages paid to the staff who manufacture the goods may be paid on the basis of production with incentives for increased productivity. It is therefore essential that records are absolutely accurate throughout the processing to ensure that every employee is paid what he has earned. Similarly any error at any point in the system may well be perpetuated causing problems throughout the organisations involved in the transaction. Checking procedures must therefore be built into any system.

Checking

Checking is expensive. It has therefore to be kept to a minimum. It is usual to use either *spot checking* which means taking work at random and checking it, or *batch checking*, which means taking batches of documents either at regular intervals or in a predetermined sequence, e.g. every tenth batch. Another method used is to check documents involving more than a certain amount of money on the basis that errors in small amounts will cost more to correct than the loss involved.

SUMMARY

1. A transaction takes place between two organisations, one buying and one selling.
2. There are four main stages in a transaction for the purchaser, each stage involving a series of procedures and a range of documents which have to be completed and processed.
3. The seller may have to work through six stages in a transaction, each stage involving procedures and processing of documents.
4. Stock control involves the setting of maximum, re-order and minimum levels of stock, stock-taking and stock recording.
5. Ordering and receiving goods must be carefully documented to ensure that stock control criteria are met and that control of budgets is maintained.
6. Purchase control and payment procedures are of the utmost importance as it is in these areas that there may be security problems.
7. The procedures and documentation involved in receiving an order, production control and credit control are closely interlinked to ensure that customers' orders are fulfilled as quickly as possible with financial safeguards for the supplier.
8. Procedures and documentation for the despatch or delivery of goods within Great Britain may vary from those involved in exporting. Export documentation is complicated and should be dealt with by experienced staff or outside agencies.
9. Sales invoicing and receiving payment must be dealt with on a carefully planned time schedule to avoid long delays in collecting payment.
10. Wages and salaries procedures involve computations of gross salary and net salary. Net salary is the "take home" pay after deductions of income tax (PAYE), national insurance contributions, pension fund contributions and other deductions agreed by the employee.

SELF-ASSESSMENT QUESTIONS

Answer all questions as quickly as possible. Do not turn back to the Chapter until you have completed this test.

1. What are the main stages in a transaction when you are buying goods?
2. What are the main stages in a transaction when you are selling goods?
3. Why is it necessary to have a system of stock control?
4. Explain maximum, re-order and minimum stock levels.
5. State three ways in which stock-taking may be carried out.
6. What information would you expect to find on each of the following documents: (*a*) goods received note; (*b*) stock record card; (*c*) order form; (*d*) discrepancies report; (*e*) credit transfer list (for payment of debts)?
7. How does documentary credit safeguard both the purchaser and the supplier in a transaction involving import/export of goods?
8. What documents may a supplier send to a customer from the point of receiving an order to the point of acknowledging payment? (Assume home trade.)
9. For what purpose is a bill of lading used?
10. What is a payroll and what information does it contain?
11. Every employee is entitled to a pay statement each week or each month, depending on the frequency of payment. What details must be given on that statement?
12. What is meant by "contracted-out" and "not contracted-out" national insurance schemes?

ASSIGNMENTS

Assignment 1

Prepare a diagram illustrating the flow of documents between the buying and selling organisations from the point where the buyer places an order with the seller to the point when the seller sends a receipt for payment.

Assignment 2

Work in groups of two or three if possible.

Refer to the diagram you have drawn for Assignment 1. After the order had been received by the supplier a complete set of documents for the transaction was produced in the usual way. The job card dropped on the floor and it was not noticed that it was missing from the set. It was later swept up by the cleaners and destroyed. All the other documents in the set were distributed correctly.

(*a*) Discuss the implications of the loss of the job card, particularly bearing in mind that a number of people would be involved in subsequent events. Consider the implications from as many aspects as possible including communications, human relations, costs, company image.

(*b*) Suggest a procedure or set of procedures which would ensure that such an occurrence could not happen again.

Assignment 3

(*a*) You are a stock records clerk at Seethru Glass Limited. Your supervisor has authorised you to purchase a new printing electronic calculator, but the cost must not exceed £100. Draw and complete an order form for this equipment which is available from Super Calculators Limited. (You may use imaginary details but all necessary information must be included on the form.)

(*b*) You are a sales clerk at Super Calculators Limited. You have received an order from Seethru Glass Limited for a printing electronic calculator. Draw and complete the documents necessary to obtain the calculator from store, despatch by registered mail and obtain payment. It is customary to charge post and packing in addition to the cost of the equipment. Terms of payment are monthly. Five per cent discount is allowed for settlement of statements within seven days.

CHAPTER FIVE

Data Processing Equipment and Methods

CHAPTER OBJECTIVES

After studying this chapter you should be able to:

* identify the equipment which may be used for processing data for different purposes;
* explain the principal use of each type of equipment;
* explain the basic methods of processing data.

DEFINITION AND PURPOSE

With the growth of business it has been necessary to advance from the manual systems of data processing, although such systems are still in use. Even the smallest organisations have some form of equipment to assist with the task of processing data. In some cases the use of equipment necessitates changes in methods, procedures and/or systems.

There is a vast amount of data flowing around and among organisations. There are machines available for every stage of processing. The major factor that is considered when deciding whether or not to install a particular machine is cost effectiveness. This usually means asking such questions as "Is the volume of work large enough?" and "Will the speed of operation be sufficiently increased?". There are also considerations of the numbers of staff which may be reduced, redeployed, etc.

Machines for receiving, reproducing and transmitting information are dealt with in the appropriate chapters. In this chapter we are concerned with machines for analysing and classifying data.

MANUAL SYSTEMS

Peg-boards

A peg-board is a useful, inexpensive device for small jobs such as sales analysis where a limited number of items are being sold. It consists of a rectangular board with evenly spaced metal pegs along the top. Forms having evenly spaced punched holes along their tops are then hung on these pegs so that each form overlaps its neighbour with one or more columns visible. The forms are fixed to a bar which is reversible and interchangeable so that both sides of the form can be used.

Edge punched cards

Cards can be punched on one or more edges using a small pair of ticket clippers. The edges of the card are divided into "fields" so that the number and position of the slots represents a value, either alphabetic or numeric.

Figure 18 shows a set of cards being lifted out of the block by using a needle slotted through a particular hole.

If these cards represented employees for example, and one wanted to find out how many female employees there were, the needles would be slotted through the hole representing female. This could be further analysed by pulling out those females aged 59, if one wanted to know how many females would be retiring during the next twelve months.

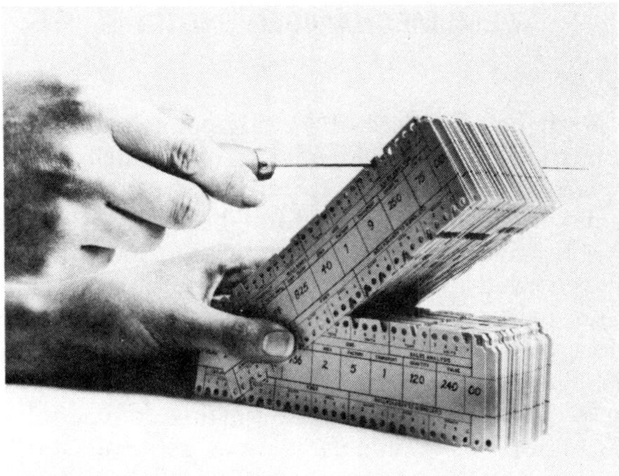

Fig. 18. *Sorting marginally (edge) punched cards. (Courtesy The Copeland Chatterson Company Ltd.)*

Slotted cards

A slotted card has a series of evenly spaced slots across and down it with a blank space at the top on which is written the details of the record. This data is then recorded on the body of the card by joining up appropriate slots with a slotting machine.

To select information from the slotted cards they are placed in a sorting "cradle". Metal rods are passed through holes appropriate to the information required. Cards which have been punched in that particular place will fall down below the others in the cradle. These cards can then be counted, listed or extracted.

Feature cards

A feature card has anything from 1,000 to 10,000 numbered positions, each denoting an item in a series. Each card represents some feature characteristic of that series. If any item in that series has the feature index on the card, then the item numbered is punched out with a hole.

With feature cards, it is possible to select and compare items, and sets of items, at great speed. It is a fairly simple system, and it is quite economic, requiring only a hand punch and the printing of the feature cards.

Feature cards may be used for membership records, operational research, personnel records, medical research, market research and other fields of analysis.

SEMI-MECHANISED SYSTEMS

Key sort

This is a mechanised system of the edge punched card system. A hand or electric slotting machine is used for punching cards which are then placed in a special selector machine fitted with a dropping platform and an automatic tabulator. This operates by sensing the punched holes and printing the numerical and alphabetical information recorded in the form of punched holes.

Calculators

There is a very wide range of electronic calculators available for every purpose from simple add-listing to scientific calculations. Calculators are available in sizes as small and slim as a credit card up to full size desk models. The small models, known as pocket calculators, are usually non-printing. The input figures and totals are shown on a register. Most desk models can be programmed to a greater or lesser degree, e.g. to calculate discount automatically on the basis of a pre-set percentage. Many calculators now have store and recall memories and dual column independent calculations.

Autographic register

Continuous stationery is used in an autographic register, or manifold machine as it is sometimes called. The forms are drawn over a hard writing surface by operating a crank handle. After writing the handle is operated emitting the top one or two copies and retaining one or two carbon copies in the box folded in concertina-style.

Imprinting machine

Whenever payment is made by credit card the sales assistant uses an imprinting machine to reproduce the name and address and account number of the customer on an invoice or bill. A card is placed in position on the machine and the document is placed on top of it in the correct position. A handle is drawn across the document and card, the pressure causing the carbon paper to create an image on the document. The card and document are then taken out of the machine and the document is completed by hand.

MACHINE SYSTEMS

Cash-register machines

A cash-register type machine is appropriate when a printed receipt is required simultaneously with a posting slip and a sales analysis. This prints every item on an audit record which is visible through a glass panel on top of the machine. Symbols are used which indicate analysis totals and identify totalling operations. This record is kept under lock and key and forms a complete unalterable record of the machine's operation. The machine can also print a unit docket, which can be used for further analysis, as a posting medium. Automatic cash registers post the information as it is fed into the machine on to another input medium such as magnetic tape for subsequent processing by computer. There are also electronic cash registers used as terminals linked to a computer. This enables the stock position to be updated at each transaction.

Accounting machines

Although many accounting operations are now computerised, electronic accounting machines are used in smaller organisations. They may be operated by keys or by some other form of input such as punched or magnetic card, magnetic tape or diskette.

An accounting machine is basically a calculator which can perform a wide variety of tasks, including invoicing, payroll and stock records. In addition to standard calculations it normally calculates extensions, credit transactions and new balances, and can analyse data. Several documents can be completed in one operation, e.g. an invoice can be calculated and printed and the sales ledger card updated at the same time.

Most accounting machines produced today are, in fact, micro or minicomputers. They may be used individually or as terminals in a computer system. This will be explained in Chapter Ten.

Machines for producing cheques

Machines can be used for writing, crossing and signing cheques. Apart from speed these machines provide protection against fraud. Cheques are completed with carbon or indelible ink and are said to be one hundred per cent proof against alteration.

The signature, or signatures, for signing cheques are printed on a metal plate which must be kept in a very safe place when not in use. Access must be allowed to one or two specified people only.

Many organisations cross every cheque as soon as it is received. The two-line crossing may contain the firm's name and the name of their bankers. This prevents anyone stealing the cheque and endorsing it fraudulently.

METHODS OF DOCUMENT PRODUCTION

One-time writing

Documents may be produced by hand. To save time it is possible to produce several documents at one writing by having the appropriate sections of each document carbonised on the back so that only the information required on each document is reproduced on it. For example, a cheque-writing and recording system allows a page of cheques and a cash book record to be made in one operation. A batch of cheques and a cash sheet are secured by notches to a collator (*see* Fig. 19). The sheet is headed with the date, and then the payee's name and the amount paid to him are written on the cheque and reproduced on the cash sheet. The amount is then written in the appropriate analysis column on the cash sheet which extends beyond the right-hand edge of the cheques.

Document sets—typewriting

In the previous chapter we saw that a number of documents may be produced when an order is received. These can be typed all together on an *invoice set*. This may consist of an acknowledgment of order, advice note, despatch note, works order and accounts copy. By having shaded areas on some of the forms only the relevant information is legible on each. The documents are usually in different colours for easy identification.

It is usual to use one-time carbons in these sets, which may be individual sheets joined at the top or in the form of continuous stationery which has carbon sheets between each layer. The sets of

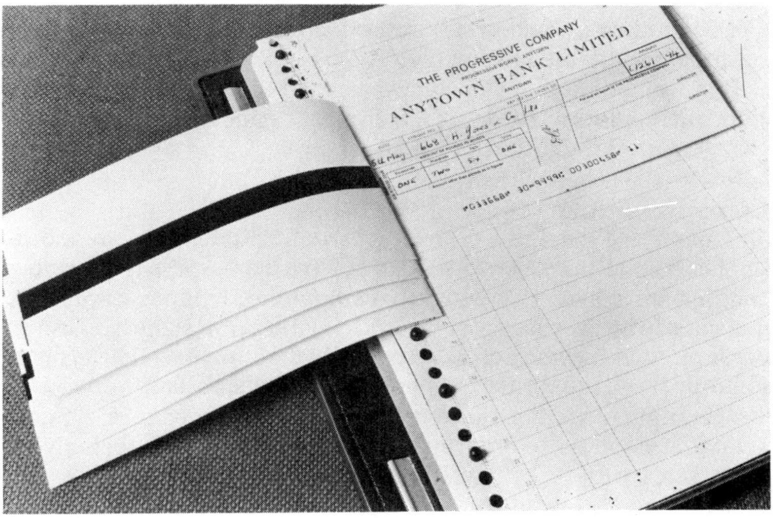

Fig. 19. *Cheque writing and recording system which provides a cash book record simultaneously with the cheque.*
(Courtesy Kalamazoo Ltd.)

documents are joined by perforations and there are bands of sprocket holes on either side. The paper is fed through a special typewriter attachment so that after typing the sheets are folded concertina-style. The documents are then "burst" at the perforations and decollated, i.e. the carbon sheets removed and the sheets separated on a special machine. Document sets may also be made in carbonless paper. The paper is treated so that an image will appear without the use of carbon paper.

Master document—spirit duplicating or copying processes

The document sets explained above are suitable for small organisations which do not need a large number of documents for each transaction. Many larger organisations do need a great many documents, and this is especially true of export orders. It is possible to prepare a master document which contains every detail about the transaction. A series of *masks* are then used to cover the data not required for each individual document. When the masked document is placed on the spirit duplicating machine only the relevant data will be reproduced on the particular form which is passed through it, e.g. bill of lading. The same process can be followed on a copying machine instead of a spirit duplicating machine. A typical master document is illustrated at Fig. 20.

The masked document for reproduction of a Certificate of Insurance is illustrated at Fig. 21.

By this method every document needed throughout the transaction, including job cards, labels for packaging, etc., can be produced from the master document.

Computer output

In Chapters Nine and Ten we discuss a computer system and its applications. Routine systems such as were discussed in the previous chapter are now very frequently computerised. Input documents still have to be prepared and accuracy is vital at this stage because an error in input may be perpetuated throughout the system causing a great deal of trouble for supplier and customer alike.

A computer system can combine many procedures in a transaction, e.g. purchase ordering with stock control and stock inventory, sales orders with credit control, production control and finished goods inventory. All the documents necessary for the transaction to be completed (including job cards, packing labels, etc.) can be prepared and produced by computer. This is explained in more detail in Chapter Ten.

METHODS OF PROCESSING

Sales orders should be processed as soon as possible, which ought to mean immediately they are received. Any shortage of stock is identified and can be ordered without delay. If production departments are involved, scheduling of the work can be arranged or adjusted to take into account orders received. If documents are produced in a set there has to be a time scale for action on the various pieces of paper. If any problem arises it is vital that the sales department is informed so that the person responsible for co-ordination can in turn inform the people concerned.

Systems such as stock control and production control must be carried out continuously. Orders must be acknowledged as they are received. It is usual to send out invoices either when the goods are sent or a few days afterwards. Statements of account are usually sent out monthly. To avoid a large volume of accounts having to be dealt with at one time in the month some organisations use a system known as *cycle billing*.

Cycle billing

Batch processing means working on similar documents or similar groups of documents in batches at predetermined intervals. This is

MASTER DOCUMENT

Start

Exporter
SITPRO EXPORT LIMITED
HIGH STREET
BURTON ON TRENT
STAFFS., DE15 1YZ, ENGLAND

Vehicle Bkg. Ref. 0415 CAN 99999
Tariff Heading 4813
Invoice No. and Date 16418 1Nov 1976
Exporter's Reference 364/B205/190
Buyer's Reference ED1814-97-10-3
F/Agent's Ref. IR76-4740
S.S. Co. Bkg. No. BU64

Consignee (If "Order" State Notify Party and Address)
SITPRO IRAN LTD.
Khiaban Takhte
Shiraz
IRAN

Buyer (If not Consignee)
SITPRO IRAN LTD.
Avenue Ferdowsi
Tehran, IRAN

Name of Shipping Line
Port Account No. 12742

Forwarding Agent/Merchant
Burton Forwarding Ltd.
210 Station St.
Burton on Trent, Staffs., DE15 4ZY

Coding for H.M. Customs ▶ **Destination** IR **ICD** **Container** **Ro Ro (a) (b)** 9 **Flag** GB **Port** LIV

Country of Origin of Goods United Kingdom
Country of Final Destination Iran

Receiving Date(s) 4 - 9 Nov 76
Dock, Container base Etc SE3 Canada Dock
Pre Carriage By Our vehicle
Place of Receipt by Pre-Carrier
Terms of Delivery and Payment CIF Bushire. Payment against sight draft accompanied by documents through British International Bank, Tehran
Vessel/Aircraft Etc Bebington
Port of Loading Liverpool
EUR1 Remarks

Enter Port Scale if Required ▼

Port of Discharge Bushire
Place of Delivery by On-Carrier Shiraz
Insured Value (state Currency) Stg £2660.00
Name of Receiving Authority British Line

Marks, Nos. and Container No.; No. and Kind of Packages, Description of Goods (specify Nature of Hazard if any)

SITPRO
ED1814A
SHIRAZ VIA BUSHIRE
Nos. 1-3
3 Cases: Refills for ballpoint pens (Cat. no. 43-746)

SITPRO
ED1814A
SHIRAZ VIA BUSHIRE
No. 4
1 Case: Electronic duplicator stencils (Cat. no. 42-648)

SITPRO
ED1814C
SHIRAZ VIA BUSHIRE
No. 5
1 Carton: Self-adhesive labels size 70mm x 50mm boxed in packs of 1000 (Cat. no. 40-070)

SITPRO
ED1814D
SHIRAX VIA BUSHIRE
No. 6
1 Case: Self-inking hand operated rubber date stamps (Cat. no. 44-101)

Tariff/Trade Code Number | **Quantity 2** | **Quantity 3**

	Gross Weight (Kg)	Cube (M³)	Net Weight
1)	186	0.126	154
2)	213	0.369	180
3)	26	0.042	24
4)	67 kg	0.175	50 kg

FOB Value (£)

X Customs Free Status | Customs Pre-Entry | Special Stowage | AGI/ATR1/CT – Form type | attached to C273 lodged Customs No. | AG1/ATR1/CT form not required

Invoice Total (State Currency) £ 2416.68
Total Gross Wt. (Kg) 492
Total Cube (M³) 0.712

We certify this invoice to be true and correct and in accordance with our books, also that the goods are of United Kingdom origin. We hereby certify that the prices stated in this invoice are the current export market prices for the merchandise described therein and we accept full responsibility for any inaccuracies or errors therein.

Cost of freight £62.40
Cost of insurance £17.55

Ocean Freight Payable at Liverpool
Number of Bills of Lading 2 Original 4 Copy
Signatory's Company and Telephone Number Sitpro Export Ltd/0283-41835
Name of Authorised Signatory H J Helliar, Chief Clerk
Place and Date of Issue Burton, 1 November 1976
Signature H.J. Helliar

Fig. 20. *Master document from which all documents for an export order can be reproduced. The format of the master is in accordance with international standards.*

(Courtesy SITPRO.)

Start

MASTER DOCUMENT

Exporter	SITPRO EXPORT LIMITED HIGH STREET BURTON ON TRENT STAFFS., DE15 1YZ, ENGLAND
Vehicle Bkg. Ref.	0415 CAN 99999
Tariff Heading	4813
Invoice No. and Date	16418 1Nov 1976
Exporter's Reference	364/B205/190
Buyer's Reference	ED1814-97-10-3
F/Agent's Ref.	IR76-4740
S.S. Co. Bkg. No.	BU64
Consignee (If "Order" State Notify Party and Address)	SITPRO IRAN LTD. Khiaban Takhte Shiraz IRAN
Buyer (If not Consignee)	SITPRO IRAN LTD. Avenue Ferdowsi Tehran, IRAN
Name of Shipping Line	
Port Account No.	12742
Forwarding Agent/Merchant	Burton Forwarding Ltd. 210 Station St. Burton on Trent, Staffs., DE15 4ZY
Coding for H.M. Customs ► Destination / ICD / Container / Ro Ro (a) (b)	IR / / / 9
Flag / Port	GB / LIV
Country of Origin of Goods	United Kingdom
Country of Final Destination	Iran
Receiving Date(s)	4 - 9 Nov 76
Dock, Container base Etc.	SE3 Canada Dock
Terms of Delivery and Payment	CIF Bushire. Payment against sight draft accompanied by documents through British International Bank, Tehran
Pre-Carriage By	Our vehicle
Place of Receipt by Pre-Carrier	
Vessel/Aircraft Etc.	Bebington
Port of Loading	Liverpool
EURI Remarks	
Port of Discharge	Bushire
Place of Delivery by On-Carrier	Shiraz
Insured Value (state Currency)	Stg £2660.00
Name of Receiving Authority	British Line

Enter Port Scale if Required ▼

Marks, Nos. and Container No.; No. and Kind of Packages; Description of Goods (specify Nature of Hazard if any)		Tarrif/Trade Code Number	Gross Weight (Kg)	Cube (M³)
SITPRO ED1814A SHIRAZ VIA BUSHIRE Nos. 1-3	3 Cases: Refills for ballpoint pens (Cat. no. 43-746)		1) 186 2) 213	0.126 0.369
SITPRO ED1814A SHIRAZ VIA BUSHIRE No. 4	1 Case: Electronic duplicator stencils (Cat. no. 42-648)		3) 26 4) 67 kg	0.042 0.175

		Quantity 2	Net Weight	FOB Value (£)
SITPRO ED1814C SHIRAZ VIA BUSHIRE No. 5	1 Carton: Self-adhesive labels size 70mm x 50mm boxed in packs of 1000 (Cat. no. 40-070)		1) 154 2) 180	
		Quantity 3		
SITPRO ED1814D SHIRAX VIA BUSHIRE No. 6	1 Case: Self-inking hand operated rubber date stamps (Cat. no. 44-101)		3) 24 4) 50 kg	

X Customs Free Status / Customs Pre-Entry | Special Stowage | AGI/ATRI/CT – attached to C273 | Form type .... lodged-Customs No .... | AGI/ATRI/CT form not required

Invoice Total (State Currency): £ 2416.68

Total Gross Wt. (Kg): 492 | Total Cube (M³): 0.712

We certify this invoice to be true and correct and in accordance with our books, also that the goods are of United Kingdom origin. We hereby certify that the prices stated in this invoice are the current export market prices for the merchandise described therein and we accept full responsibility for any inaccuracies or errors therein.

Cost of freight £62.40
Cost of insurance £17.55

Ocean Freight Payable at	Liverpool
Number of Bills of Lading	2 Original 4 Copy
Signatory's Company and Telephone Number	Sitpro Export Ltd/0283-41835
Name of Authorised Signatory	H J Helliar, Chief Clerk
Place and Date of Issue	Burton, 1 November 1976
Signature	H.J. Helliar

Fig. 21. *Masked master for reproduction of a Certificate of Insurance. (Courtesy SITPRO.)*

explained in more detail on page 220. An adaptation of batch processing is cycle billing.

Cycle billing means sending out statements of account throughout the month. A certain group of accounts are dealt with each day. This may be scheduled on an alphabetical basis, e.g. accounts of all clients whose names begin with the letter A are dealt with on day 1, B on day 2 and so on throughout the month. It could be organised on the basis of account numbers, e.g. accounts 001–100 on day 1, 101–200 on day 2, etc. The advantages of this system are that the work load is spread throughout the month, avoiding month-end peaks; money is coming in throughout the month; equipment and staff are effectively employed throughout the month.

SUMMARY

1. The system used for processing data depends to a great extent on the volume of work to be done, on the resources available and the objectives, i.e. information required from the processing.

2. Machines range from those which are manually operated to electronic machines including computers.

3. Documents may be produced by handwriting, typewriting, copying, duplicating and computer methods.

4. Two methods of processing are batch processing and cycle billing.

SELF-ASSESSMENT QUESTIONS

Answer all questions as quickly as possible. Do not turn back to the Chapter until you have finished the test.

1. Name three manual data processing systems. Briefly outline the operation of two of them.

2. What information is given on a "master document" from which all documents needed for a transaction are to be produced?

3. What is

(*a*) an autographic register; and

(*b*) an imprinting machine?

4. What is a cash-register machine? What facilities are provided by:

(*a*) an automatic cash register; and

(*b*) an electronic cash register?

5. Name three tasks which might be carried out on an accounting machine.

6. Cheques can be produced by machine.

(*a*) What machines are available?

(*b*) What is the main advantage of these machines?

7. What is meant by the term "one-time writing"? Give an example of its use.

8. Documents raised when an order is taken are often produced in sets.

(*a*) How many methods are there of producing these sets?

(*b*) Give the names of the methods.

(*c*) Explain two of the methods.

9. What is batch processing?

10. What is cycle billing?

ASSIGNMENT

Each person in the class or group is to prepare a list of 25 numerical values containing up to eight digits including two decimal places. Each list is to be reproduced so that everyone in the group may have a copy. (The reproduction should be by the cheapest method possible.)

The lists are then distributed so that every member of the group has a complete set. Each list of figures is to be totalled, the totals being inserted. The list totals are then added together to give a grand total which is to be inserted.

(*a*) In the first round the calculations are to be carried out mentally. Everyone is to start when the tutor says "go". As soon as the calculation is completed each person puts up his hand so that his finishing time can be noted by the tutor. When everyone has finished the accuracy of the results is checked. The winner is the person with the fastest accurate work.

(*b*) The same exercise is to be repeated using calculators. The totals are to be checked off this time. If the total on the machine is different from the written total the new total is to be inserted.

When both exercises have been completed compare the time taken by each individual to work mentally and using the machine, and compare the accuracy. Compare the time taken and accuracy of the group as a whole.

Draw conclusions relating to individuals and to the group.

CHAPTER SIX

Storage and Retrieval of Information

CHAPTER OBJECTIVES

After studying this chapter you should be able to:
* list the types of records on which information is stored;
* choose appropriate methods of storing the various types of records;
* identify and use the standard classifications by which records may be arranged, including sorting documents in accordance with alphabetical filing rules;
* know and keep up-to-date the documents and records involved in maintaining a storage and retrieval system, including control of file and record movements;
* explain the principal methods of indexing.

DEFINITION AND PURPOSE

What is a storage and retrieval system? It is a means of storing documents and records of all types and information contained in any form so that they are:

(*a*) secure from fire hazards, industrial espionage and unauthorised access;
(*b*) easily retrievable by authorised people;
(*c*) kept in good condition for as long as they are required;
(*d*) capable of being added to or subtracted from as necessary;
(*e*) cost a minimum amount of money consistent with the first three criteria mentioned above.

The "system" includes the location, equipment, methods of arrangement, the procedures for storage and retrieval, control of access, and retention policy.

Why are records stored? So that they can be referred to quickly at any time.

TYPES OF RECORDS

What is stored? Records are sets of information about categories of people or things, for example personnel records in a business organisation, financial records, stock records, and correspondence about all manner of topics. These sets of information may be recorded on card, on paper, on film or on a magnetic medium such as tape or disk. Magnetic media will be dealt with in Chapter Nine.

The list below indicates records commonly found in business organisations. It is not comprehensive and you will be able to add to it.

Correspondence: Internal and external letters, memoranda, telegrams, telexes.

Notes of conversations (face-to-face and telephone) and informal meetings.

Minutes of meetings with supporting documentation.

Reports.

Financial transactions and accounts documents.

Forecasts and budget—revenue, expenditure, cashflow, etc.

Legal documents, including insurance policies, contracts, agreements, property deeds.

Company documents including Memorandum and Articles of Association, shareholders register, etc.

Plans, drawings, diagrams, charts.

Production and sales statistics.

Machine maintenance and break-down details.

Lists of stock.

Lists of staff, students, members of associations, etc.

Mailing lists.

Press cuttings.

Information file in which are kept any items of information such as advertisements, names and addresses of maintenance people, e.g. plumbers, and services, e.g. courier, which may one day be useful.

STORING RECORDS

Folders and binders

How are records stored? With the exception of cards, most documents are stored in a folder or binder before being stored in a cabinet. There are many types of such covers to cater for the wide variety of documents which are kept as records, from small scraps of paper to A3-size computer printout. These include plastic and manilla folders, ring binders, lever arch files, ledger binders, suspension binders and box files.

There are three basic types of storage in which folders and binders may be kept—vertical, lateral and horizontal.

Vertical storage

Cards or files are placed one behind the other in boxes, drawers, on or in "wheels", or round drums. Files may be stored in suspension pockets in cabinet drawers. All these methods are illustrated in Figs. 22 to 26.

Fig. 22. *Individual tabbed suspension pockets. Different coloured wafers can be placed on the tabs for colour coding.*
(Courtesy Twinlock UK Ltd.)

Fig. 23. *Linked flat-top suspension pockets (concertina style) with removable individual folders.*
(Courtesy Twinlock UK Ltd.)

Fig. 24. *Rotadex "wheel" card index.*
(Courtesy Rotadex Systems Ltd.)

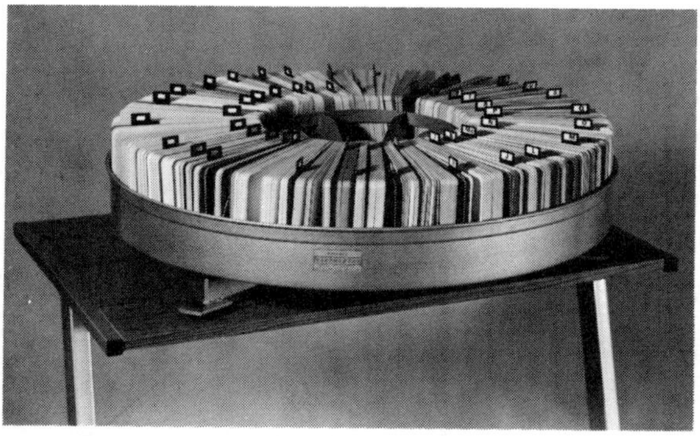

Fig. 25. *Horizontal "wheel" which can accommodate large quantities of index cards.*
(Courtesy Rotadex Systems Ltd.)

Fig. 26. *T-cards can be obtained in different colours and sizes to fit various sizes of board.*

(Courtesy Sasco Ltd.)

For people who need to refer constantly to records, e.g. ledger cards, training records, mobile cabinets are available (*see* Fig. 27).

Lateral storage

Files are placed side by side on shelves or in suspension pockets. The great advantage of lateral filing over vertical filing is the saving of space. Cabinets can be higher and no space is needed for pulling out drawers. Also, lateral cabinets can contain a variety of different types of file, e.g. file folders, lever arch files, printout hangers, etc. A lateral cabinet is illustrated in Fig. 28.

Lateral filing cabinets can be stationary or mobile. Mobile cabinets are mounted on rails on which they can be moved by operating a wheel either mechanically or electrically. Thus several cabinets can be mounted without walking space between them: they are then moved to allow walking space in front of the particular cabinet required. Mobile cabinets are used for systems containing many thousands of files (*see* illustration in Fig. 29).

Rotary lateral shelves are available for lever arch files, which are usually wider at the spine than at the outside edge. The files are placed round a centre spindle, thus saving a lot of space (*see* Fig. 30).

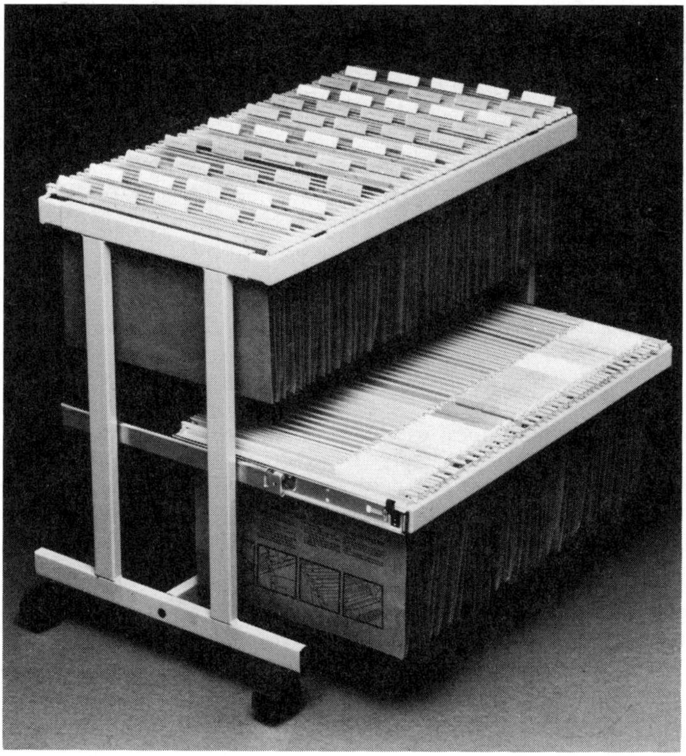

Fig. 27. *Mobile vertical filing trolley.*
(Courtesy Twinlock UK Ltd.)

Horizontal storage

Documents may be laid on top of each other in a pile. Plans and drawings are often stored in this way in cabinets of shallow drawers. Individual documents or files may be stacked in pigeon holes one on top of another, e.g. mail awaiting collection or in the process of being sorted. Documents awaiting filing are usually placed in filing trays, as are papers pending action.

Fig. 28. *Lateral filing cabinet showing the flexibility of this method of filing. (Courtesy Flexiform Ltd.)*

Electrically operated storage

When vast numbers of records have to be stored and retrieved this mammoth task can be made easier and faster by means of electrically operated storage cabinets.

Cards are arranged in trays which are suspended round a drum inside the cabinet. The operator has a control panel of push buttons, and the depression of a particular button brings the required tray to operating level so that the card or cards required can be retrieved. An electrically operated record card storage cabinet is illustrated in Fig. 31.

Similarly, files can be stored laterally on racks which are operated in the same way as the trays of cards. Electrically operated storage cabinets for files are usually at least 10 feet high but can be built through two stories of a building. An electrically operated storage cabinet is illustrated in Fig. 32.

Microcopy storage

The various types of microcopy will be discussed later in the Chapter. They can be stored in standard filing cabinets with special

Fig. 29. *Mobile lateral filing cabinet.*
(Courtesy Herbert Zippel (UK) Ltd.)

Fig. 30. *Rotary lateral, or "roundabout", shelves for lever arch files.*
(Courtesy Rotadex Systems Ltd.)

Fig. 31. *Electrically operated filing cabinet for record cards.* *(Courtesy Kardex Systems (UK) Ltd.)*

sections in them or, better, in cabinets made specifically for the purpose.

INDEXING

An index is anything that "indicates" and is commonly used as a guide to the location of information. Indexes may point to individual items, groups or categories of information and may themselves contain information which eliminates the necessity for further reference. A typical example is a personnel record card, which indicates the number of the file for a person and also gives his or her name and address, perhaps date of birth and other details which are commonly needed.

There are five main types of index, viz. page index, vertical card index, visible card index, strip index and rotary index.

Page index

A page index may be a book or loose-leaf binder with one or more pages for each letter of the alphabet. This type of index is commonly used at the front or back of the minute book, ledger or miscellaneous correspondence file.

Vertical card index

The information is written or typed on small cards, usually A6 or A7, which are then stored in boxes, drawers, or rotary wheels (*see*

Fig. 32. *Electrically operated file storage. The control panel enables the operator to "call for" whichever tray or cradle is required.*
(Courtesy Kardex Systems (UK) Ltd.)

page 78). The cards are normally divided by guide cards, A to Z or numerical, to make location of individual cards easier.

With card indexes it is easy to remove or add cards as required.

Visible card index

The principle behind all kinds of visible card indexes is that the cards overlap, so that one line of entry on each card projects and is visible, thus forming a one line index (*see* Fig. 33).

The card usually contains full details of a particular person or item, e.g. members of staff, customer credit, stock, client contract details, etc.

T-cards, as shown in Fig. 26, can be used for indexing, e.g. trainees enrolled for short courses. As soon as the course has been completed the cards are removed and new ones can be inserted.

Visible loose-leaf binders

For smaller indexes a visible loose-leaf binder serves the same purpose as a visible card index, but at less cost. It is used in the same way and for the same purposes as visible record cards.

Strip index

In every type of office, whatever the organisation, lists of names or numbers are needed for the provision of simple one-line data—telephone numbers, accounts numbers, addresses, minute references. The strip index is specially designed for this purpose.

Fig. 33. *Visible card index allows a single line at the bottom of the card to be used for identification.*

(Courtesy Twinlock UK Ltd.)

The line of information is written or typed on a strip of card which can easily be placed into or removed from a frame which may consist of a series of leaves on a free-standing base, or be attached to a wall, or form pages of a book. The frames or pages can be indexed alphabetically or numerically. A strip index is illustrated at Fig. 34.

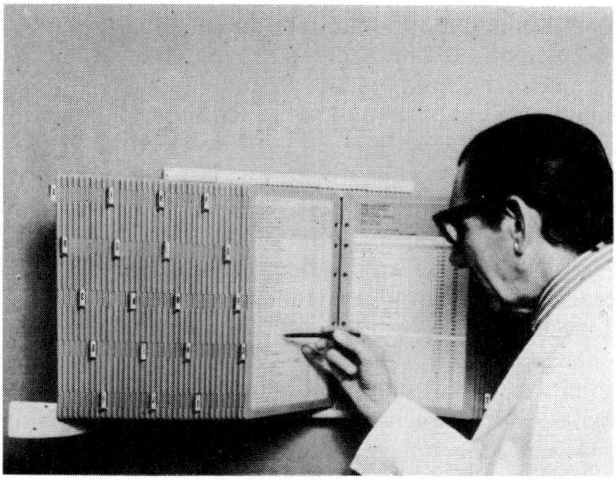

Fig. 34. *Strip index—wall unit. These indexes are also available in book form or as desk stand units.*
(Courtesy Twinlock UK Ltd.)

Signalling

Signalling is used as a method of drawing attention to specific items of information on records. It often takes the form of a coloured transparent wafer which is slid on to the edge of a visible index card or a strip index. Different colours may represent different items of information, e.g. a red wafer may indicate membership of the pension fund on staff records, a blue signal may indicate retirement in the current year. The applications are endless and include stock positions, production controls, credit controls.

LOCATION

Where are records stored? Records may be located in one central place in an organisation, usually known as the file registry. This is common in governmental organisations. They may be stored centrally in a department or they may be held by individuals. The advantages and disadvantages of centralised systems are listed below.

Advantages

(*a*) The procedures of this system can be uniform.

(*b*) All documents relating to one topic are filed together, regardless of the source.

(*c*) Properly trained filing clerks are employed.

(*d*) Access to files can be strictly controlled.

(*e*) The condition of files can be monitored.

(*f*) Equipment can be used more cost-effectively.

(*g*) Filing is more likely to be kept up to date.

Disadvantages

(*a*) There may be a delay in obtaining files.

(*b*) Lack of technical knowledge on the part of filing staff may result in misfiling of some documents.

(*c*) If a document is lost it is difficult for secretarial staff to help find it because of their limited knowledge of the filing system.

In the case of departmental filing, access by managers and other staff may create problems because they frequently will not co-operate by indicating the loan of a file. This point is discussed below under procedures and records.

The main disadvantage of individual filing is that copies of documents are kept by several people, none of whom have a complete record. It also results in a great deal of duplication. Sometimes this may be necessary when various people need to refer constantly to the same documents in the course of their work.

CLASSIFICATION

Documents may be stored and retrieved either by direct or indirect methods. Direct filing means that the documents can be stored or retrieved without reference to an index. Documents and files are arranged in alphabetical order by name, by subject or by geographical location. Indirect filing means that reference has to be made to an index before a document or a file can be located. Each file is allocated a number and is then placed in numerical order. Index cards are filed in alphabetical order. Alternatively a combination of letters and numbers may be used and this is known as alpha-numeric. Again the arrangement may be by name or by subject. Some examples of the various classifications are shown below. There are many variations, of course, but it is wise to use the simplest classification compatible with the type of material. Chronological filing, i.e. the arrangement of documents in date order, is often combined with some other arrangement.

The chart on pages 94–5 shows some of the uses for which each classification is useful, together with its advantages and disadvantages.

Alphabetical classification by name

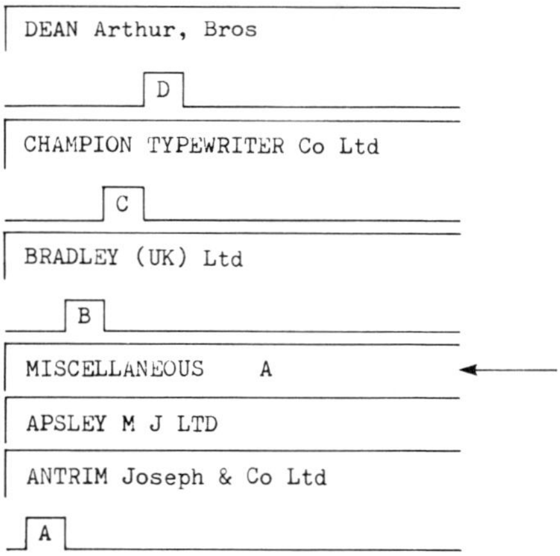

A "Miscellaneous" file is provided when there are very few documents relating to a particular name. Several such sets of documents are filed together.

Note the use of "guide cards" for easy identification of each group of files

Alphabetical classification by subject

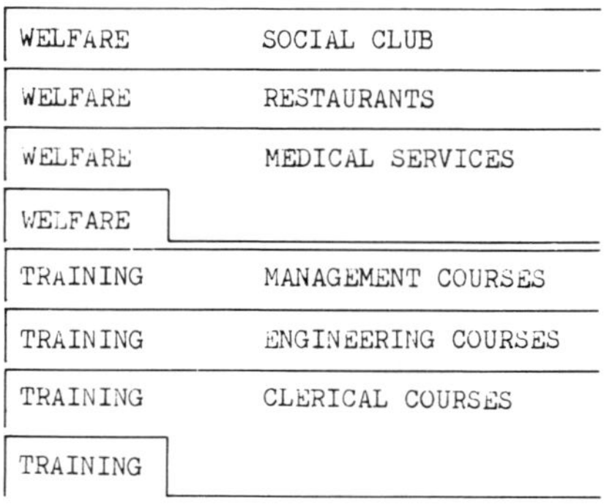

Colour coding can be used, each "tab" being in a different colour and the folders for all topics filed under one subject-heading in a similar colour.

Alphabetical classification by geographical location

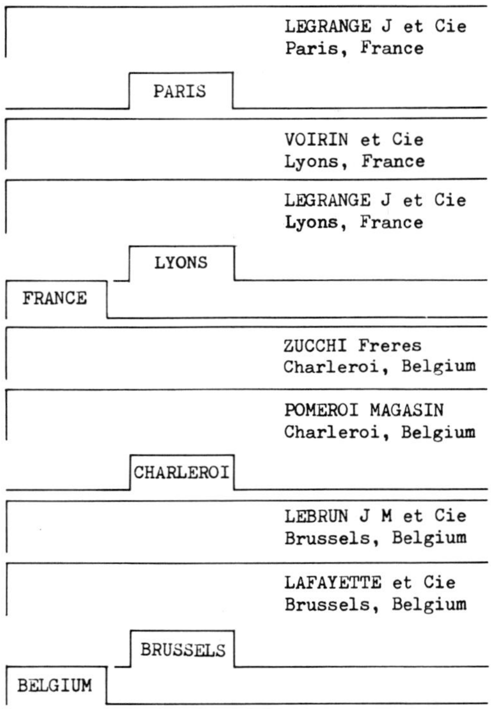

Again colour coding can be used, e.g. a different colour for each country or coloured strips representing countries and towns. This makes the replacement of files in the correct position easier.

Numerical–sequential classification

Files

PRINTRITE PLC	4
ALBERT TRENT ESTATES	3
VICHY FIZZ Co Ltd	2
GENERAL STORES Ltd	1

Index Cards

VICHY FIZZ Co Ltd	2
PRINTRITE PLC	4
GENERAL STORES Ltd	1
ALBERT TRENT ESTATES	3

Numerical–subject classification

File list (or accession register)
(Files would be arranged in
numerical order.)

TRAINING		16
MATERIALS		16.1
Visual Aids	16.1.1	
Supplies	16.1.2	
COURSES		16.2
Clerical	16.2.1	
Management	16.2.2	
Engineering	16.2.3	

Index Cards

	VISUAL AIDS	16.1.1
*	TRAINING	16
	SUPPLIES	16.1.2
†	MATERIALS	16.1
	MANAGEMENT COURSES	16.2.2
	ENGINEERING COURSES	16.2.3
	COURSES	16.2
	CLERICAL COURSES	16.2.1

* The main subdivisions should be listed on the index card.

† The topics within the subdivisions should be listed on the index card.

Alpha-numeric–sequential classification

Files		Index Cards	
LINDEN HOTELS GROUP	L3	LONDON TRADING Co Ltd	L1
LAWSON N M & Co	L2	LINDEN HOTELS GROUP	L3
LONDON TRADING Co Ltd	L1	LAWSON N M & CO	L2
KASTELER WINESHOPS Ltd	K2	KINGSWAY CHEMISTS Ltd	K1
KINGSWAY CHEMISTS Ltd	K1	KASTELER WINESHOPS Ltd	K2

Alpha-numeric–subject classification

The topics are arranged alphabetically before numbers are allocated.

61 Sales
- 61.1 Export
- 61.2 Home

62 Social welfare
- 62.1 Medical Services
- 62.2 Social Club
- 62.3 Sports Club

Terminal digit

File numbers are in groups of two or three read from *right to left*, each group representing a particular location or some other coding.

For example:

Number 123 456 089
could mean the document will be found in
file 089
behind guide card 456
in drawer 123.

Number 076 018 397
could mean
Policy document number 397
in All Risks 018
First taken out in 076 (1976)

Number 06 78 19
Document 19
will be found in file 78
in drawer 06

PROCEDURES

The ultimate aim of any filing system is the quick and accurate retrieval of documents. This can be achieved only when specific procedures for the operation of the system are established and adhered to. Procedures should be worked out in consultation with both operators and users of the system and should cover:

(*a*) storing documents;
(*b*) borrowing files (by the user);
(*c*) retrieving and lending files (including access);
(*d*) passing on files from one office to another;
(*e*) opening new files;
(*f*) closing full files and opening continuation files;
(*g*) segregating active, semi-active and non-active files;
(*h*) transfer of non-active files;
(*i*) destruction of unwanted documents and/or files;
(*j*) movement of and access to confidential files.

Filing clerks should be adequately trained in the procedures and given the authority to enforce them. The users of files should be informed of the procedures and their co-operation in following procedures laid down should be insisted upon.

ALPHABETICAL FILING RULES

The most commonly used method of classification is alphabetical. When this is applied to names of people or organisations there are certain rules which must be followed.

(*a*) File by surname first—initial letter and each subsequent letter:

Sanders
Smiles
Smith

(*b*) File by initial when surnames are the same:

Sanders A
Sanders B D
Sanders B N

(*c*) "Nothing" comes before "something":

Sanders
Sanders D
Sanders Albert

Classification	*Examples of application*	*Advantages*	*Disadvantages*
Alphabetical by name. Note: British Standard BS 1749: 1969 "Specification for Alphabetical Arrangement and the filing order of numerals and symbols" sets out the rules for placing alphabetical files in sequence	Clients/customers. Students. Personnel/staff. Index cards for numerical files and cross-reference	Direct filing. Simple to operate. Maximum flexibility for insertion and extraction of files	Subdivision possibilities limited: if files are grouped, e.g. customers, staff, there is a danger of misfiling unless some form of coding, e.g. colour, is strictly observed. Cross-reference may be necessary
Alphabetical by subject	Products. Supplies/Purchases. Services. Projects, contracts, etc. Index cards for numerical–subject files and subject cross-reference	Direct filing. Subjects can be subdivided	Care must be taken that subdivisions do not overlap other subject areas. Not suitable for a large number of files. Cross-references may be necessary
Alphabetical by geographical location	Sales territories. Import/export. Survey areas. Provision of services. Mail order. Insurance	It is not necessary to remember the names of individual firms. No cross-references likely to be needed	File list necessary when there is a large number of files

Numerical–sequential	Customers, etc. Subjects—where no subdivision is required	Provides a file reference. A block of numbers can be allocated to a particular department	No subdivision possible. Files cannot be grouped in any way. Index essential. File list or Accession Register necessary if volume of files is large
Numerical–subject	Products. Supplies. Services. Functions of an organisation	Flexibility—easy to subdivide and add topics. Can be combined with alphabetical or numerical coding for departments/ sections of the organisation	Index essential. File list or Accession Register necessary. Danger of misfiling when contents of a document are not understood by filing clerk
Alpha-numeric–sequential	Names—clients, trainees, etc. Single topics, i.e. subjects which require no subdivision	Provides a file reference	Index essential. File list or Accession Register necessary. Time consuming unless number of files is very small
Alpha-numeric–subject	Technical material	File groups are preconceived to meet specific needs	Index essential. Flexibility very limited. Trained filing clerk essential
Terminal digit	Customers' accounts and mortgages. Case records. Insurance policy numbers. Contract numbers	Easy to add new files. Easy to identify a misplaced file	Index essential

(*d*) Include prefix as part of name:

De Havilland
Le Marquand
McAlpine

(*e*) Treat M', Mc, Mac as Mac:

McAllister
Macdonald
M'Mahon

(*f*) Treat St and Saint as Saint:

St Andrew's College
Saint Catherine's Hospital

(*g*) Ignore titles of people and "The" and "Co":

Andrews A (Mrs)
Bell J (Prof)
Cash Company Ltd (The)
Cash and Carry Ltd

(*h*) File names consisting of initials before whole names:

NMOS Services
New Milton Dress Co

(*i*) Treat numbers as words:

3001 Services Ltd
2000 Supermarket

(*j*) File by key word of department and ministry names:

Energy, Ministry of
Environment, Dept of the
Foreign Office

RANDOM ACCESS

Electronics have now been applied to filing, in the form of random access. Cards—opaque, aperture, microfilm jackets or transparent envelopes containing microfiche—are edge punched to indicate a letter code. Combinations of letters can be devised ad infinitum to produce new codes. The codes are recorded and the punched cards placed at random in the trays. When a particular item of information is required the relevant code letter keys are depressed and all the cards containing that information are automatically ejected. The system consists of trays (capacity 2,000 cards), a push-button

Fig. 35. *Electronic random access storage. The cards are edge punched by a coder. Any group of cards can be selected within three seconds from up to 20,000 in the storage trays.*
(Courtesy Herbert Zippel (UK) Ltd.)

console and a coder which is activated by the console to edge punch the cards. One console can be used to select from up to ten trays (i.e. 20,000 cards), which can be searched simultaneously in three seconds (*see* Fig. 35).

Random-access filing has many applications, including hospital records, insurance records, intelligence, documentation, inventory control and personnel records.

FILING PROCEDURES AND RECORDS

Storing documents

The following steps are followed when documents are stored.

(*a*) Filing should be done daily, preferably at a set time of day, whenever possible.

(*b*) Documents should be "signed off" for filing in some way, e.g. the supervisor's initials in the right-hand top corner.

(*c*) Documents for filing should be kept in a filing tray or rough sorted into an alphabetical or numerical concertina file until filing time.

(*d*) Prepare the documents for filing by removing unwanted staples and paper clips.

(*e*) Indicate the file reference if it is not already on the document (numerical classification), and the subject or the name under which the document is to be filed.

(*f*) Punch the documents ready for insertion into files.

(*g*) Sort each individual batch, e.g. all documents in "A", ready for insertion in files. This means sorting into individual names or subjects and usually into chronological order as well within each name.

(*h*) Insert into files ensuring the documents are placed in chronological order, if necessary removing documents already filed and replacing in correct sequence.

Opening a new file

When a new file is required, decide the kind of folder or binder to be used and check the colour if colour coding is used. Identify the folder or binder either by writing or typing the number and/or name on the folder or preparing a label to be stuck on it.

If suspension file pockets are used insert a new pocket in the correct sequence in the drawer or cabinet, label it and insert the new file.

New files should be opened only when necessary. Many filing systems are bulging with files which are simply duplicating others in the system.

When a filing system is centralised it is usual to have a form on which the opening of a new file is requested. The request may have to be authorised, by a head of department and/or by the file registry supervisor, to ensure that a file is not already in existence, or that the new file is given the correct name or number.

When a new file is opened it must be included on the file register (or file list), and if the system is not alphabetical it must be included in the index as well.

Opening a continuation file

When a file is filled—an average of 150 to 200 standard pages is usually as many as can be handled easily—a continuation file should be opened. The first file should be marked "Vol. 1", and the date of the first and of the last document should be written on the front cover. The continuation file should be marked "Vol. 2", and so on.

Lending a file

When a file is handed out on loan a record must be made, either by inserting an "out" card in place of the file or in a book. The "out" card should contain the details of the file number or name, the name or designation of the person who has borrowed it and the date on which it was lent (*see* Fig. 36). Where only a few people have access to the files, coloured cards can be used, a different colour for each person. This encourages co-operation since it does not involve writing anything and is quick.

OUT

File Identification	Date borrowed	By whom	Clerk's Initial's	Date Returned
Johnson & Co.	29.9.80	CA	[illegible]	30.8.80.
Chipmunk Eng	2.10.80	DCA	[illegible]	6.10.80
Simple Dress Co.	15.10.80	Prodn. Mgr.	[illegible]	

Fig. 36. *An "out" card should be completed and inserted in the place of any file out on loan.*

In a small suspension filing system a small "out" card, with the file number or name on it, can be kept in each pocket so that only the initials of the person who borrows it and the date need be recorded.

The advantage of recording files on loan in a book is that they are in chronological order and it is easy to check regularly which files have not been returned. On the other hand, if a file is wanted and is not in the cabinet it is necessary to check through the book to see who borrowed it.

Passing slip

When a file is lent it may be passed on from one person to another. This can cause considerable delays in locating files, particularly when the system is centralised. This difficulty can be solved if the person passing on a file completes a passing slip which is sent to the file registry. The filing clerk can then update the "out" card or loan book. A passing slip is illustrated in Fig. 37.

Access control

Certain files are "classified", i.e. secret or confidential, and may be seen by certain people only. There should be an access control list which indicates which files have limited access and the names of the people who may see them. In some cases files may be seen by certain people but not removed from the room in which they are stored.

Removing a document from a file

Documents should not be removed from a file, although occasionally it is essential to do so. A substitution note should then be

FILE PASSING SLIP

To: File Clerk

Please note that File 16/7A

has been passed to Sales Mgr.

at 3 ~~am~~/pm on 31.8.80

Signed P.R. Jones.

Fig. 37. *A passing slip should be completed by any member of staff who passes a file on loan to any other member of staff. The slip is then sent to the filing clerk so that the "out" card can be amended.*

inserted in the file in place of the document. It should contain the name and address of the sender, date, subject, date borrowed and by whom borrowed. The substitution note should then be flagged so that the filing clerk will notice it when carrying out regular file checks and can ensure that it is returned as soon as possible.

Normally when someone needs to borrow a document it should be photocopied and the original replaced in the file immediately.

ACTIVE/SEMI-ACTIVE/NON-ACTIVE FILES

Retention policy

A retention policy means having a list of the types of documents stored with the length of time for which they must be kept. Some documents concerned with the establishment of the organisation and annual accounts, for example, must be kept permanently. Other financial documents concerning the transactions have no statutory retention period but it is recommended they should be kept for six years. A complete list of recommended retention periods can be obtained from the Institute of Chartered Administrators and Secretaries, 16 Park Crescent, London W1.

Active files

Files which are in current use are known as active. These must be readily available in the central filing registry or offices. Active files always contain the current year's documents but may carry more years depending on the type of organisation/department and the type of document.

Semi-active files

In many departments files containing documents from several years back may be referred to—this is particularly true of technical documents. Since such files are referred to irregularly and not as frequently as current files they should be separated from the active files and stored in separate cabinets or on separate shelves. This separation of active from semi-active files means that current files are condensed into a smaller section and are therefore accessible more quickly and more easily.

Non-active files

Many files become non-active, i.e. they are not referred to, after a year or two. They must, however, be kept until the expiry of the retention period laid down. These non-active files should be taken from the semi-active section and stored in sequence in storage boxes. The boxes are then sent to a storage place, often referred to as "archives". This storage place may be a basement, or attic, or a separate building. The files can always be recalled for reference when necessary.

In some organisations documents in non-active files are microcopied and then destroyed, unless they must be kept permanently. Microcopying is explained later in the chapter.

Dead files

When a file is closed, e.g. a particular project is finished, the file is dead and can be sent to archives. Until the file is totally destroyed its number should not be used for any other file.

Segregating files

Files should be "spring-cleaned" at least once a year. Some types of records can be moved annually from active into semi-active, and from semi-active into non-active. This is usually possible with financial documents once the annual accounts have been prepared and audited. Any other types of work may have to be carefully scrutinised, certain files being retained in the active area even though their contents range over several years.

Transitory files

There are many documents which do not need to be filed once the subject has been dealt with or has passed: e.g. memoranda concerning holidays—except in the personnel department; invitations and replies—the addresses can be noted. Any document which is unlikely to be needed permanently on a file can be placed in a transitory file for the current month. At the end of the month the documents are sorted and those not wanted any longer are destroyed. The remainder are sorted again after two months and again after three months. Any documents still wanted after three months should be stored in the permanent files. It will generally be found there are very few documents left for permanent filing. It must be stressed that this system is suitable in certain types of organisation only. An example is a professional institution with thousands of members. Once correspondence from the members has been dealt with it may never be needed again.

FOLLOW UP

An efficient follow-up system is essential. This means that incoming documents may be acknowledged only and dealt with after information has been obtained. Out-going documents may have to be "chased" for a reply. When a document is to be brought forward (or brought up) for action, or for any other reason, the required "bf" date should be written in the right-hand top corner. The filing clerk or secretary then ensures that it will be brought forward by:

(*a*) noting the document/file name/number in a diary at the appropriate date (it is best to keep a diary specifically for this purpose); or

(*b*) noting the details at the appropriate date on a diary card—a card for each month of the year, divided up for the days (suitable for a small amount of bring forward); or

(*c*) making a copy of the document or writing a note and placing it in a diary file, which may be a concertina type or a series of folders; or

(*d*) making a note on a pre-printed slip which is then filed in chronological order of "bf" date.

Concertina file

The concertina file has pockets labelled 1 to 31 with a spare pocket at the back. The documents to be brought forward in the current month are placed in the appropriate pocket; those to be brought forward later are placed in the pocket at the back.

Diary files

Diary files consist of a separate file for each day, 1 to 31, and a separate folder for each month, January to December. Copies of documents or notes are placed in the appropriate numbered file for the current month and the appropriate file for subsequent months. It may even be necessary to have files for more than one year ahead. A diary filing system is suitable when there is a great deal of "bring forward" material, e.g. in personnel and training departments and in financial work.

A further advantage of this system is that other items can be filed in "bring forward", e.g. reminders to prepare documents for meetings, make reservations, etc.

Follow-up slip

In organisations where filing is centralised, an excellent system is for the person requiring a file to be brought forward to complete a small diary slip giving the file identification, date required and by whom. The slips are passed to the filing clerk who files them in chronological order of "bring forward" date. Each day the filing clerk removes the slips for that day and obtains the files required, attaches the slips to the relevant files and sends them to the people who requested them.

This system could be operated by an individual who would keep slips to note "bring forward" requests and file them chronologically.

DESTROYING DOCUMENTS

Documents are normally destroyed either at the expiration of the established retention period or when they become non-active and can be microcopied (*see* below).

Non-confidential documents can be made into scrap pads. Those which are unsuitable for further use can be torn up. (It is a good habit to tear up any unwanted paper: this ensures that nothing gets thrown away in readable form.)

Confidential documents are either burned—some companies have an incinerator for this purpose—or are shredded. Shredders vary in size, depending on the volume of paper to be processed. The shredded paper can be used for packing material. A large volume shredder is illustrated in Fig. 38. When operating shredders it is essential to follow safety instructions to the letter. A gentleman has been known to lose his tie while leaning over the machine!

MICROCOPYING

Microcopying or microfilming is simply a means of retaining information by photographing records to reproduce them as miniature films. The films are negative copies and after developing are stored as a permanent record often instead of the records themselves. To view documents which have been microfilmed a machine called a "viewer" or "reader" is used, which projects the film on to a screen for reading. When a hard copy, i.e. a copy on paper, of the document is required the relevant film is processed by a "reader/printer".

Fig. 38. *Large volume shredder for disposing of computer printout and other bulky documentation.*

(Courtesy Rexel Ltd.)

Preparation of records for microcopying

Records which are to be filmed must have all fasteners removed and should be arranged in the exact sequence in which they are required. Batches of documents must be clearly identified so that the name/number of the file can be printed on the microcopy.

Filming the records

Records are photographed by a camera, sometimes referred to as a "recorder". The film is then processed. Each sheet, roll or cassette of film is marked with the appropriate identification. A special camera called a "plan camera" is used for large documents such as drawings.

Types of microcopy

There are five types of microcopy.

Roll

All film is usually first made in a continuous roll, so this is the cheapest and easiest storage method, but with a large number of frames to a 200 ft (61m) roll of film, reference might be slow.

Cassette

The roll of film is housed in a plastic box which is just clipped into the machine. It is slightly more expensive than single-spooled roll film, but gives better security against dust and is quicker to insert into the machine.

Jacket

Small strips of film are slid into channels of a transparent folder, which offers a neat, easy way of keeping consecutive frames of a small series; it can be added to from time to time, e.g. medical case histories, correspondence on particular subjects, etc. Each jacket is thus equivalent to a folder with a variable number of frames. Up to seventy-five images of letter-sized documents can be stored in one jacket. Jackets are available in various sizes with channels arranged in different ways to cater for a wide range of documents.

Microfiche

This is a rectangular sheet of microfilm with rows of images. A standard A6 fiche (105 × 148 mm) normally contains sixty to ninety-eight images, depending on the reduction ratio, but can hold up to 3,000. This is the kind used extensively for parts lists in big store departments, aeroplane parts at airports, etc. Until recently microfiche could not be updated but a new technique has been developed to make this possible.

Aperture cards

An individual microfilm (35mm or 70mm) is mounted in an aperture in a punched card, which can be punched with related information and later extracted as required. This is widely used for engineering drawings, and proved invaluable for communicating the 300,000 drawings made in connection with the Concorde project between the UK and France. Quick retrieval is possible by using a punched-card sorter.

The various types of microcopy are illustrated in Fig. 39.

Any form of microfilm can be read on a machine called a microfilm reader. The individual page required is presented on a screen. A hard (paper) copy can be reproduced if needed on a reader/printer such as the machine illustrated at Fig. 40.

Advantages of microcopying

(*a*) Space is saved by replacing bulky files by compact cartons of film. A 100ft reel of 16mm film recording 3,200 letters takes about 131 cubic centimetres of space, compared with the equivalent 8,125 cubic centimetres needed for six and a half reams of paper—a saving of 98 per cent. Filing equipment is also substantially reduced.

(*b*) Time is saved by copying documents at great speed—as much as six or seven times faster than by any other method.

(*c*) Safety of original documents is ensured by substituting microfilm records for those in general use.

(*d*) Durability of records is increased, as film is more wear-resistant than paper.

(*e*) Business systems make use of microfilming by photographing current records instead of making carbon copies of them.

(*f*) Where constant reference to microfilmed records is required, thousands of microfilm records can be accommodated in a desk, thus saving the movement of staff to filing cabinets.

(*g*) COM (computer originated microfilm) processing allows documents to be produced as micro images which can be retrieved on a special terminal to a computer. The image can be printed out full size if required. More information on the integration of computer-assisted image processing into a system is given in Chapter Nine.

(*h*) Low cost distribution: if information has to be sent by airmail, which is expensive, microcopying can reduce postage costs substantially.

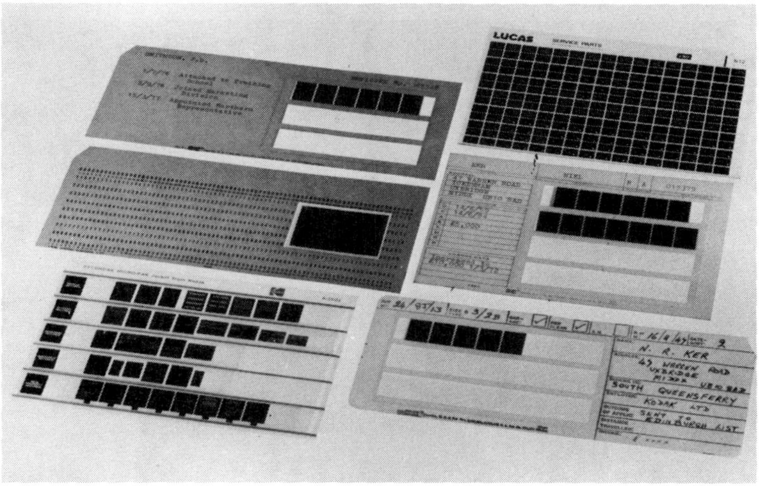

Fig. 39(a). *Microfilm—unitised formats. Left (front to rear): a jacket, an aperture card and a Tab-Jac; right (front to rear): a translucent Tab-Jac, an "Ektawrite" film folio and a microfiche.*

Fig. 39(b). *Microfilm—roll film formats. Front left: open spool 16mm; front right: open spool 35mm; back left: open spool 16mm in "Ektamate" self-threading magazine; back right: open spool 16mm in "Thread Easy" magazine; centre: 16mm microfilm in magazine.*

(Courtesy Kodak Ltd.)

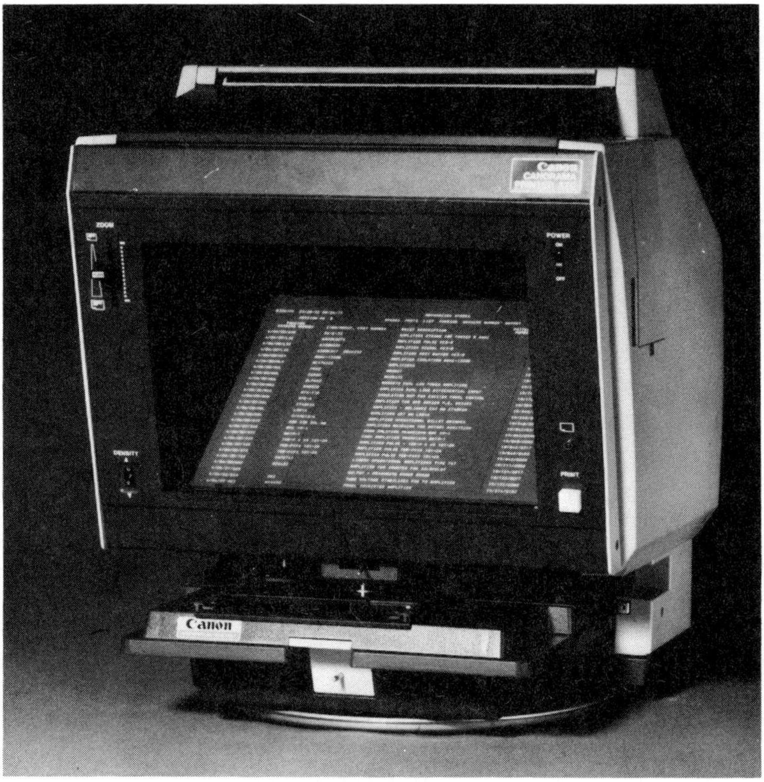

Fig. 40. *Microfilm reader/printer.*
(Courtesy Canon Business Machines UK Ltd.)

(*i*) There is fixed file continuity. This means that it is not possible to misplace or misfile any of the records on microfilm, as it would be with loose papers in a folder.

Disadvantages of microcopying

(*a*) If frequent reference is required, it may be relatively slow, because the film has to be viewed through the reader.

(*b*) On many microfilm readers, location of a particular frame may be difficult, causing further delay and frustration.

(*c*) It is an advantage that microfilm cannot be altered, thus preventing fraudulent alteration, but sometimes it is necessary to make corrections or insertions to the stored information. Not all types of microfiche can be updated.

(*d*) Film may be unreadable due to poor originals, e.g. indistinct carbon copy or processing with stale chemicals.

(*e*) The labour involved in sorting papers, removing pins, etc., may make a microfilming project very expensive, in which case cheaper storage space might be more advisable.

(*f*) Unless care is taken in the matter of choice, the reduction ratio of some documents can be so extreme as to make them difficult to read on the reader.

(*g*) Records on coloured paper are sometimes difficult to reproduce.

Applications of microcopying

Because of the enormous saving of space when documents are microcopied the most obvious application is photographing of non-active records so that originals can be destroyed. Microcopying is also used for information in current use. Some examples are given below.

(*a*) Technical and professional articles to be sent to a world-wide readership.

(*b*) Maintenance manuals, e.g. for motor car distributors and agents.

(*c*) Cycle billing. The sales, receipts and return vouchers are filed as they come in until the appropriate cycle date comes round. The details from the vouchers are then entered on a statement, which is prepared in duplicate. The carbon copy of the statement is kept in the files to give the pick-up balance (if necessary) for the next month's statement. The top copy of the statement together with the vouchers are then microfilmed, and as soon as the film is processed, statement and vouchers are sent to the customer. The records are photographed in chronological and alphabetical order so that it is easy to locate any one of them on a reader should it be necessary to refer to them.

Legality of filmed records

It is now generally accepted that if an organisation has a microcopying system for all or major sections of its records, microcopied documents are acceptable in a court of law as evidence.

REORGANISATION OF A FILING SYSTEM

When undertaking the reorganisation of a filing system it is essential to investigate fully the requirements of the new system before taking action. The questions below indicate the lines on which the investigation should be carried out.

Is it essential to store all documents?
What type/s of documents are to be stored?
What number of each type of document is to be stored?
From where does each type of document emanate?
Who will refer to the stored documents?
For what purpose will the stored documents be referred to?
For how long does each type of document remain:
active?
semi-active?
For how long must each type of non-active document be retained? (Refer to official suggested periods.)
What is the delay tolerance for retrieval of each type of document?
Who should have access to the stored documents?
What security is needed?
Who should have the authority to store and retrieve documents/files?
Are the retrieved documents/files passed from one person to another? If so, what file movement control is necessary?
Is the system likely to be enlarged in volume and/or expanded to take in new types of documents over the next 3 to 5 years?

Answers to these questions should form the basis on which to decide

(*a*) suitable folders/binders for each type of document
(*b*) appropriate location for each type of document
(*c*) suitable storage shelves/cabinets
(*d*) control procedures for access to files, storage and retrieval of documents, opening new files
(*e*) retention policy
(*f*) control procedures for destruction of non-active documents.

When analysing the requirements it may be found helpful to use a chart such as the one illustrated on pages 112–13.

Retention Policy

When a decision has to be made about retention periods for various types of documents it may be helpful to prepare a chart. The chart illustrated below indicates specimen periods for active, semi-active and non-active retention.

Type of document	*Active*	*Semi-active*	*Non-active*
General Correspondence	1 yr	1 yr	3 yrs
Technical Correspondence	3 yrs	3 yrs	7 yrs
Invoices	1 yr	1 yr	4 yrs
etc.			

Documents may be microfilmed at any stage though semi-active or non-active stages may be more appropriate for general business documents.

SUMMARY

1. A storage and retrieval system consists of records, loose or in folders or binders, arranged in appropriate sequence in cabinets located either in a central registry, at a central point in a department or in individual offices, with control procedures prescribed for access, file movement and retention.

2. Records may be stored vertically in filing cabinets with drawers, laterally on shelves or suspended on racks, horizontally in trays, pigeon holes or shallow drawers. Lateral filing cabinets can be mobile so that only one aisle is provided for several cabinets which can be moved as required, thus saving space. Electronically operated cabinets allow large quantities of cards or files to be stored together with easy retrieval by operation of control buttons.

3. There are five main methods of indexing which may be used when direct filing is not possible, for example when information on individual items—parts of a machine, people (personnel, training, medical records) is needed, or when reference to specific pieces of information may be sought, e.g. minutes, sections or topics in a report.

4. The three principal classifications are alphabetical, numerical and chronological. Combinations of these classifications, e.g. alpha-numerical, may be used. Most files have the documents

Analyse the Requirements

Materials	*People*	*Location*	*Equipment*
What categories of materials are to be filed?	Who needs to use each of the categories of documents?	Where are they stored?	What protection is needed? Fire Confidentiality
What documents, etc. need to be filed? (Prepare a list.) Source Quantity Frequency of receipt Frequency of retrieval Size Type—original carbon copy, etc.	Purpose of retrieval? (Time factor may be involved.)	Where are they needed?	What equipment is used now?
	Who does the filing?	What is the tolerable delay for each type of document?	
	Who *needs* access?	What would be the ideal location for each type of document?	
	Who should *not* be allowed access?		

How are they currently filed?

When are they filed?

Why are they filed?
Reference only?
Working documents?

When do they become
semi-active?
non-active?
(For how long are they active?)

Is highlighting needed, e.g. retrieval for specific purpose? (Colour coding)

Anyone colour blind? (Men)

arranged chronologically within them. Standard alphabetical filing rules should be followed when storing according to the names of people and organisations.

5. Filing procedures and records should be established for storing documents, opening new and continuation files, access control and file movement.

6. Files should be segregated into active, semi-active, non-active and dead (or closed). A retention policy should be established by which different kinds of record are kept for a specific period and then destroyed.

7. A follow-up system is essential and may be operated with a diary (book), diary card or diary files (concertina or file folders).

8. Non-confidential documents can be destroyed by using them for scrap pads, or tearing up. Classified and confidential documents should be destroyed by burning or shredding.

9. Microcopying saves a vast amount of space so is frequently used for non-active records. Various types of microcopy are used for active and semi-active records because reference is quick and storage problems are solved.

10. There are five main types of microcopy, each of which has particular advantages for specific applications.

SELF-ASSESSMENT QUESTIONS

Answer all questions as quickly as possible. Do not turn back to the Chapter until you have completed this test.

1. Refer to the list, page 76, of the types of records which may be found in an organisation. Try to add at least five other types of record.
2. What advantages has lateral filing over vertical filing?
3. What is suspension filing?
4. For what purposes is horizontal filing used?
5. Explain the term "indexing".
6. If an index is kept on separate cards, size A7, how might they be stored?
7. Describe a visible card index and suggest three uses of it.
8. List the advantages and disadvantages of a page index and a card index.
9. What is "signalling"? For what purpose is it used?
10. What are the advantages of a central filing system within an organisation?
11. List ten alphabetical filing rules, giving an example to illustrate each rule.

12. Explain briefly with examples of application: (*a*) direct filing; (*b*) numerical–subject classification; (*c*) terminal digit classification; (*d*) random access; (*e*) alpha-numerical–sequential classification.

13. Imagine you are explaining filing procedures to a new colleague. Explain: (*a*) how to open a new file; (*b*) an "out" card and its purpose; (*c*) a passing slip; (*d*) a file register; (*e*) an access control list.

14. Six people in your office need to borrow files which are in your care. They have refused to co-operate by completing "out" cards. What possible remedies are there?

15. What is meant by the term "retention policy"? Why is it necessary to have a retention policy?

16. What is a dead file?

17. Not every piece of paper needs to be filed permanently. By what method can you ensure such documents are kept for as long as they might be wanted without actually storing them in the system?

18. What is a follow-up system and what methods of operation are there?

19. Why is a follow-up system vital to the smooth running of an organisation?

20. Your supervisor asks you to destroy the contents of a confidential file. What steps would you take?

21. What is microcopying?

22. Briefly explain the five main types of microcopy.

23. If you are asked to send a file of records for microcopying how would you prepare them?

24. What are the disadvantages of microcopying?

25. Under what circumstances are microcopy records acceptable as evidence in a court of law?

ASSIGNMENT

You start work in a new job in which you have responsibility for the storage and retrieval of all records on paper and card. There is a system in existence but after studying it carefully you find you cannot understand it. There are some files with names of people and organisations and some with subject names. There is a drawer of files with numbers, for which you can find no index. There is no file register. Some files are very thick, others contain only one or two documents. Some files date back eight years with the last document being several years old.

Documents are stored in plastic folders, manilla folders, spring clip files, lever arch files—the latter on a shelf. There is a four-drawer filing cabinet and a lateral filing cabinet. Cards are in six separate boxes.

You speak to your supervisor who says that normally reference is made to records up to eighteen months, possibly two years, old. Some records need to be kept for longer. You are given "carte blanche" to reorganise the system. If you need new equipment the expenditure would have to be authorised.

Consider carefully how you would set about the task of re-organisation and write down, step by step, exactly what you would do.

CHAPTER SEVEN

Reproducing Information

CHAPTER OBJECTIVES

After studying this chapter you should be able to:
* explain the methods of reproducing data and documents;
* identify the appropriate method of reproduction in given circumstances;
* compare the cost of different methods of reproduction.

DEFINITION AND PURPOSE

What is the reproduction of information, or reprography, as it is known? It is the production of more than one copy of a document by a means which produces facsimile, i.e. identical, copies, thus obviating the need for checking each copy.

Why is it done? People who send documents or information of any kind to other people may need to refer to the originals from time to time. Therefore a copy must be kept. Copies of documents are often needed by several people within and/or outside the organisation. The purpose of reprography is therefore to distribute identical information, presented in identical format, to a number of people wherever they may be.

There are two main categories of document reproduction. They may be produced simultaneously with the document, or they may be reproduced from a prepared master.

SIMULTANEOUS REPRODUCTION

Simultaneous reproduction involves the use of some form of carbon. It can be used when a document is being produced in handwriting, on a typewriter, or on a printer linked to a word processor or computer.

Carbon paper

There are various weights and types of carbon paper. The best type of carbon paper for typewritten copies is a film-based solvent carbon. As the carbon is transferred on to the copy paper when the type segment strikes it, the carbon is redistributed from the surrounding area. This greatly lengthens the life of the carbon. It is also cleaner to handle than the older type of carbon paper made with a mixture of waxes, oils and pigments.

Types of carbon include the following.

One-time carbon
These are normally pre-collated in sets of forms. This sort of carbon is thrown away after use, although many typists find they can use them subsequently two or three times for letters.

Carbon backing
Carbon is deposited on the back of a specific area of a form from which information is required on copy forms.

Carbon-free paper
There are two types of carbon-free paper which can be used for simultaneous copying. Chemical carbonised paper is made with two kinds of coating. When one copy only is required the top sheet is coated on the back with an emulsion consisting of millions of tiny capsules containing colourless dyes. The bottom sheet is coated on the front with a special clay. When pressure is applied the capsules burst and the dye penetrates the clay surface of the sheet beneath, producing an image. When more than one copy is required intermediate sheets are inserted which have both an emulsion coating on the back and a clay coating on the front. Carbon-free paper is made in a variety of colours.

Another type of carbon-free paper can be used with plain paper top sheets. A deposit consisting of dye capsules and chemical on the front of the copy paper produces a coloured image when struck by a type segment. Although more expensive than ordinary copy paper used with carbon paper, the time saved in collating carbon packs should more than offset the difference.

Some examples of the use of carbonised paper are given below.

(*a*) Insurance—proposal forms.

(*b*) Garages—work dockets, forecourt credit account invoices, stores requisition.

(*c*) Catering and hotel trade—hotel bills, breakfast order to be hung on bedroom door, booking forms, two or three-part registration forms.

(*d*) Retail electrical trade—three-part repair tickets, goods inward advice notes, stock control.

(*e*) Police—charge sheets.

(*f*) General—purchase orders, invoice sets with advice note, despatch note, etc., credit notes, statements, salary advice slips, requisition forms for personnel, stationery, etc., internal memoranda, hire purchase agreements, customs declaration slips.

Copies can be reproduced using a carbon or carbon-free paper method when only a small number of copies is required. The number of legible copies which can be obtained depends on a number of factors, including the weight of the carbon paper, the weight and finish (smoothness) of the typewriting paper, the hardness of the typewriter platen or cylinder, the type style and the type of ribbon used—better copies are usually obtained from carbon ribbons than from ribbons made of material such as nylon.

REPRODUCTION FROM A PREPARED MASTER

Types of reprography which require a prepared master (either handwritten or typewritten) include spirit duplicating, ink duplicating, offset duplicating and printing, and copying.

Spirit duplicating

Art paper with a shiny surface is used either with a sheet of coloured hectograph carbon (sometimes called a transfer sheet) or a hectograph ribbon on the typewriter. Spirit masters may be handwritten or typewritten and can also be prepared on a thermal (heat) copier. The transfer sheet is placed behind the master sheet, carbon face up so that an image is created on the back of the master. This master is then placed on a rotary spirit duplicating machine with the carbon image outside so that as the drum is turned a sheet of paper is fed under it, transferring an image from the master on to the paper. This process is achieved by moistening the paper with spirit as it is passed under the roller. The image on the master is gradually eroded until it becomes too faint for reproduction.

It is a quick and cheap method of reproducing documents, particularly suitable for schools, restaurants, factory offices, clubs, etc. It is the only method of reproduction by which a variety of colours can be reproduced simultaneously. This is achieved by using different-coloured transfer sheets when preparing the master. Both manual and electric duplicators are available.

Ink duplicating

Ink duplicating requires a stencil master which has to be "cut". This is done either by hand, using a special stylus pen, on a typewriter, with the ribbon switched to non-operation, on a word processor, thermal copier or electronic stencil cutting machine (also called an electronic scanner). A stencil cutting machine is particularly useful when copies of complicated drawings or designs are required and when material consists of a variety of items which may be cut from journals, etc. An electronic stencil cutter is illustrated in Fig. 41.

A stencil consists of a wax sheet and a thin card backing sheet attached to a card head on which is punched a pattern of holes. These holes allow the stencil to be attached to a drum on an ink duplicating machine. When the drum is turned, paper is fed under the drum and ink is squeezed from behind the stencil through the images which have been cut into it, thus reproducing a copy on the paper.

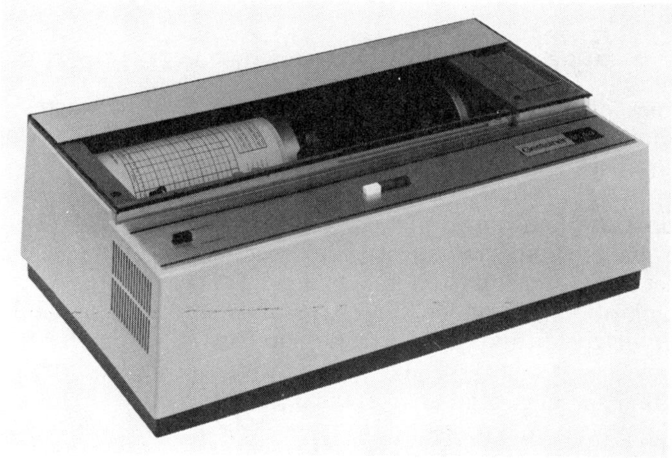

Fig. 41. *Electronic scanner for cutting a stencil from an original document. (Courtesy Gestetner Ltd.)*

Colour reproduction is possible, but a separate run is necessary for each colour, and parts of the machine and the ink have to be changed for each run. A special semi-absorbent paper has to be used to avoid the off-setting of the printed image from the copy underneath after running off, as the ink dries fairly slowly. If copies on non-absorbent paper are wanted it is possible to use a special attachment containing interleavers, which are released one at a time on top of each copy, thus avoiding the offsetting.

Duplicating machines are made to take standard width stencils, i.e. to produce copies on A4 and foolscap paper, and are also made to take double size stencils to produce copies on A3 and brief size paper. A fully automatic ink duplicating machine is illustrated at Fig. 42.

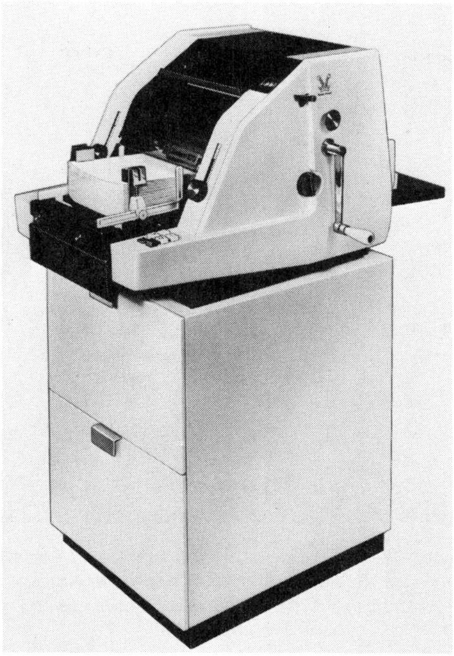

Fig. 42. *Fully automatic ink duplicator controlled by operating push-button keys.*

(Courtesy Roneo Alcatel Ltd.)

Ink duplicating is suitable for materials used internally and for reports, training materials, etc., which are to be distributed outside the organisation, provided sufficient attention is paid to the standard of reproduction.

Another application of ink duplicating is addressing machine "plates". Some of the stencil plates are guaranteed for 10,000 applications. An electrically operated addressing machine is illustrated at Fig. 43.

Offset lithography

Offset lithography has been used for almost two hundred years and is still carried out on the same basic principle, i.e. the antipathy of grease to water. A greasy image is produced on the master, known as a plate, by writing, typewriting, photography and certain copying processes. The plate is affixed to a cylinder on an offset machine. The roller comes in contact with inked cylinders and water, and the

Fig. 43. *The Roneo Neopost Stielow 5400 electrically operated addressing machine. Accepts cassettes of master stencil cards and automatically prints up to 7,500 addresses an hour on to envelopes or labels. Selective addressing can also be done.*

(Courtesy Roneo Alcatel Ltd.)

image is then offset on to another roller (known as a blanket) on which it produces the negative impression. Paper is then fed between the blanket and an impression roller and receives a positive imprint. The offset process is illustrated in Fig. 44.

Plates are made of metal, plastic, paper and parchment. Metal plates are prepared photographically from an original. They are either made from copper, which is expensive but gives an unlimited number of copies, or aluminium, which can give up to 25,000 copies.

Parchment, paper and plastic plates can be prepared by hand, on a typewriter or word processor printer, or on a special machine called a "platemaker". From 1,000 to 10,000 copies can be obtained from a plate, depending on its quality.

Offset machines range from simple duplicators which can be operated by any office worker, to complex and sophisticated printing machines which need specially trained operators. Offset reproduction has a professional appearance which may be lacking in other duplicating methods.

An automatic offset duplicator is illustrated at Fig. 45.

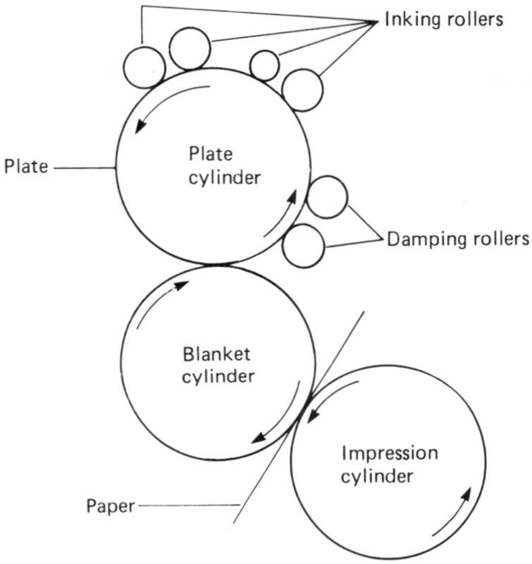

Fig. 44. *The offset process.*

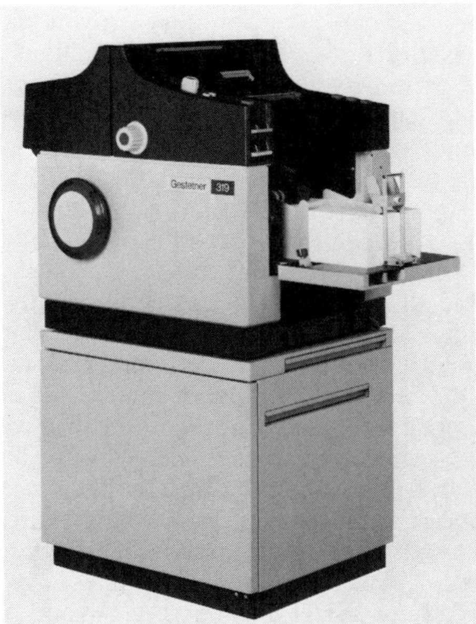

Fig. 45. *Gestetner Model 319 automatic offset duplicator.*
(Courtesy Gestetner Ltd.)

Copying

There are eight basic copying processes, some of which are more commonly used than others. The eight processes are:

(*a*) reflex;
(*b*) diffusion transfer;
(*c*) gelatine transfer;
(*d*) direct positive;
(*e*) dyeline;
(*f*) electrostatic;
(*g*) thermal; and
(*h*) dual spectrum.

It is possible to produce a facsimile hard copy, i.e. paper copy, by any of these methods except dyeline. Microcopying is also a copying process but is not included here as it is primarily a means of storing information and data rather than of producing additional copies.

Of these eight processes only electrostatic copies and thermal copies can be made directly from an original. The other six processes all involve the production of a negative master from which a copy or number of copies are made.

The most commonly used method in offices today is one of the two electrostatic processes. These are xerographic, or plain paper, copying, which is a dry process, and dry copying on to sensitised paper, known as electrofax. On the latest machines the quality of reproduction is extremely good. The speed of reproduction varies from about eight copies a minute up to 120 copies a minute on a sophisticated high-speed copy-duplicator.

Nearly all the latest machines allow copying from any original, handwritten, typewritten or printed. Most of them are not "blind" to any colour, although blue presents a difficulty with some machines and yellow is often difficult to reproduce clearly. It is usual to be able to copy from books. This facility is known as flat-bed copying. Many facilities are now available including reduction and enlargement of originals, simultaneous double-sided copying, multiple feed which allows a number of originals to be stacked in a hopper feed so that as the number of copies required off each original is completed a new original is fed on to the platform; runs can be interrupted so that another master can be copied and then the original run can be continued. Many plain paper copiers are versatile enough to reproduce on to paper varying from 65gsm to 130gsm or even heavier card. Some machines have twin cassettes which hold two different sizes of paper, e.g. A4 and A3. A button is pressed to select the size required for any particular copy or run of copies. The density of the image can also be controlled to make it darker or lighter. It is possible to produce items as small as A6 on some machines. A number of machines take A3, but many more take up to B4 only, which is adequate for accounts and legal work. Overhead projector transparencies can also be produced on plain paper copiers. A copier which has many of these features, the Xerox 9200, is illustrated at Fig. 46.

Fig. 46. *Xerox 9200 copying machine. Every operation has push-button control, including enlargement, reduction, double-sided (or reverse) copying and collation.*

(Courtesy Rank Xerox Ltd.)

On many of the copiers using sensitised paper, the paper is in a roll which is cut to the required size as each copy is made.

One important application of copying is the reproduction of sets of masters from one original. This is achieved by masking the unwanted data so that only the data required on a particular document is reproduced. The mask is called an "overlay".

Colour copying

Reproduction of colour printing is now possible in colour. The copying is achieved by an electronic process so the machines are expensive (£30,000+) and have to be maintained by a skilled operator. There is some concern about copyright and security aspects of colour copying. Because the reproduction is so faithful there could be implications for the worlds of art, publishing and finance, among others.

Summary

The methods of preparing masters, the advantages and disadvantages of the various reprographic processes and their applications are summarised on pages 129 to 132.

CHOICE OF COPIER

For general office use electrostatic copying is now general, the plain paper copier (PPC) being most widely used. There are many machines on the market, each manufacturer claiming some "extra" useful facility. Choosing a machine can be difficult. A full knowledge of requirements is essential before a decision is made. Some of the factors which must be considered are:

(*a*) the size and nature of originals to be copied;
(*b*) the density of the original and the density of print required;
(*c*) whether copying is required on both sides of the paper from one or double-sided originals;
(*d*) the number of copies required at a run, and the number likely to be required per month/year;
(*e*) the cost of copy paper for different types of machine;
(*f*) the cost of maintenance;
(*g*) space available for the machine;
(*h*) who will operate the machine;
(*i*) ancillary requirements, e.g. reduction/enlargement of the original, collation;
(*j*) whether reproduction on offset plates, overhead projector transparencies is required as well as on paper;
(*k*) the capital cost of the machine in relation to the use that will be made of it.

Copying costs

To an office clerk 0.9p seems an inconsiderable sum to "make a fuss about". Because of the low cost of copying and the ease with which copies can be made, there tends to be a lack of cost-consciousness where copying is concerned. Making a few extra copies, "in case they are needed", of nearly every document may mean only a penny or two but if several hundred staff do it several times a day the total waste can be astronomical over a year. Sometimes extra copies are made because the location of the copying machine involves several minutes' walk. Also there may be a queue at the machine. If machines are provided on every floor several may be out of order—the penalty for allowing all "hands" to use them—which means time to locate one that is functioning. These frustrations cost money, of course—perhaps more than a few extra copies.

It is essential therefore that the organisation of copying should be well thought out so that the service fulfils its purpose without creating problems of time consumption and cost. Volume copying should normally be the province of the reprographics section or print room. Many organisations have a rule that when more than a certain number of copies, usually ten, is required the job must be sent to the printing department. Copiers are provided in various locations for individual small-volume copying. The problem that most frequently arises is the delay in obtaining work from the printing department. Consequently if twenty copies are required a secretary will go to the machine twice rather than pass out the job!

TYPESETTING

There are several methods of preparing a master for reproduction. Most of them involve the use of a typewriter or a keyboard.

Direct typing

The master is prepared on the typewriter. This applies to spirit masters, ink duplicating stencils and offset plates (paper and parchment).

Cold-type composing

The preparation of a master from which an offset-plate may be produced by a photographic process is known as cold-type composing. This can be done on any electric typewriter, a composer or word processor.

Photo-typesetting (or photo-composition)

The text is "keyed into" a photographic machine. Different sizes and styles of print are "selected" by pressing an appropriate key. The text is seen on a small display screen.

Interface equipment is available which allows text prepared on a word processor to be transferred directly on to a typesetter. Some typesetting editing is necessary but it does avoid the necessity for keying in twice and proof reading each text input.

"Hot metal" typesetting

The printer sets individual metal blocks for each letter into a block. It is a very slow process, requiring great skill.

Computer typesetting

The text is "keyed into" the computer via a terminal which may be a word processor with a visual display unit. The process is explained in Chapter Ten.

CHOICE OF REPROGRAPHIC METHOD

It is not possible to lay down which method is most suitable for certain purposes as there are so many variable factors. A particular process which may seem expensive to run may prove to be economical if it is installed for another purpose in addition and if the maximum use is made of the machine.

Many of the special features of the various processes have been mentioned. A summary is given below of the factors which should be considered when deciding on the appropriate duplicating process for a particular task.

(*a*) Number of copies required.
(*b*) Likelihood of reprints being required.
(*c*) Speed of reproduction—sometimes the speed is most important.
(*d*) Type of copy paper—perhaps a good writing surface is needed.
(*e*) Whether half-tone illustrations, line drawings, and/or text are to be reproduced.
(*f*) Economy of operation—cost of materials and of operator.
(*g*) Whether it is wished to enlarge or reduce the size of originals.
(*h*) Whether variable details on pre-cut forms are needed.
(*i*) Number of colours required.
(*j*) Durability of image and of master.
(*k*) Whether typewritten appearance is desired.
(*l*) Whether printed typeset appearance is preferred.

Relative costs

The relative costs of the various methods of reproduction depend on the quantity required off one original or master and whether or not a master has to be produced.

Number of copies	*Cheapest method*	
1–6	Carbon paper or carbon free paper	
1–20	Copying, if from existing document	
7–200	Spirit duplicating	
7–7,000	Ink duplicating	
30–1,000	Offset duplicating	where very good quality reproduction is required
1,001 up	Offset printing	where very good quality reproduction is required

Methods of preparing masters for reprographic processes

Method	*Process*
Handwriting	All (in some cases certain inks and colours will not reproduce)
Typewriting	All
Word processor	All
Electronic scanner	Ink duplicating
Platemaker	Offset
Reflex copying	—
Diffusion transfer copying	Offset and dyeline
Gelatine transfer copying	Offset
Direct positive copying	Dyeline
Dyeline copying	—
Electrofax*	Offset
Xerographic*	Offset
Thermal*	Spirit duplicating Ink duplicating
Dual spectrum*	—

*Overhead projector (OHP) transparencies can also be produced by these processes.

PRINCIPAL APPLICATIONS OF REPROGRAPHIC PROCESSES

Process	*Applications*
Carbon paper	Correspondence. Reports. Business documents. (Can be used with continuous stationery)
Carbon free paper Carbon processed paper	Memo sets Business documents
Spirit duplicating	Internal circulars and notices. Business documents including export documents. Lesson notes and tests. Coloured charts, diagrams, maps. Addressing

Process	*Applications*
Ink duplicating	Circulars for external distribution. Reports. Training materials. Forms
Offset duplicating	Circular letters. Sales literature, brochures, etc. Reports. Letterheads, forms, etc.
Reflex copying	Black and white copy of any type of document including half-tones and colours
Diffusion transfer copying	Offset litho plates. Translucent masters for dyeline copying
Gelatine transfer copying	Paper copies. Offset litho plates
Direct positive copying	Dyeline masters
Dyeline (diazo) copying	Plans, drawings. Business document systems, e.g. sales order documentation
Electrofax copying	Paper (sensitised) copies. Offset litho plates. OHP transparencies
Xerographic copying	Plain paper copies. Offset litho plates. OHP transparencies
Thermal copying	Paper (sensitised) copies. Spirit masters. Ink duplicating stencils. OHP transparencies. Laminating (creating a shiny protective surface on paper)
Dual spectrum copying	Paper (sensitised) copies. OHP transparencies

ADVANTAGES AND DISADVANTAGES OF THE COMMONLY USED REPROGRAPHIC PROCESSES

Process	*Advantages*	*Disadvantages*
Carbon paper	No master required	Limited number of copies. Collating and decollating of carbon pack takes time. Error correction on carbon copies is time-consuming
Carbon free paper	No master required. Time saved by not collating and decollating carbon packs	Copies fade quite quickly
Spirit duplicating	Quick and cheap to produce. No special pens or tools required. Simultaneous colour reproduction. Master can be stored for further use up to 500 copies. Complete set of documents can be prepared from one master by using masks. Masters can be amended after use	Error correction on masters not easy. Limited number of good copies. Quality of reproduction is not very high. Printed copy fades quickly in the light
Ink duplicating	Excellent quality reproduction can be obtained from well-prepared stencils. Any size of material can be reproduced from postcard size to brief/A3 size	Expensive when few copies are required from one master. Interleaving is necessary if copies are required on non-absorbent paper.

Process	*Advantages*	*Disadvantages*
	(depending on size of duplicating machine). Many different types of lines, drawings, etc., can be drawn. Errors on stencils can be corrected easily before use. Master can be stored for further use up to maximum number of copies	Separate runs have to be made for each colour, necessitating changing parts of the machine
Offset duplicating	Fully professional reproduction. Reproduction of photographs. Up to 10,000 impressions an hour on some machines. Cheap reproduction for large quantities and/or large volume of work. Any type of paper can be used. Plate can be stored for further use up to maximum number of copies	Trained operators required for some machines. Capital outlay is high. Separate runs have to be made for each colour, including bi-colour machines. Correction of errors on typewritten plates is not easy
Electrofax copying	Reproduction from coloured originals. Suitable for large-volume work	Sensitised paper required
Xerographic copying	Uses ordinary paper. Good quality reproduction. Variety of size	Repeated maintenance may be required. Will not copy all colours equally well on some machines
Dual spectrum copying	Will copy ballpoint-pen ink	Slow process

SELF-ASSESSMENT QUESTIONS

Answer all questions as quickly as possible. Do not turn back to the Chapter until you have completed this test.

1. What are the main advantages of spirit duplicating over other methods of reproduction?
2. Describe two types of carbon-free paper used for making a duplicate copy when producing a document.
3. What is the basic principle on which offset lithography works?
4. What is the main difference between offset duplicating and offset printing?
5. What kind of carbon paper has the best wearing qualities?
6. Copying can be used for producing trading documents. What method is used to ensure that each document contains only the information required for that document?
7. What reprographic processes are there by which copies can be reproduced in colour?
8. By what method could you prepare an ink duplicating master to reproduce a diagram of a machine?
9. If you wanted to produce a copy of a page you had "mocked up", i.e. prepared by pasting photographs, pieces cut from newspapers, etc., what reprographic process would be most suitable?
10. Name and briefly explain three methods of typesetting.

ASSIGNMENTS

Assignment 1

Your office manager has asked you to find out what make/s and model/s of office copier meet his requirements. These are:

(*a*) it must be quiet in operation and have a quick warm-up time (not more than 2–3 minutes);

(*b*) it must copy from any original, which may be on coloured paper, printed in colours, be written in ink or with ballpen, or be typed or printed;

(*c*) it must be capable of copying any size from A5 to A3;

(*d*) it must have an "interrupt" facility so that if a run is interrupted to run off an odd copy it is possible to know how many more copies have to be run off to complete the number required;

(*e*) it should preferably have the capacity to load two cartridges of paper at the same time, e.g. A4 and A3 with interchangeable use;

(*f*) it should have adjustable density control to make copies lighter or darker;

(*g*) it must be capable of producing copies at not less than 20 per minute;

(*h*) it must have very high quality reproduction.

What would be the cost of a suitable machine:

(*a*) if purchased outright?
(*b*) if leased over a period of five years?

Assignment 2

A large head office has decided to replace its copying machine and wishes to install a Mitsucopiwonder. This is available either to rent or buy. The following alternatives are available:

Buying—£3,000

(*a*) The cost is to be repaid over five years, an interest charge of 10 per cent being levied on the amount outstanding at the beginning of each year.

(*b*) The maintenance costs are estimated at £200 per annum.
(*c*) The cost of paper is £20 per 1,000 sheets.

Renting—£1,100 per annum (maintenance included)

(*a*) Copies are charged at the rate of £20 per 1,000 copies up to 100,000 and then £10 per 1,000 copies thereafter.

(*b*) The cost of paper is £5 per 1,000 sheets.

The problem

Will it be cheaper to rent or buy if in the next five years the number of copies is expected to be a total of:

(*a*) 100,000 copies?
(*b*) 500,000 copies?
(*c*) 1,000,000 copies?
(Ignore inflation)

Having established the financial facts on which to base a decision, what other major factor must be taken into account before making a final decision?

Assignment 3

Overleaf is a chart indicating the various reprographic processes and their main features. Working in groups if possible, complete the chart as shown in the first line, indicating a "yes" by a tick, a "no" by a blank, or by inserting an appropriate number. The first question has been answered, as an example.

	Carbon paper	Carbon free paper	Spirit duplicating	Ink duplicating	Offset duplicating	Dyeline	Electrofax copying	Xerographic copying	Thermal copying	Dual spectrum copying
How many copies can be produced simultaneously?	Up to 20	Up to 5	1	1	1	1	1	1	1	1
How many copies can be produced from one master?	1-6	1-6	500	5000	25000	UNLIMIT	"	"	-	
Can copies be produced from an original hard copy master?	NO	NO	YES	NO	NO	NO	YES	YES	YES	
Can copies be made on coloured paper?	YES	YES	YES	YES	YES	YES	YES	YES	YES	YES
Can copies be made from all colours of printing?	NO	"	YES	NO	NO	NO	YES	YES	YES	
Can copies be made from all types of printing?	NO	"	YES	NO	NO	NO	YES	YES	YES	
Can colours be produced simultaneously?	NO	"		NO	NO	NO	NO	NO	NO	
Can colours be produced on separate runs?	YES	NO	NO	YES	YES	NO	NO	NO	NO	
Are copies fade-proof?	NO	"	NO	YES	YES	NO	YES	YES	YES	
Can the master be stored after use and used again?	NO	"	YES	YES	YES	YES	YES	YES	YES	

CHAPTER EIGHT

Transmitting Information

> CHAPTER OBJECTIVES
>
> After studying this chapter you should be able to:
> * list and know the uses of systems, equipment and facilities available for transmitting information both internally and externally
> * compare the costs of the various systems and facilities
> * explain the advantages and disadvantages of the various systems and facilities
>
> Note: computerised transmission systems are discussed in Chapter Ten.

DEFINITION AND PURPOSE

What is a transmission system? Information must be sent from one person to another and from department to department within an organisation; it must also be sent from one organisation to another. Transmission of information can be by word of mouth or in some form of documentation. In either case it must be sent, and received, by mail, telegraph, telecommunication or data transmission system of some kind. Internal and external systems are devised to provide a service appropriate to specific needs. There are many facilities for external transmission of information which are provided to meet the requirements of individuals and of organisations both nationally and internationally.

When choosing the method of transmission for a particular piece of information various factors must be considered.

The type of information

(*a*) Is it classified or open?
(*b*) Is it written?
(*c*) Does it contain a lot of figures?
(*d*) Does it need to be discussed?

The way it is presented

(*a*) Is it on paper?
(*b*) Can it be microcopied?

Speed

(*a*) Is it urgent?
(*b*) Is there any time change between countries?

Accuracy

Does it contain technical information, figures, foreign words?

Security

(*a*) Is it classified, confidential?
(*b*) Has it taken many hours of work to produce?
(*c*) Can it be sent as microcopy, or on a magnetic medium such as a floppy disk, so that it is easily replaceable if lost?

Cost

What is the cheapest method compatible with the foregoing criteria?

SYSTEMS

Every organisation has established internal systems for transmitting information and every organisation uses a variety of external systems. It is essential to look at the transmission of information as one operation so that the various services and facilities used can form an integrated communication system for the whole organisation. This is a relatively new approach born of the computerisation of systems in recent years. It is now possible to have virtually instantaneous transmission of information, i.e. the sending and receiving of a document across the world in a few seconds. Many large organisations are still in the process of integrating mailing, telegraphic and telecommunication systems. This is discussed in Chapter Ten.

TRANSMITTING SPOKEN INFORMATION

Face-to-face communication

You have dealt in detail with face-to-face communications in the module "People and Communication" so you know the pitfalls and problems, advantages and disadvantages. Within an organisation it is used a great deal between individuals and in groups. The shorthand-typist takes dictation from an individual. Two people (sometimes more) are involved in interviews which may be concerned with recruitment, disciplinary matters, grievances, briefing, debriefing, on-the-job training, etc. Groups of people hold meetings to exchange ideas, be trained, find solutions to problems, plan projects, etc. Since face-to-face communication involves people's time it is an expensive method of communication, but is essential in some circumstances. Very often though people talk to each other unnecessarily and a less expensive method would be equally suitable for the particular piece of information involved.

TELEPHONES

A wide range of telephone equipment, services and facilities is available. Equipment can be obtained from British Telecom and several manufacturers: services and facilities are provided solely by British Telecom.

It is important that the right equipment is provided for the needs of individuals and departments within an organisation. It is equally important that each person in the organisation uses the equipment cost effectively. Everyone should know the services available and be able to ascertain the cost.

Telephone equipment

Telephone equipment includes direct line telephones, multi-line telephones, switchboards, extension instruments. A brief summary of the various types of telephone equipment and the facilities provided by them is set out in the table below.

Equipment	*Description*	*Facilities*
Manual Direct line	Single telephone line with its own number to an ordinary telephone. Instrument has dial, or push button known as "keyphone" Many types of instrument available	Up to 7 extension telephones with bells, or with bells which can be switched off. Extension instruments may be with or without dial or keys. Incoming calls can be taken on any instrument
Keymaster (*see* Fig. 47)	One- or two-line telephone connected to five or ten extensions respectively	Bell on extension instruments can be switched off. Incoming calls can be taken on any instrument. Calls can be transferred from one extension to another. Three-way conversation can be held. Intercommunication

Equipment	Description	Facilities
Key and lamp unit (*see* Fig. 48)	Ten or twenty circuits connected to exchange lines, extensions or private circuits. Incoming calls indicated by a flashing light. Steady light indicates a line in use. A call is received or made by switching a key	Calls can be received on any unit on the circuit. Particularly useful where all staff in an office receive outside calls constantly, e.g. a travel agent, sales order office. Can be installed to by-pass a switchboard or as an extension to a switchboard
Private manual branch exchange (PMBX)	2 + 6 (two exchange lines with six extensions), 3 + 12, 4 + 18. Operated by lever-type keys	All calls, internal and external, made by extension users must be routed through the switchboard operator

Fig. 47. *Keymaster—two exchange lines plus ten extensions if required. (Courtesy British Telecom.)*

Equipment	*Description*	*Facilities*
Automatic		
Private automatic branch exchange (PABX)	Various combinations of exchange lines and extensions. Smaller switchboards can be rented from British Telecom; larger installations must be bought from manufacturers	Direct dialling from one extension instrument to another for internal calls. Direct dialling of external calls from extension instrument, usually by dialling the digit 9 to obtain the use of an exchange line, and then the subscriber's number

Fig. 48. *Key and lamp unit. An incoming call is indicated by a flashing lamp. An engaged line is indicated by a steady lamp.*
(Courtesy British Telecom.)

Equipment	*Description*	*Facilities*
Private internal automatic exchange	10 to 600 exchange lines with up to several thousand extensions (can be bought from manufacturers, not rented)	Installed in very large organisations when internal telephone traffic is very heavy in comparison with external traffic
Electronic systems		
Switching— Ambassador	2 + 3 (max)	Various facilities including some or all of the following:
Call connect— Ensign	2–6 exchange lines 6–10 extensions	Repeat last number (to save redialling an engaged number)
Herald	2–18 exchange lines 4–20 extensions	
Senator	5 + 10 (max)	Repertory calling (store of numbers)

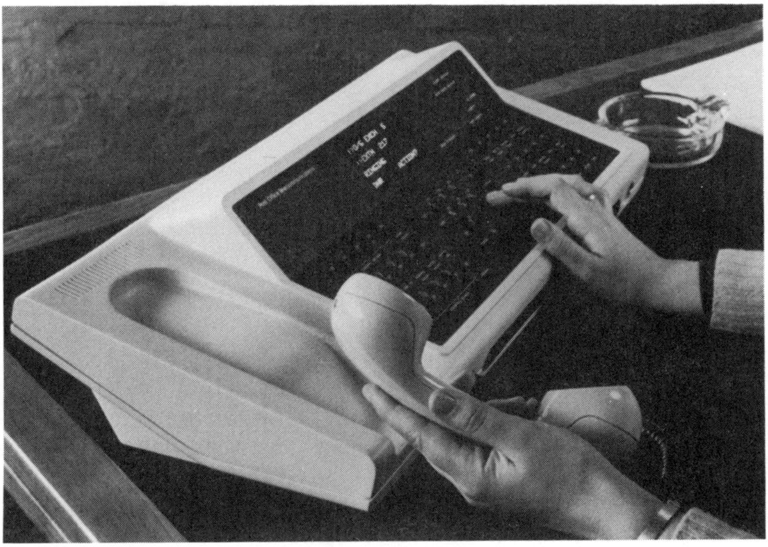

Fig. 49. *Monarch 120 all-electronic telephone system. It is designed on a modular basis so that it can be enlarged to serve about 20 exchange lines and 120 extensions.*

(Courtesy British Telecom.)

Equipment	*Description*	*Facilities*
Kinsman*	8 + 32 12 + 48	Call diversion (re-routeing of incoming calls)
Monarch* (see Fig. 49)	2 + 4 to 30 + 120 (max)	Conference calls
Viceroy*	8 + 16 (max)	Call barring for various types of outgoing call
Regent*	24 + 134 (max)	Abbreviated dialling

*These systems have an operator console

Private datel exchange	Similar to an electronic switchboard but used for controlling transmission of data between computers and terminals or computers and computers	*See* Chapter Ten
Internal telephone system	*See* page 154	Various numbers and types of extension. Teleconference
Extension instruments	Similar to a direct line instrument. Various types of instrument available	With or without dial or push buttons. With bell, or "bleep" which is softer. Various "plans" available to cater for specific needs
Plan 105/107 (*See* Figs. 50 and 51)	A direct line or extension to a switchboard, which allows calls to be received and made by the main instrument and then switched through to the subsidiary instrument or can be received and made directly on the subsidiary instrument	Plan 105 has two extensions. Plan 107 has one extension. Intercommunication between the main and subsidiary instruments

Equipment	*Description*	*Facilities*
Radio-telephone	Telephones allowing two-way conversation between a central point and moving vehicles (equipment must be purchased)	Radiophone service provided by British Telecom
Answering machine	Can be rented or purchased	Subscriber records the message for callers (the caller cannot record a message)

Fig. 50. *Plan 105/107 extension or direct line instrument which allows calls to be "filtered" to a supplementary extension.*
(Courtesy British Telecom.)

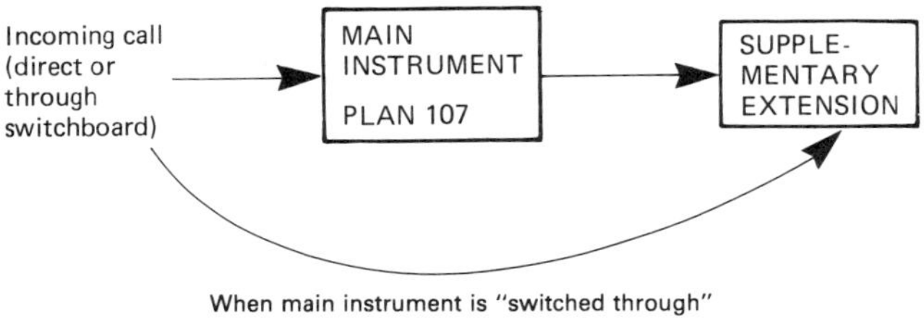

Fig. 51. *Plan 107 call routeing.*

Equipment	*Description*	*Facilities*
Answer-recording machine	Can be rented or purchased	Subscriber records the message for callers who can then record a message to be played back by the subscriber. Can be used for routine operations such as receiving orders for parts, etc., taking names and addresses of applicants for jobs
Heavy duty telephones	Special weather-proof container for use outside buildings	
Payphones	Direct line telephone with coin box	Free calls for emergency (999), directory enquiries and to the British Telecom operator
Loudspeaking telephones	An instrument which allows the person using it to listen and speak without using the normal telephone hand-set so that the hands are free Various types available	Handset can be used for confidential calls when other people are in the room
Speakerset	It can also be used so that a number of people can hear	Only incoming speech can be routed through the speakerset. Call is restored to set at press of button. Extension speaker set available

Equipment	*Description*	*Facilities*
Separate bells	For use in places which are too noisy or distant from the telephone, e.g. machine rooms, nursery gardens	
Automatic dialling devices	Press button callmakers are available on rental from British Telecom. Allow subscribers' numbers called regularly to be dialled automatically	*Tyne callmaker:* stores up to fifty numbers, each one having a calling button which is depressed as appropriate. Each number stores up to 18 digits. Callmaker is plugged in to a normal electrical plug socket. Standby battery which maintains telephone number store for 72 hours in the event of electricity mains failure. *Trent callmaker:* As Tyne plus: Display of telephone number keyed. On-hook dialling. Call progress monitor loudspeaker. Call times 24-hour clock and date display.

Equipment	*Description*	*Facilities*
Call meter (*see* Fig. 52)	A device to indicate the cost of a call	With or without printer. Programmed to take account of day of the week, time of the day, charge band and VAT rate
Videophone	A television type screen linked to the telephone so that the speakers can see each other	Not yet commonly available. It is very expensive because a very high quality transmission line is needed
Logging	Connected to PABX switchboard to monitor out-going calls	Produces a report which gives details of calls made on each extension including date; number called; town or country; time, duration and cost of call

Fig. 52. *Telephone call meter indicating charges when calls are being made. (Courtesy Monitel Ltd.)*

System X

British Telecom is converting the public telephone network over a period of years to System X. Telephone exchanges will be digital instead of electro-magnetic. This will mean a much higher quality of transmission than at present and many additional services will be available to subscribers. The first System X exchanges have been installed in Colchester, Cambridge and Liverpool and are fully operational. British Telecom plan to install another 41 such exchanges by March 1985. Ultimately System X will allow subscribers to use one link for various facilities, e.g. facsimile, electronic mailing, instead of having separate links as at present.

Types of call

British Telecom provides a wide range of facilities which are summarised below.

Type of call	*Facilities*
International direct dialling (IDD)*	Direct dialling to most overseas countries (see telephone code directory)
Subscriber trunk dialling (STD)	Direct dialling to almost anywhere within the country (see telephone code directory)
International call through the telephone exchange operator*	Pre-book (which may be necessary several days in advance for some countries)
Trunk call through the telephone exchange operator†	Personal (person-to-person/particular person) call. Fixed time call. Transferred (reverse) charge call. Advice of duration and charge (ADC) (to be notified to operator before giving number required). Freefone call (the person called pays the charge). Credit card call.
Local call	Direct dialling (see telephone code directory for exchanges within the area but outside own exchange)

* Remember the time difference between countries.
† More expensive than direct dialling.

Type of call	*Facilities*
Local exchange operator services	Fault reports. Number unobtainable enquiries. Alarm (morning) call. Freefone (the caller states the Freefone number required). Freefone Name (the caller states the name of the organisation required). International exchange. Telemessage (dial 100)/International telegram (dial 193) (dictated to the operator; transmitted within one hour; addressee receives written message). Other facilities as for trunk calls through the operator
Local direct dialling services	Emergency service (999). Time. Weather conditions on roads. Principal events of the day in major cities (in English, French, German, Italian, Spanish). Test match scores. Raceline. Business news summary (FT Index). Recipes. Dial-a-disc. Bedtime story

Teleconference

It is now possible for a "meeting" to be held by more than two people over the telephone or by television. Most electronic telephone systems have the facility whereby a discussion can be held simply by the people concerned sitting at their desks and using the telephone extension.

Orator is a new teleconference system designed to link two groups of up to six people over private circuits, PBX extensions or the public telephone network.

Videoconference

In certain large cities in the UK (London, Birmingham, Bristol, Glasgow and Manchester) it is possible to rent British Telecom television studios in which to hold meetings between groups of people in two or three different places. Each member of the group sits in front of a microphone. Television screens are in view so that the speaker can see the people to whom he is talking (*see* Fig. 53). It is also possible to screen documents which may be important for technical meetings. Mobile studios are also available.

Although the cost of videoconference is high, the cost of travel of one or two of the groups is saved, together with the cost of the people's time, which might be much more expensive than the studio rental charge. The meeting must be very well prepared to ensure maximum utilisation of studio time. Costs are based on distance.

Telephone directories

There always seems to be a shortage of telephone directories in offices. It is not practical to provide every extension user with a complete set of directories but everyone should have quick access to the directories he needs to use frequently. It may be that a complete set can be made available for each section or department.

British Telecom provides to all subscribers a directory for their

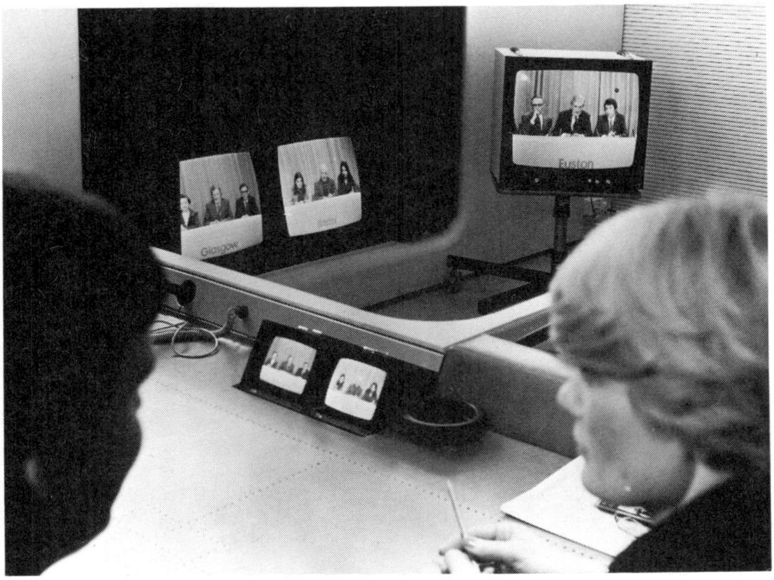

Fig. 53. *Videoconference studio—a three-way "meeting" in progress. (Courtesy British Telecom.)*

area. The directory contains information including how to dial, services and charges. Subscribers are listed in alphabetical order of name in the white page section and by alphabetical order of type of business (and alphabetical order of names within the appropriate business section) in the yellow page section. The yellow pages are produced as a separate directory in many areas.

A telephone code directory is issued at regular intervals listing the codes to dial before the subscriber's number when making calls outside the local exchange area. International direct dialling (IDD) codes are included.

Every subscriber is entitled to an entry in the white page section of the directory without charge, and a business subscriber is entitled to have his name printed in the yellow page section under the appropriate heading free of charge. In both sections, if entries are required in bold print, a small charge is made.

Additional copies of directories for the local area and other areas of the country are available at a small cost. The telephone directory contains a form on which to apply for the directories required.

Radio paging

British Telecom has developed a radio paging system which works on the same lines as the wireless call system explained on page 156. This extended paging service means that a person can be provided with a pocket receiver which will "bleep" when called. If, for example, a secretary receives an urgent message for her executive, she dials the appropriate radio paging code. On hearing the "bleep" the person wanted would call his office for the message. It is also possible to have a coding system so that on hearing one "bleep" a doctor, for example, would call his hospital and two "bleeps" his surgery.

Group calling is also available whereby up to 99 pagers can be alerted simultaneously by dialling one paging number.

This system is in operation in certain areas of the British Isles and is being extended to cover the whole country in the foreseeable future.

Telephone procedures

The cost effective use of the telephone depends upon each person using his or her equipment correctly and following procedures which will ensure that:

(*a*) the best possible corporate image is established and maintained;

(*b*) communication within, into and out of the organisation is effective;

(*c*) costs are kept to a minimum consistent with efficiency.

Telephone switchboard

1. Incoming calls

(*a*) Greet pleasantly.

(*b*) Identify the organisation correctly.

(*c*) When the caller states whom he wishes to speak to, repeat the name of the person wanted.

(*d*) Ask the name of the caller if he has not identified himself ("May I know your name please?").

(*e*) Ask him to hold the line ("Will you hold the line please Mr X?").

(*f*) Ring the person wanted.

(*g*) When the extension user answers inform him of the caller's name.

(*i*) Call accepted: inform caller he is being connected ("Mr X, I am putting you through to Mr A").

(*ii*) Call not accepted: apologise to caller ("I am sorry Mr X, Mr A is not available at present"). Offer alternative—speak to someone else/Mr A to ring back/Mr X to leave a message. Note the name and number of Mr X if Mr A is to call back. Take down the message or pass to suitable person to take message. (Message should include name of person wanted, name of caller, organisation, telephone number, extension number, time and date, the message, initials of recipient.)

(*h*) Extension wanted engaged: inform caller ("I am sorry Mr X, Mr A is engaged. Will you wait?"). Keep in contact with caller about every thirty seconds. If the delay is likely to be long offer to call back and take the name and telephone number of the caller.

2. Calls from extensions

(*a*) First calls of the day—greet the extension user.

(*b*) "Number please."

(*c*) Write down and repeat the number or extension required.

(*d*) Ask for the extension number of the caller (automatic switchboards only).

(*e*) Ask the extension user to hold the line if a connection can be made immediately; if not say "You will be rung later."

3. Making calls

(*a*) Dial: when answered check the number and/or name of

the organisation and ask for the person and extension number required.

(*b*) When answered by the extension user, greet, identify, explain who is calling.

(*c*) Connect to the originator of the call and inform him who is on the line.

(*d*) Cross the number off the list of calls to be made.

(*e*) If the number is engaged, or the person wanted is not available, inform the originator of the call. Try the engaged number again after three to five minutes.

4. Records

(*a*) An alphabetical list of organisations called frequently, with telephone numbers, and, if possible, names of contacts and their extension numbers.

(*b*) A list of trunk calls, overseas calls, etc., with date and time for checking against bills.

(*c*) Fault book in which faults are recorded with the date and time when reported to the British Telecom Engineers and the date and time of follow-up reports.

5. Closing duties

(*a*) Switch to night extension or connect answering machine.

(*b*) Remove headset or handset and lock away.

(*c*) Cover switchboard.

6. Opening duties

(*a*) Disconnect answering machine or return switchboard to normal operation.

(*b*) Connect headset or handset.

(*c*) Dust switchboard.

(*d*) Check for faults; record and report faults.

Notes on telephone switchboard procedures

1. (*d*) and (*g*) (*i*). These points may be omitted on automatic and electronic switchboards to save time.

1. (*g*) (*ii*). Telephone operators on busy switchboards should not be expected to take messages other than brief ones. A typist or clerk can be designated to undertake this duty if there is no receptionist. A simple message form suitable for use by telephone operators is shown in Fig. 54.

2., 3. If the switchboard is automatic, extension users normally dial their own calls (*see* below).

Extension user (automatic switchboard only)

1. Receiving calls

Greet and identify yourself or identify, and then greet after the caller has identified himself.

2. Making calls

(*a*) To extensions, dial the extension number.

(*b*) To other subscribers.

(*i*) Check the code and number of the organisation and extension number of the person wanted.

(*ii*) Dial for a line (this may be the digit 9); await the dialling tone and then dial/key the number required. Dial correctly, allowing the dial to return freely by itself, or key slowly.

(*iii*) When answered, wait for identification and then greet, identify yourself and ask for the name and extension number of the person wanted. If you get a wrong number apologise, replace the receiver and check the code and number. Repeat item (*ii*).

(*iv*) If the person wanted is not available give your own name, number and extension number to be rung back; or ask for someone else; or leave a message, e.g. with a secretary.

Notes on extension users' procedures (automatic switchboard)

1. Though incoming calls are passed through the telephone operator it is normal for an automatic/electronic switchboard operator not to announce callers. This can be done, but one of the objectives of installing such a switchboard is to save time.

2. The operator can be asked to make calls but again it saves time if you dial directly. However, in some countries telephone connections are not made easily and it may be rather time-consuming to dial your own calls.

When devising the procedures for extension users, costs should be borne in mind as well as the corporate image. Whatever type of telephone system is installed, the following points should always be incorporated and emphasised.

(*a*) Preparation of calls: list the main points to be discussed before dialling.

(*b*) Keep a personal telephone directory (a small alphabetical notebook is adequate) for numbers called frequently.

(*c*) Check the direct line and extension numbers before dialling and dial or key correctly.

(*d*) Avoid making calls during the peak charging period: 9.00 a.m. to 1.00 p.m.

(*e*) Avoid busy hours if possible—mid/late mornings and early afternoons.

(*f*) Keep the conversation to the point and be as brief as possible, without being discourteous.

(*g*) Use telephone message forms. A specimen is illustrated at Fig. 54.

If the system is electronic make sure that you know

(*a*) all the facilities available, and

(*b*) how to use them.

Co-operation between extension user and switchboard operator

It cannot be stressed too strongly that the efficiency of the organisation's telephone system depends on the efficiency of all the people who use it. Co-operation between the operator and the extension user ensures that people calling into the organisation will get fast service. For example, if the extension user notifies the operator when he or she is leaving the office, callers can immediately be told that this person is not available—would they like to speak to somebody else? Better still, arrange for someone else to take the calls. Where electronic telephone systems are installed unanswered calls can be picked up by another extension or are automatically transferred from one extension to another on a circuit. The last extension on the circuit should be the point at which messages are taken.

Another way to ensure swift connections is to answer calls promptly, and of course, never go on talking to someone else while holding the receiver.

The Code Decoder

This booklet is obtainable from British Telecom Enterprises, Freepost, Newport, Gwent NP1 7YY, price £2.50. If you receive a message with a telephone number only (no name or first name only), you can identify the part of London or of the country where the message originated by checking the code.

INTERCOMMUNICATION SYSTEMS

Apart from intercommunication provided by PMBX, and PABX electronic systems, internal telephone systems can be purchased or rented from British Telecom. These are sometimes referred to as multi-cord telephone systems, where no central exchange is involved. The different instruments in such a system are all interconnected by multi-cord cable, and contact can be made from any one

Message For ____________________

Date ____________ Time ____________

WHILE YOU WERE OUT

Name ____________________

Organisation ____________________

Phone No ____________________

Telephoned		Please ring him	
Called to see you		Will call again	
Wants to see you		Urgent	

Message:

Signature ____________

Fig. 54. *Telephone message form suitable for use throughout the organisation.*

station to another by the simple depression of a key, but none of the extensions is connected to the external telephone system. Conversations on these internal systems are often non-secret, i.e. a conversation between two extensions can be "listened in to" by a third extension.

Internal telephone systems can vary from five extensions upwards. The British Telecom "Proteus" system can accommodate up to 24 extensions or, in another version, from about 20 up to 64 extensions. Various types of extension instruments are available. Many internal systems have teleconference facilities (*see* page 148).

There are many systems available with a variety of facilities, including one-way only, i.e. a person can speak on the master set but the extensions can receive calls only and not speak. The extensions from the masterset may be one-way only, i.e. they cannot initiate calls but can only receive them from the masterset; they may be able to call the masterset but not other extensions; or they may be able to receive and make calls from and to the masterset and all other extensions as required.

PAGING SYSTEMS

In large organisations it is often necessary to find a member of staff quickly. Managers in a factory, departmental chiefs in a store, or doctors in a hospital may all be wanted urgently. Many paging or staff-location systems are available, the suitability of each system depending on whether it is required for office, factory, hospital or store.

There are four main types of paging systems:

(*a*) public address;
(*b*) bells and buzzers;
(*c*) light signals;
(*d*) wireless call.

A public address system involves the installation of loudspeakers at various main points in the organisation and announcements are made over it usually, though not necessarily, from the telephone switchboard room. Bells and buzzers work on a coding system, i.e. each person on the "call list" has a code of long and/or short buzzes, rather like morse code. The disadvantage of both these systems is that every one must stop and listen.

Light signals work on coding also. Each person on the "call list" has a code of still and/or flashing colours which are illuminated on the lights which are placed at strategic points throughout the organisation. In some cases the system is based on lighted numbers. The disadvantage is that people may not notice the lights.

A wireless call system consists of a central transmitting station (usually at the telephone switchboard) and the allocation of a portable receiver to each member of the staff to be called (*see* Fig. 55). Each receiver picks up only its own particular frequency; thus when a member of the staff is wanted, a wireless signal is transmitted and is received by that member of staff *only*. The signal, usually a bleep, is unmistakable, it cannot be ignored, and the person receiving the call has to telephone the switchboard to see why he is wanted; it does not disturb any other person in the building and the signal will reach the person called wherever he may be within a certain radius.

Call systems which allow two-way speech are also available but in most cases it may be advisable to use the bleep system so that the

Fig. 55. *Wireless call system which enables a person within a fixed radius of a central calling point to be paged at any time.*
(Courtesy Cass Electronics Ltd.)

person called has to telephone for the message. The only disadvantage is that unco-operative members of staff do not always answer the call, but this applies equally to any other paging system.

TRANSMITTING WRITTEN INFORMATION

Written communication comes in many forms, most of which involve physical movement of documents within the organisation and to and from others outside the organisation.

TELECOMMUNICATIONS

Teleprinter

A teleprinter is a machine which resembles a large typewriter with a telephone dial. The operator dials the number of the organisation to be contacted and, when a signal is received to indicate that the connection is made, types the message which is simultaneously reproduced on the distant teleprinter (the answer-back code is transmitted automatically provided the machine is free). The message is printed on a roll of paper, normally in duplicate. The completed message is torn off the roll using a perspex guide as a cutting edge. If there is an operator at the receiving end it is possible to have a "conversation" if necessary. Provided a machine is switched on it can receive messages at any time of the day or night without an operator in attendance. This is one of the major advantages of teleprinters.

To attract the attention of an operator on a receiving machine the transmitting operator can press a key marked "bell" which operates a bell or buzzer on the receiving machine. This might be done if a question is being transmitted which the receiving operator can answer immediately.

Many teleprinters have a punched tape attachment. The message is typed and reproduced on punched tape without being transmitted (Fig. 56 shows a specimen punched tape). After checking the copy, which is produced in the normal way, the punched tape is "fed through" the machine for transmission. This ensures the accuracy of the message and is faster. Transmission speed from typing is approximately 35 words per minute; from punched tape the speed is approximately 66 words per minute. Machines are being developed which will be able to transmit about 260 words per minute when linked to a computer.

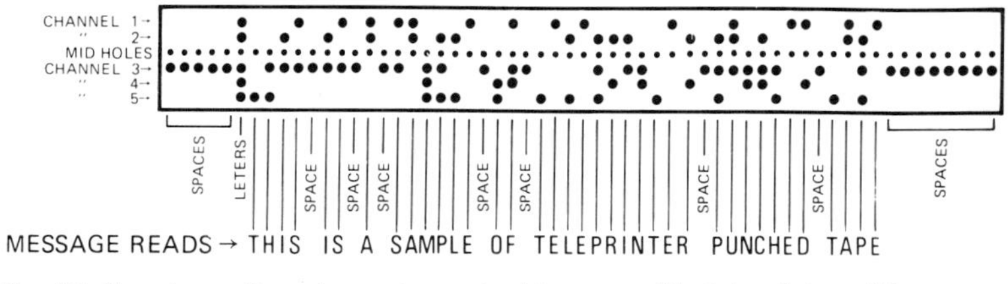

Fig. 56. *Specimen five-channel punched tape used in teleprinters. The message is in the international punched tape code.*

The "Cheetah" (*see* Fig. 57), a British Telecom electronic telex machine, enables the operator to check and edit messages before transmission; correction of errors is simple. It has facilities for justifying, short code calling (similar to abbreviated telephone dialling), automatic pagination and fault diagnosis. An electronic memory stores messages for later transmission. British Telecom have produced an electronic machine with a VDU to meet the special needs of central London customers.

Private teleprinter networks are installed within organisations, e.g. between branches of a company. It is possible to have a receiv-

Fig. 57. *"Cheetah" electronic telex terminal.*
(Courtesy British Telecom.)

ing-only teleprinter installed to obtain information from a central point, e.g. stock prices. In the UK, many stockbrokers have a teleprinter service from the Stock Exchange which gives constant updating of prices.

Apart from the time element and cost factor the teleprinter has the great advantage of providing a written copy and is used a great deal for orders between branches of an organisation, instructions, queries, etc.

Telex service

The telex services provided by British Telecom enable subscribers to rent one or more teleprinters so that they can contact other telex subscribers anywhere in the world. Direct dialling is possible to many countries. Transmission of messages is charged on a time basis—fast punched tape transmission is therefore an advantage. The 24-hour service is especially useful when transmitting to countries with a wide time difference, e.g. the Far East. Telemessages can be sent by telex to British Telecom for onward transmission and can also be received on telex.

Telex users who have heavy traffic between two or more points can hire a private circuit from British Telecom. The telex system can also be linked to a computer for the transmission of data (*see* Chapter Ten). The machine is then referred to as a "teleprinter terminal".

For the benefit of users in the City of London British Telecom provide a Telex Plus service. This provides for the storage of messages until off-peak times and will automatically retry for a connection which cannot be established when transmission is required. The same message can be sent to up to one hundred different addresses and files of addresses can be held for regular multiple users.

Advantages

Telex has the following advantages over the telephone.

(*a*) It is generally cheaper, though as tariffs change from time to time careful scrutiny of costs is necessary.

(*b*) The content is expressed in telegraphic style, saving the time of the originator and operator as well as the cost of transmission.

(*c*) The written record can avoid costly mistakes which can occur orally.

(*d*) The distraction of a telephone call when one is in the middle of another task is avoided

(*e*) When information is needed for an answer the caller does not have to "hold on" while it is being obtained.

(*f*) Messages cannot be extended into non-business discussions.

There are, however, times when discussion is necessary and the telephone is obviously the more suitable medium on these occasions.

Distribution of incoming messages

It is essential to have a good back-up service with the teleprinter/telex facilities. Incoming messages must be distributed as a matter of urgency. If there is a regular internal mail delivery service the messenger should include the telex room in his round. Incoming messages marked urgent should, however, receive special attention. The telex operator should telephone the addressee and either read the content or ask for collection of the message. If there is no internal mail delivery some means of delivering telex messages quickly must be devised.

Because telex is now being used a great deal more in place of telephone calls and letters there tends to be a lack of urgency in handling and processing the messages. Any message marked urgent should be dealt with immediately.

Facsimile copiers

It is often important for technical and professional people to be able to send formulae, drawings and other diagrammatic information quickly over a distance. A teleprinter or telex machine is not suitable for transmitting such documents.

A facsimile copier is a special copying machine which is linked to a telephone. The subscriber to whom the document is to be transmitted is dialled in the normal way and, providing he has a compatible machine attached to his telephone, the telephone is then switched to the facsimile copier into which the document is fed. An A4-size document can be transmitted in from one to six minutes depending on the type of machine.

A conversation can be held before and after the copying process. It is possible to send virtually any form of document or drawing, whether typed, printed or handwritten. The copy is always black on white.

The advantages are that no skilled operators are required; transmission can be over any distance, provided there is telephone communication; transmission can be selective from any part of the document in the machine; transmission can be to two or more receivers near or far; a stack of documents can be fed into the machine from a hopper feed; and the facsimile copies received are of good quality and can be reproduced.

The only disadvantage is that not all types of machines are compatible. Machines are now made to specifications known as Group I, II, III or IV. A new machine may be compatible with more than one group.

British Telecom International provide a Bureaufax service which enables most non-compatible facsimile machines to transmit and receive documents from other countries. This service is obtained by dialling 01–250 1117 between 8 am and 7.30 pm, Monday to Friday.

Telewriters

A telewriter (*see* Fig. 58) is attached to a telephone in a similar way to a facsimile copier. By pressing a switch either of the people holding a conversation can stop talking and write with an electronic pencil on the paper in the machine. The writing or drawing is copied simultaneously on the telewriter of the other subscriber who can later amend or add to the written material. Constant interchange of speaking and writing is possible.

Examples of the use of this facility are technical discussion, when sketches and diagrams are necessary to make the conversation meaningful, and for instant written confirmation of spoken agreements, discussions, etc.

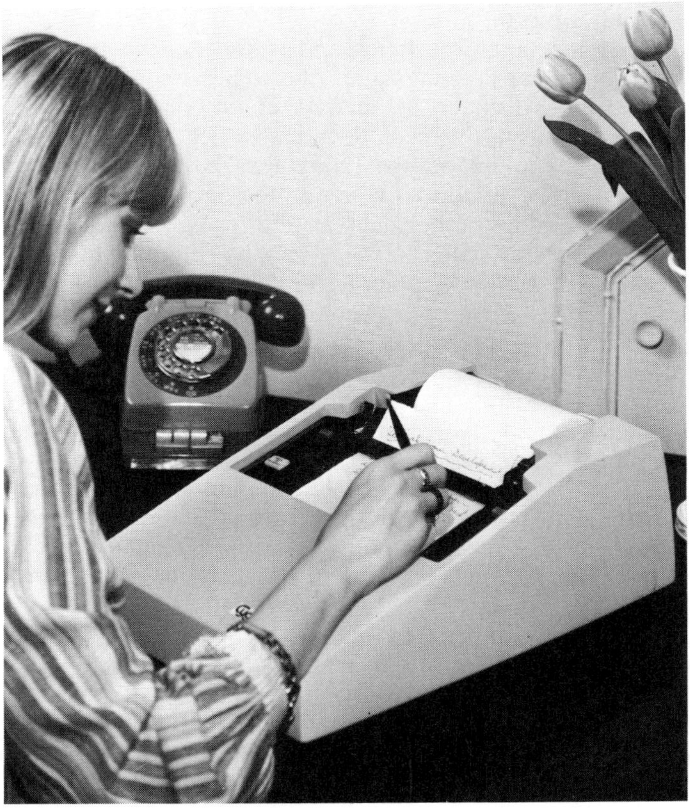

Fig. 58. *Telewriter. Connected to a telephone this gives complete interchange of spoken and written communication over any distance.*
(Courtesy Feedback Instruments Ltd.)

Prestel

Prestel is a British Telecom service by which constantly updated information is available from a computer database on specially adapted television sets. Details of this and other similar services, known as *teletext*, are given in Chapter Ten.

MAIL SERVICES

There are a number of mail (non-Post Office) services available within and outside an organisation. These are summarised below.

Mail Service	*Description*	*Uses*
Messenger	Letters, packets, etc., taken by hand at prescribed times during the day from the mail registry to individual offices from where mail for other offices and external organisations is collected. Messengers may also deliver to nearby addresses	Internal External
Company transport	When two or more parts of an organisation are in different locations a regular transport service is often available for the movement of staff and mail from one location to another. There is a set time for the last delivery of the day	Internal
Taxi	Taxis are used quite frequently in big cities by organisations which have an account with a taxi company. The driver is asked to deliver a package	External
Courier	City, national and international couriers collect letters/packages, etc., from an address and deliver them either to the addressee's address, or to a pre-determined collecting point. Couriers normally carry items themselves so that there is no chance of them getting lost in baggage	When normal postal services would take too long, items are delicate, or maximum security is required
Mechanical	Internal lifts, overhead wires, gravity belts, conveyor belts, and	Irregular delivery requirements, space limited for the

Mail Service	*Description*	*Uses*
	pneumatic tubes are used for transmitting documents on certain routes which are used very frequently	movement of messengers, limited access to documents for security reasons
Electronics	Carriers on tracks controlled by microprocessors	In place of messengers

POSTAL SERVICES

Communications are generated in the industrial or works offices as well as in the administrative offices. The volume and type of communication varies from office to office and the times of highest output are likely to be different from one part of the organisation to another. The basic precept for developing a sound mail handling system is to collect the communication from the place of origination and deliver it to its destination with minimum delay at minimum cost.

Collection and delivery

In the UK the Post Office offers the facility of a Post Office box or private bag. In this case the mail has to be collected from the Post Office. This is useful if mail is required early so that it can be sorted and distributed before or soon after opening time.

The normal mail service is also available, of course, and large organisations may find it useful to have the mail pre-sorted into departments by the Post Office staff. Organisations which normally receive more than twenty letters a day have an individual postcode.

Similarly, outgoing stamped mail may be posted in a post-box, while franked mail may be taken to the Post Office or collected once or twice a day by Post Office mail-van. A docket is completed for each collection. Arrangements can be made for special collections of outgoing parcels as the need arises. Incidentally, it is helpful to the Post Office if they are warned of unusually large volumes of outgoing mail when these occur only occasionally.

Inland Mail

(*a*) First-class inland mail—when delivery is essential within 48 hours.

(*b*) Second-class inland mail—normal delivery may take up to four days.

Security

(*a*) Recorded delivery—provides proof of posting and delivery, and compensation for loss up to the value of £18 on letters and packets.

(*b*) Registration—provides proof of sending and delivery of any first-class letter, and compensation for loss up to a maximum of £1,750 depending on the fee paid.

(*c*) Compensation fee (CF)—provides compensation for loss of goods sent by parcel post up to a maximum of £350 depending on the fee paid.

(*d*) Insurance—this is available to countries to which mail cannot be registered. There is compensation for loss up to a maximum of £1,000 depending on the fee paid.

Urgency

(*a*) Special delivery—delivered by special messenger if the letter is received at the delivery office on the next working day after posting but too late for normal delivery that day. Items must be posted at post office counters in advance of the latest recommended posting times for next day delivery.

(*b*) Swiftair—a similar service to special delivery, but used for Europe and other overseas countries. Accelerated handling is given in both the country of posting and the country of delivery.

(*c*) Expresspost—urgent packages are collected and delivered the same day by messengers in major cities in the UK. There are also same day intercity links between Expresspost centres. Expresspost is not available in Cornwall and Devon, Northern Ireland, Isle of Man or the Channel Islands.

(*d*) Railway letter—available on private railways only: handed in at nearest railway station and sent by next passenger train, to be collected at the station by the addressee or posted in area of destination. First-class postage plus a railway fee.

(*e*) Airway letter—available on certain airlines only (including British Airways): handed in at certain airports or air terminals to be sent by next direct flight, to be collected at the airport or air terminal or posted by the airline. First-class postage plus an airline fee. Available on domestic flights only.

(*f*) Nightrider—overnight delivery of parcels in an area stretching from Egham in the west to Gravesend in the east, and from Croydon in the south to Enfield in the north, is now available in the London postal region to organisations needing to send goods regularly. Charges are negotiated on the basis of operating costs, not solely on weight. (Details from Marketing and Customer Division, London Postal Region, 148–66 Old Street, London ECN 9HQ, tel. 01–250 2888.)

(*g*) Exchangepost—A fast and inexpensive service enabling firms in the City of London, Cardiff, Derby, Glasgow and Newcastle to exchange their mail in their respective cities. There is a flat annual fee which varies from city to city. An additional fee of 2p is charged for each item too large for the boxes: these items are held by the Post Office until collected.

(*h*) Datapost Scheduled service (inland)—an overnight door-to-door delivery service within the United Kingdom for urgent packages. Regulations concerning size, weight and contents are similar to letter post. A contract is negotiated with the Post Office for a regular service on a daily, weekly or monthly basis or for a schedule of dates.

(*i*) Datapost On Demand service (inland)—available to senders with irregular demand for the service. Payment of an initial annual contract fee allows datapost packages to be handed in at a nominated posting centre at any time. Alternatively items can be handed in at almost any main post office and be paid for at the time of posting.

(*j*) International Datapost, scheduled contractual service—next-day delivery available to thirteen countries including USA (by Concorde on Tuesdays and Fridays providing same day delivery for central New York). Second and third-day deliveries after collection are provided to many countries. For up-to-date details ring the telephone exchange operator and ask for FREEFONE DATAPOST.

(*k*) International Datapost, On Demand service—may be on a contractual or non-contractual basis as for the inland service and is available to most of the countries to which the scheduled service operates.

(*l*) Intelpost—a high speed facsimile service for the transmission of urgent copies of documents up to A4 size. Available between over 50 Intelpost centres in the United Kingdom and certain towns in Canada, Netherlands and the USA. Full details of this service are obtainable from the Postal Services Representative or by telephoning FREEFONE INTELPOST.

(*m*) Franc de droits service—overseas customs duty and other charges can be paid in advance by the FDD service which is available to many countries.

(*n*) Customs clearance for letters and parcels from overseas—the Post Office provides customs clearance services for which handling charges are payable. Priority clearance of goods can be obtained by a personal visit to the depot where the goods are held.

Bulk

(*a*) Parcel collection—regular or special collection of parcels by the Post Office from the sender can be arranged. A minimum number of parcels is stipulated for free collection—20 for regular collection, 100 for special collection. A fee is charged for smaller quantities.

(*b*) Second-class letters posted in bulk—when 4251 or more second-class letters of identical shape and size are posted at the same time by the same sender a sliding scale of rebates on the postage is payable by the Post Office, provided certain conditions are fulfilled. This does not apply to addresses in the Irish Republic, Channel Islands or Isle of Man.

(*c*) Prepayment for Post Office franking—letters requiring identical postage and prepared in bundles of fifty can be handed into the Post Office with the appropriate amount of postage. The Post Office will then frank the letters.

(*d*) "Paid" franking—postal packets and parcels, not bearing any indication that postage has been paid, may be accepted at certain post offices for franking "Paid".

Certain discounts are available for one-off second-class postings of 5,000 or more for mail pre-sorted into towns. Fully post coded addresses attract a larger discount than mailings which are not post coded. There are contractual discounts for consistent mailings throughout the year.

Licensed services

Licences to use the services outlined below must be obtained from the Head Postmaster.

(*a*) Business reply service—first- or second-class letters or cards may be received from senders without prepayment of postage. The envelopes or cards have to be printed in the style required by the Post Office and include the licence number. For each item a fee of ½p is charged to the licensee in addition to the postage.

(*b*) Freepost—similar to the business reply service but the sender uses a plain envelope or card and addresses it to FREEPOST plus a postcode. A fee of ½p in addition to the postage is payable by the licensee.

(*c*) Postage forward parcel service—the sender may despatch a parcel without paying postage, which is paid with an additional fee by the addressee.

There are two services which may be valuable to an organisation which has a large volume of outgoing mail. By arrangement with the Head Postmaster it is possible to have a Post Office sorter on the premises. This speeds up the processing at the Post Office sorting office.

Secondly, a Postal Services Representative is available for consultation at every Head Post Office. His advice can be sought on means to obtain the most suitable, efficient and economic postal service for the organisation.

Post Office Directories

Post Office Guide

The *Post Office Guide*, issued annually, contains full details of the facilities offered by the Post Office including postal services, telecommunications, giro, etc. It gives guidance as well as regulations and is a valuable reference book. By completing the post-paid card provided with the *Guide*, supplements can be received throughout the year. The *Guide* is available at main post offices for a small charge.

Postcode directories

Copies of the postcode directories covering the United Kingdom are available for reference at main post offices. These directories are useful for ensuring that address lists include the postcodes.

Postal addresses and index to postcode directories

The addresses for over 20,000 places in the United Kingdom are given in the *Directory of Postal Addresses*. The names of villages and towns are listed alphabetically. The appropriate postal town is given in capital letters. It also indicates whether or not it is necessary to include the county in the address. Finally, the relevant postcode directory is shown.

London Post Offices and Streets

This is a directory giving the address of every Post Office in London and a list of streets.

MAIL PROCEDURES

Incoming mail

Each organisation has its own routine for handling incoming mail, which may be collected from the Post Office (private bag) or delivered to the premises. It may then be sorted and distributed unopened, except for mail addressed to the company which must be opened to identify which department or person should deal with it. In other organisations the central mail registry may open all except "classified" (secret and confidential) mail. Whoever deals with the mail at various stages should follow certain procedures, depending on the requirements of the organisation or department.

Procedure	*Purpose*
Sorting	Envelopes marked "personal" and "confidential" are sorted aside and the remaining ones are faced (turned the right way up for reading), checked that they are addressed to the company or someone in it, and arranged in piles according to size
Opening	The envelopes are slit with a paper knife or on a letter-opening machine (*see* Fig. 59)
Removal of contents	The contents of each envelope are removed from the envelope, the letters are checked for enclosures which are attached to the letter if loose. Missing enclosures are noted on the letter. The inside address is also checked to ensure that the document has been sent correctly
Date stamping	Each document is date stamped, preferably under the date typed on the document, to indicate when it was received—useful proof if there has been postal delay
Distribution stamping	A distribution stamp may be used to indicate the person or people to whom the letter is to be sent for action or information
Copying	If the document should be seen quickly by more than one person it should be copied, a copy being sent to each person
Previous correspondence	The incoming document is attached to the relevant file or previous documents if appropriate

Procedure	*Purpose*
Cash handling	Each amount of cash (money and cheques) received is entered in a special cash book after checking the amount against the incoming document, e.g. remittance advice. The book and the cash is sent by hand to the cashier as soon as the mail opening has been completed

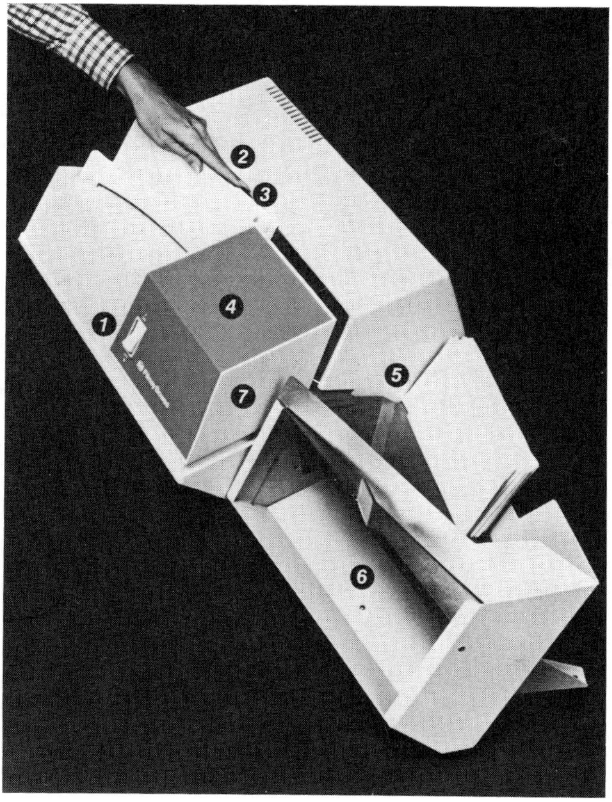

Fig. 59. *A letter opening machine for slitting envelopes. Indicated on the photograph are: (1) the power switch; (2) envelopes being placed in the feed deck; (3) feed roller feeds envelopes along the feed path; (4) cover door protecting the cutting wheels; (5) opening envelopes in the letter stacker; (6) chip bin for collecting paper chips; and (7) trim-adjustment control for adjusting the depth of paper cut off the envelope.*

(Courtesy Pitney Bowes Ltd.)

Procedure	*Purpose*
Distribution	Documents are sorted into piles for distribution. They may then be (*a*) placed in pigeon holes for collection by individuals; (*b*) collected by the messenger or junior who will take them round; (*c*) delivered by an electronically controlled system.
Registration	Details of each document are written in an inwards mail register (this is time consuming but in some organisations is useful as proof of receipt when documents are passed from one person to another). If the correct distribution is not identifiable the letter is passed to the supervisor in a large mail registry or the person responsible for office services in a smaller organisation

Outgoing mail

It is usual to have a central point in an organisation for co-ordinating the outgoing mail. In some cases mail is prepared for despatch in the individual offices, only franking and despatch being dealt with in the registry. In other organisations the mail is sent to the registry open (unless it is classified) where it is enveloped, etc.

Procedure	*Purpose*
Checking	The document must be scrutinised to ensure that it has been signed and dated, that the inside address is correct and matches the address on the envelope, that enclosures are attached, and that the envelope is the right size
Folding	The documents are folded to fit the envelope. This may be done by hand or by a folding machine

Procedure	*Purpose*
Preparation of envelopes	It is usual for secretarial staff to type envelopes for the correspondence they prepare. In a large organisation bulk documents such as invoices, statements, sales literature may be sent to the registry for envelopes to be printed on an addressing machine. Alternatively, window or aperture envelopes may be used
Insertion of folded documents and sealing of envelopes	Documents are inserted in the envelopes by hand or by machine, and the envelopes are then sealed by hand, using a damp sponge (if they are not self-sealing), or by machine
Weighing	Envelopes are weighed on a special weighing machine which indicates the cost of postage depending on whether the letter is to be sent first or second class, inland, or overseas by surface or air mail. The cost of any service such as registration must be added. The letters are sorted into piles according to cost of postage
Stamping or franking	Postage stamps are affixed by hand (they are kept in a book separated according to denomination) or the letters are passed through a franking machine (*see* Fig. 60). The machine has a "credit" which has been paid at the Post Office, either by cheque or special credit card. Every time a letter is franked the credit is reduced and the amount used is increased by the amount of postage. A daily record is kept of the credit balance. An electronic system for updating the credit of your franking machine is now available from Pitney Bowes. The Remote Meter Resetting System

Procedure	*Purpose*
	(RMRS) comprises an electronic franking machine and a data pad. A deposit is paid to Pitney Bowes from which the required credits are deducted. When you need more postage credit on your machine you telephone the RMRS data centre, which gives nation-wide coverage. A cup from the data pad is then attached to the telephone handset and you key in your account and meter numbers and the franking machine register readings. A voice response from the RMRS data centre then gives you an exclusive resetting number for your meter. Entry of this number on your keypad then unlocks the meter so that you can reset the required credit. This system eliminates the need to take the franking machine register to the Post Office for renewal of credit
Registration	Outgoing mail may be listed in a postage book (*see* Fig. 61)
Bundling	If large quantities of letters are to be franked at the Post Office they should be tied up in bundles of 50. The cash must be paid when the envelopes are delivered to the Post Office. Franked letters should also be bundled according to delivery area
Despatch	Stamped letters may be posted in a post box. Franked letters must be handed in at a Post Office or may be collected by Post Office van. Alternatively, letters may be delivered by messenger or collected by courier (*see* page 163). It is usual to have a fixed time ot day by which all outgoing correspondence

Procedure	*Purpose*
	should be received in the mail registry to ensure despatch the same day. Parcels are dealt with in a similar way but must be wrapped and addressed, preferably using labels. If mail is franked the postage is indicated on an adhesive label which is affixed to the parcel

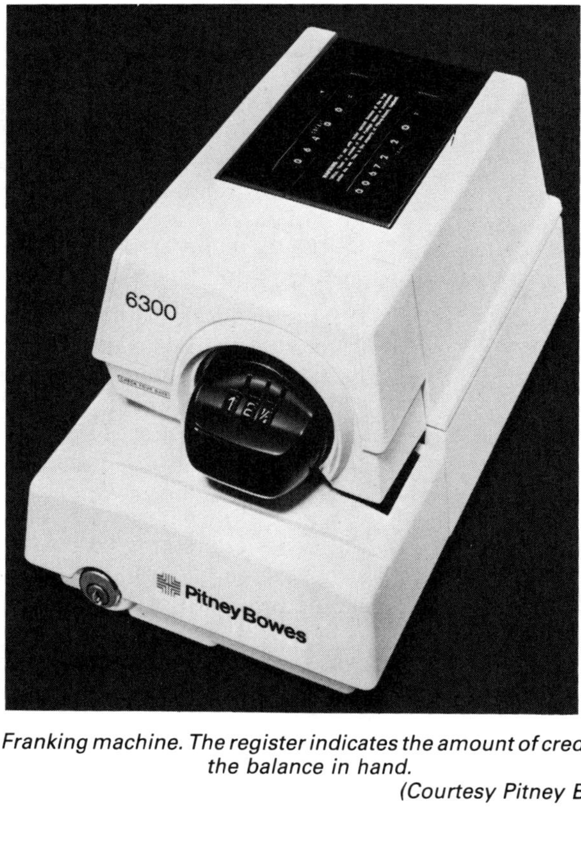

Fig. 60. *Franking machine. The register indicates the amount of credit used and the balance in hand.*

(Courtesy Pitney Bowes Ltd.)

Dr. £		Date		£	Cr.
20	—	1.8.81	Cash received		
			Bullimore, Hartlepool	—	14
			Smith, Cardiff	—	14
			Peters, Bournemouth	—	11½
		2.8.81	42 brochures @ 11½p	4	83
			Davies, Lymington	—	26
		3.8.81	Balance, c/d	14	51½
20	—			20	—
14	51½	3.8.81	Balance b/d		
5	48½		Cash received		

Fig. 61. *Postage book. Note that bulk items are recorded in a single entry.*

MAILROOM LAYOUT AND EQUIPMENT

The size and arrangement of the mailroom and equipment provided depends on the size and locations of sections of the organisation serviced and the volume of mail to be handled. In a small to medium organisation all incoming and outgoing mail including parcels may be handled in the same room. In a large organisation it is usual for parcels to be dealt with either in a special mailroom or by the despatch department.

Layout

Space is needed for:

(*a*) work surfaces for receiving mail and for machines;
(*b*) bag racks, skips, trays or baskets for sorted outgoing mail;
(*c*) pigeon-holes, trays, baskets or wire mesh systems for sorted mail for internal delivery;
(*d*) a tray or basket for private, stamped mail;
(*e*) movement of mailroom personnel.

All sorting stations, baskets, etc., must be properly labelled. The layout is determined by the flow of mail, internal and external, by the location of doors and windows, and by the number of staff and their area of responsibility. The flow of incoming and outgoing mail and a typical mailroom layout in a large organisation is shown in Fig. 62.

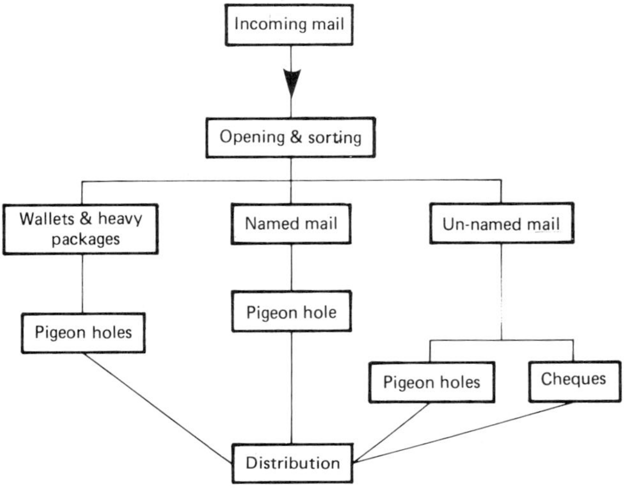

Fig. 62(a). *Typical incoming mail flow.*

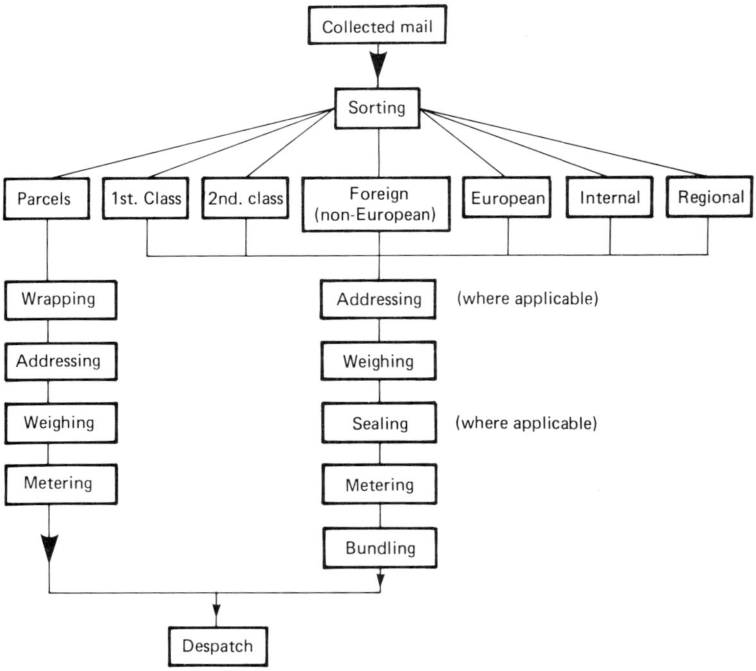

Fig. 62(b). *Typical outgoing mail flow.*

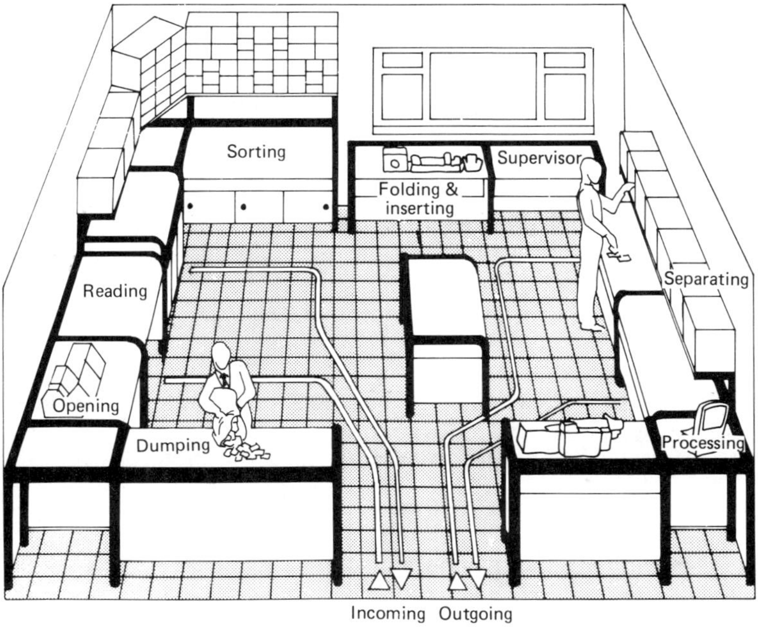

Fig. 62(c). *Typical layout of a mail room in a large organisation to ensure systematic physical progression of mail as it is processed.*
(Courtesy Pitney Bowes Ltd.)

Equipment

Equipment can range from a paper knife and a sponge for damping envelopes and stamps to a complete battery of machines that will handle every operation in the mailroom except sorting. Machines available include the following.

Weighscales—letter and parcel
These can be obtained with faces to show weights only or weights and charges (time-saving when a lot of overseas mail is involved).

Letter-opener
Envelope slitters or guillotines are available.

Mail-sorter
Sorts incoming mail into sizes at speeds up to 30,000 an hour; can also open mail.

Franking machine
With a meter or using a "credit card" (*see* page 172). Available for

various thicknesses and sizes of envelope. Can also seal and stack franked letters.

Folding and inserting machines
Available with a range of folds.

Lightbox
For checking that used envelopes are empty (can be home-made).

Self-adhesive labelling machine
To stick computer-produced labels on envelopes.

Addressing machine
A wide variety are available, from the small hand-operated spirit duplicating system to a fully computerised system which includes address selection and updating facilities (*see* Chapter Ten).

Many of the machines can be "banked" to feed letters on from one operation to another. It must be stressed that most machines, apart from the franking and small addressing machines, are economically worth while only for large-volume mail.

COSTS

The transmission of information, whether spoken or written, costs money whichever method is used. There are circumstances in which an expensive means of transmission is justified, e.g. a telephone call overseas costing £100 to clinch a million-pound contract, or a confravision meeting to solve a problem costing an organisation £10,000 a day in lost production.

In normal circumstances the cheapest method should be used. In assessing the cost the time involved must not be overlooked, because it is an expensive commodity. The real average cost of a letter at the present time (1984) is approximately £10. It may therefore be cheaper to telephone. If total accuracy is vital a letter may be more appropriate.

SUMMARY

1. The method of transmitting information should be chosen on the basis of the type of information, the way it is presented, urgency, accuracy, security and cost.

2. Face-to-face communication is expensive in time so should be used only when necessary.

3. There is a wide range of telephone equipment and services to meet the needs of individuals and organisations. Maximum use should be made of British Telecom advisory services.

4. Telephone services include calls, confravision, directories and radio paging.

5. Procedures should be established throughout the organisation for telephone switchboard operators and extension users.

6. Efficient telephone communication depends on co-operation between the switchboard operator and extension users.

7. Telecommunications written media include teleprinter, telex, telecopiers, telewriters, viewdata (Prestel, Ceefax, Oracle).

8. There is a wide variety of mail services available from the Post Office and other sources. The user must choose the right services for regular and occasional needs, bearing in mind cost, speed, accuracy and security requirements. Post Office advisers are always willing to give guidance.

9. Procedures should be established for incoming and outgoing mail to ensure the quickest and most accurate mail handling system.

SELF-ASSESSMENT QUESTIONS

Answer all questions as quickly as possible. Do not turn back to the Chapter until you have completed this test.

1. When choosing the method of transmission for a particular piece of information, what six factors should be taken into consideration?

2. Why is face-to-face communication an expensive method of transmitting information?

3. What are the main differences between private manual branch exchange (PMBX) and private automatic branch exchange (PABX) from the point of view of: (*a*) the switchboard operator, and (*b*) the extension user.

4. What type of telephone equipment would you have installed: (*a*) so that a secretary could "filter" calls for her executive; (*b*) so that one of several people could answer incoming enquiries in the Parts Department of an engineering company; (*c*) if you were self-employed, had only a part-time clerk/typist to do your office work, and were frequently out "on-the-job"; (*d*) so that staff would know how much their telephone calls (outward) were costing the company; (*e*) if you wanted to monitor telephone calls with a view to identifying the heavy users and cutting costs?

5. Briefly explain the following abbreviations: STD; DDI; IDD; PABX.

6. List and briefly explain five types of trunk call which can be made through the telephone exchange operator. (Refer to a telephone directory if necessary.)

7. Give brief explanations of: (*a*) confravision; (*b*) radio paging; (*c*) viewdata; (*d*) telex.

8. What are the three main telephone directories issued to subscribers by British Telecom?

9. You are asked to explain to a newly recruited employee, a school-leaver, how to answer calls on an extension. List the points you would include in your explanation. The switchboard is a PABX.

10. What details should be given when asking for a message to be passed to someone who is not available to speak when you telephone?

11. What is the cheapest time of day to make a call during office hours?

12. State two ways in which you can help the telephone operator to be more efficient.

13. What is an intercommunication system?

14. Briefly explain four methods of paging.

15. What is the difference between a facsimile copier and a telewriter?

16. What postal services might you use to ensure the safe delivery of: (*a*) a letter to an inland address; (*b*) jewellery to the value of £500 sent to an inland address by first-class letter post; (*c*) a parcel containing a machine worth £150 to an inland address; (*d*) a package containing a book worth £50 to an overseas country to which mail cannot be registered?

17. Briefly explain: (*a*) special delivery; (*b*) Swiftair; (*c*) Datapost On Demand; (*d*) Nightrider; (*e*) Expresspost.

18. What is the difference between the Business Reply Service and Freepost?

19. Explain to a junior mailroom clerk the procedures for: (*a*) receiving and distributing incoming mail; (*b*) receiving and despatching outgoing mail.

20. List five machines which may be used in a mail room.

ASSIGNMENTS

Assignment 1

You are the Senior Clerk in charge of the Sales Order Office at Cuddly Toys Ltd. You supervise 25 order clerks, most of whom spend at least fifty per cent of their time on the telephone taking orders, receiving complaints about late delivery, etc. You consider that the company is losing business because of the clerks' telephone manner and general lack of efficiency in dealing with customers.

You discuss the matter with your superior, Mr John Allen, the Sales Manager. He suggests you devise and carry out a training programme and gives you authority to go ahead. Before you actually start training he would like to see your proposals.

Prepare for Mr Allen the following:

(*a*) a list of points you will include in the training for
- (*i*) receiving calls from customers all over the world,
- (*ii*) taking orders,
- (*iii*) receiving and dealing with complaints,
- (*iv*) making calls, about 25 per cent of them being overseas;

(*b*) an outline plan for training the 25 order clerks over a period of one month. Mr Allen has suggested that not more than 5 clerks should be taken for training at any one time, and not more than three hours a day should be spent in training.

Assignment 2

The Chief Accountant of Crystal Lighting Ltd. is complaining about the amount of money spent on postage. There are also complaints from many members of staff about the collection and delivery of mail internally. They say it is haphazard and unreliable. One case has been quoted of a very urgent letter being placed in an "Out" tray at 2.30 p.m. and not being collected until 10.30 a.m. the next day.

As you are the Mail Room Supervisor you bear the brunt of these complaints. It is obviously time you reviewed the mail handling system and procedures throughout the organisation. You have one clerk in the mail room who also acts as messenger to collect and deliver mail to the offices. It takes approximately 30 minutes "to do the round" of the building. Five to ten minutes of this time is spent in walking into the sections of the offices to the mail trays, which are usually placed on window sills. The offices are open plan with an aisle down the middle. Many offices have mail addressed to the same companies, though to different people within them. These are all posted separately at present. All mail is sent 1st class unless indicated otherwise.

Mail is delivered to you by Post Office van at approximately 0900 hours and 1200 hours. The postman who delivers also collects at 1200 hours and again at 1700 hours. The average day's mail consists of the following:

0900 hours	approx. 250 incoming letters and 20 packets/parcels
1200 hours	approx. 50 incoming letters and 10 packets/parcels
	approx. 100 outgoing letters and 6 packets/parcels
1700 hours	approx. 300 outgoing letters and 15 packets/parcels

(*a*) Prepare a daily time schedule for mail room activities indicating those which you will undertake and those which will be carried out by your assistant.

(*b*) Write a memorandum to the Chief Accountant suggesting how you propose to reduce postage costs.

(*c*) Write a circular memorandum to the staff explaining the new procedures as they affect the staff. Also suggest any suitable means by which staff can help speed up collection and delivery of mail.

CHAPTER NINE

A Computer System

> CHAPTER OBJECTIVES
>
> After studying this chapter you should be able to:
> * describe the main parts of a computer system;
> * describe the processes involved in electronic data processing;
> * describe the differences and relationships between hardware and software.

DEFINITION AND PURPOSE

What is a computer? When this question is asked a variety of answers will be forthcoming. Here are a few examples.

(*a*) An electronic brain controlled by a man.
(*b*) A means of storing information/data.
(*c*) A piece of machinery which, with the aid of software, can carry out a vast amount of work in the least amount of time.
(*d*) A large electrical arithmetic machine with storage capacity.
(*e*) A machine with endless possibilities.
(*f*) A machine which does exactly what it is told.
(*g*) A machine designed to make complicated and laborious jobs easier.

All these answers are correct. The dictionary definition of a computer is "electronic calculating machine". The machine itself makes calculations in accordance with instructions. The most complex operations are reduced to arithmetical form for the computer to handle.

What is a system? Any system, be it manual, mechanical, electrical or electronic, is simply the arrangement of activities into a pre-determined sequence.

A computer system is therefore a series of activities processed electronically. To achieve this there must be input devices, the central processing unit (CPU) and output devices. These various pieces of machinery are known as the hardware. The instructions which tell the machinery what to do are contained in a program which is known as the software.

When we discussed storage and retrieval of information in

Chapter Six we included the people who stored information, the people who retrieved it and the purpose for which it might be wanted, the equipment needed and its location, the type of information contained on various kinds of media, retention periods, etc. All these factors make up the system whether that system be the familiar manilla folders and filing cabinets or cupboards or the latest electronic equipment. A very simplified diagram (Fig. 63) illustrates the system of charging and receiving payment for electricity supply, using the computer as a tool within the system.

It is important to realise that a computer very rarely makes a mistake. Faults usually occur as a result of inaccurate or inadequate input, which is a human responsibility.

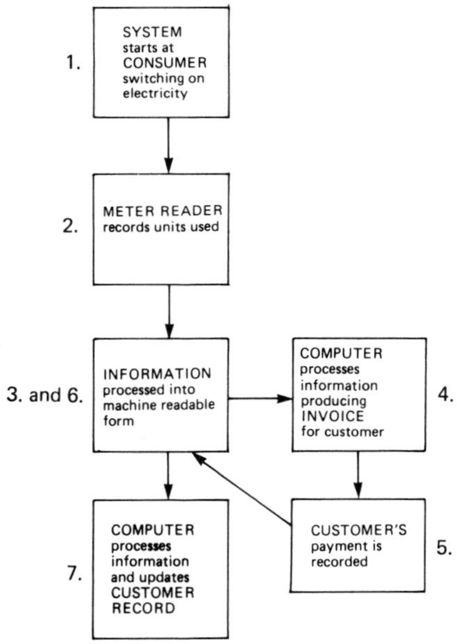

Fig. 63. *A diagrammatic illustration of a system.*

THE CENTRAL PROCESSING UNIT

The "heart" of the computer system is the central processing unit (CPU) or "mainframe" as it is frequently called.

Components

The CPU consists of three components, viz. the control unit, the arithmetic unit and the core store or memory.

Control unit

The control unit controls the input and output devices, commonly called peripherals, and the sequence in which the activities of processing are carried out.

Arithmetic unit

The arithmetic unit does the actual calculations. It can add, subtract and divide. Multiplication is carried out by addition. All other calculations, e.g. percentages, square roots, are calculated by application of the three basic principles.

Memory

The memory contains the programs which control the computer. It also contains compilers and assemblers which interpret the programs it is instructed to work on. These are explained below. The control program, compilers and assemblers are known as resident programs or firmware. In addition the memory has to hold the programs, or parts of them, and the data which is being worked on at any given time. There may be a range of programs in operation—this is known as multiprogramming—because many users may be accessing, inputting, updating and/or amending information at the same time.

Compiler

The compiler is a program which converts programs written in a high-level language, often similar to human readable language, into machine code, i.e. binary arithmetic.

Assembler

The assembler is a program which converts "assembly language", which consists of a series of symbols, into machine code.

Binary arithmetic

The computer operates on the basis of varying combinations of two digits, 0 and 1. Binary arithmetic works on the basis of doubling, so $1 \times 2 = 2$, $2 \times 2 = 4$, $4 \times 2 = 8$, etc. If these values are written in sequence from the right of the page we get

256 128 64 32 16 8 4 2 1

Each of these values is given a binary value of 1. In order to write the figures in binary form we have to indicate how far along the line we have moved from the right by placing a 0 for a value we do not want. Thus

Decimal	*Binary*
1	1
2	10
4	100
8	1000
etc.	

The intermediate numbers are made up of combinations of these values.

1 + 2 = 3	11	
1 + 4 = 5	101	(2 is not represented, thus 0)
2 + 4 = 6	110	
1 + 2 + 4 = 7	111	
1 + 8 = 9	1001	
2 + 8 = 10	1010	
1 + 2 + 4 + 8 = 15	1111	
1 + 16 = 17	10001	

These binary figures are known as bits, from BInary digiTS. Bits are usually combined into a series, of which there are three.

Character
A character consists of six bits which give sixty-four possible combinations of bits. This size of group has been virtually superseded by the eight-bit byte—see below.

Byte
A byte consists of eight bits which gives 256 possible combinations. (The French word for a byte is *un octet*, which indicates the number 8.)

Word
Computer words may consist of from sixteen to thirty-six bits, which greatly expands the range of possible combinations of bits. In some machines the length of the word is flexible according to the needs of each instruction. Whether the bits are combined into bytes or computer words depends on the make, model and age of the computer.

Numbers used in denary or decimal arithmetic can easily be converted into binary arithmetic. Letters of the alphabet are coded arithmetically, i.e. each letter is given a representative numerical value. This can then be converted into binary digits. There are standard codes for the conversion of letters, punctuation signs, symbols, etc., into machine code.

Computer capacity

The "size" of a computer is its capacity, that is to say the number of bytes or words which the CPU memory can hold. It is common to talk of 16K, 32K, 256K computers. Because we are using binary arithmetic K represents 1024, unlike the decimal k, which represents 1,000. A 32K computer can store 32 × 1024 bytes or words), i.e. 32,768 bytes. As the physical size of computers becomes smaller in relation to capacity you hear people saying "We have 32 megabytes", i.e. 32 million bytes, or 33,554,432 bytes in binary value. The capacity of the memory is important because it regulates the amount of data which can be processed at any one time.

PROGRAMMING

A computer has to be told what to do. These instructions are given in the form of a *program*. Because the computer cannot think the instructions have to be precise, absolutely accurate and be able to deal with any situation which might arise. The steps in the program must be in a carefully thought out sequence and provision must be made for every possible activity which may be required, whether frequently or only occasionally.

Types of instruction

There are four types of instruction which a computer can carry out.

Input, output and file instructions

An input instruction tells the computer to read the next input item, e.g. the next punched card or the next item on a magnetic tape or disk. The output instruction indicates that a line is to be printed on paper, a microfilm image is to be produced or a line presented on the visual display unit. The file instruction tells the computer to include the information on the file storage device, e.g. write to the magnetic tape or disk.

Internal transfer instructions

This tells the computer to move data around from input information to file records, to withdraw information from the file record for updating, etc.

Arithmetic instructions
These tell the computer to calculate.

Logical instructions
These provide for the comparison of one value with another, the identification of errors and the action to take when an error is found.

Preparing instructions

When an instruction or a series of instructions is given to a computer the programmer must analyse in minute detail exactly what has to be done, and provide a separate instruction for each item. We will take an example of something we all do frequently, washing our hair. If we analyse this task the steps will be:

(*a*) wet hair;
(*b*) apply shampoo;
(*c*) rub hair and scalp;
(*d*) rinse;
(*e*) repeat (*b*);
(*f*) repeat (*c*);
(*g*) repeat (*d*);
(*h*) part dry with towel.

These instructions would not be adequate for a computer. In the first place you cannot wet your hair until you have leaned over the basin (first step) and turned on the tap (second step). After wetting the hair we ought to turn off the tap. We cannot apply the shampoo unless we pick up the bottle, unscrew the cap and so on. The analysis must be very detailed and it must also be absolutely logical. Any mistake in the logic may result in the program "going into a loop". This means that it keeps going round in a circle from one point in the program to another. This can be shown diagrammatically in Fig. 64, using our washing hair example.

Narrative program

Programs can be written in narrative form. An example of a very simple program to update stock records is set out below. The transactions would include: new stock items, an addition referred to as Type A; change of balance (an issue or receipt), referred to as Type C; and deletion of a stock item referred to as Type D.

Specimen program to update stock records files by transaction
(1) Open master file (MF).
(2) Open transaction file (TF).

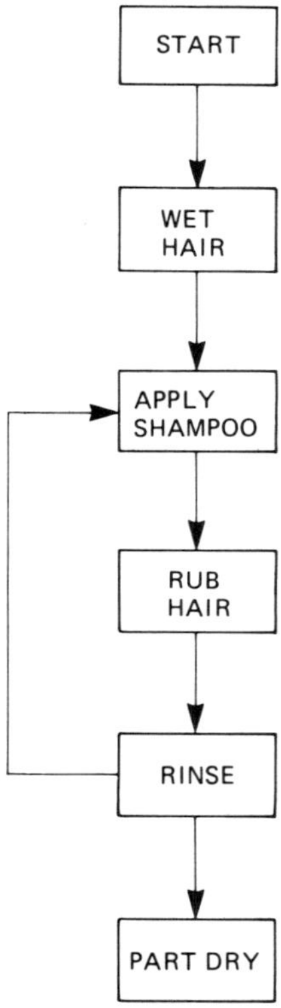

Fig. 64. *Steps in a computer program. At the Rinse point the program would keep going round and round because there is no step to stop it after the first repeat of steps 3, 4 and 5. Therefore the second application of shampoo, rubbing hair and rinsing would have to be repeated in the program instruction.*

(3) Open new master file (NMF).
(4) Check master file operational.
(5) Check transaction file operational.
(6) Check new master file operational.
(7) Read first stock code on TF.
(8) Read and identify first type on TF.

IF TYPE A
(9) Read first stock code on MF.
(10) Compare MF and TF stock codes.
(11A) If MF stock code less than TF stock code, transfer all information under MF stock code to NMF.

(11B) If MF stock code same as TF stock code, print error report: "stock code already exists".

(11C) If MF stock code greater than TF stock code, transfer all information and TF stock code to NMF.

IF TYPE C

(9) Read first stock code on MF.

(10) Compare MF and TF stock codes.

(11A) If MF stock code less than TF stock code, transfer all information under MF stock code to NMF.

(11B) If MF stock code same as TF stock code, update relevant information under MF stock code and transfer existing and updated information to NMF.

(11C) If MF stock code greater than TF stock code, print error report: "no stock code exists".

IF TYPE D

(9) Read first stock code on MF.

(10) Compare MF and TF stock codes.

(11A) If MF stock code less than TF stock code, transfer all information under MF stock code to NMF.

(11B) If MF stock code same as TF stock code, proceed to next TF stock code, step (14).

(11C) If MF stock code greater than TF stock code, print error report: "no stock code exists".

IF ELSE

(9) Print error report: "transaction type not valid".

(12) Read next stock code on TF.
Repeat steps (10) to (13) until all master and transaction file items have been compared.

(13A) Process remaining transaction file items if any.

OR

(13B) Transfer remaining MF codes (if any) to NMF.

END OF RUN

Flow chart

To check the logic of a program it is usual to prepare a flow chart. The narrative program above would be shown as in Fig. 65.

The computer cannot be asked to make a choice. Therefore each step must consist of a single question to which the answer is "Yes" or "No". Depending on what the answer is so the next step is programmed.

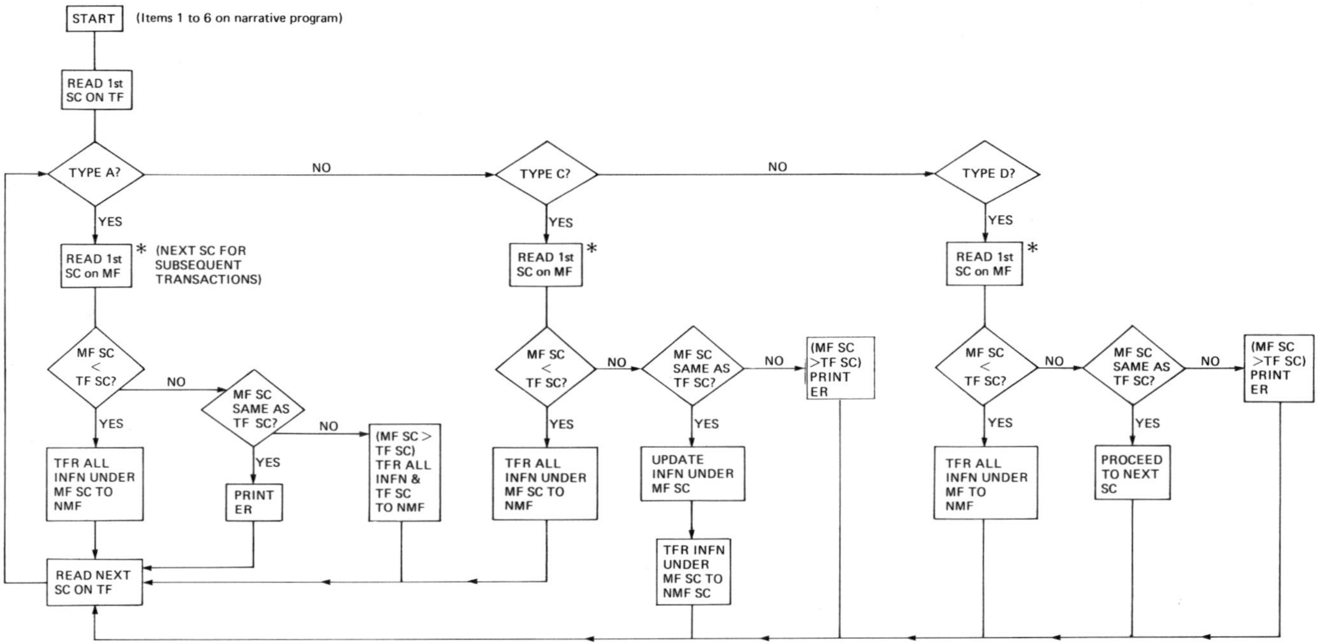

KEY: MF = Master File
SC = Stock Code
TF = Transaction File
NMF = New Master File
ER = Error Report (Refer to narrative program to identify)

Fig. 65. *Computer program flow chart.*

Languages

So far we have discussed the preparation of a program in human readable form, either using words to explain the steps to be taken, or combining words with diagrams to indicate progressions. The standard computer cannot understand plain language so special languages have been developed which they can understand.

There are three main categories of computer language, viz. machine language, low-level languages and high-level languages.

Machine language

Machine code is rarely used by programmers except for special tasks which cannot be programmed by any other means. Machine code is a set of binary code instructions. Unfortunately this method is wide open to human error.

Low-level languages

Low-level languages are really series of abbreviations which represent standard functions carried out on a computer. For example, a frequent operation is to retrieve information from the memory of the computer. A standard abbreviation enables the programmer to give the necessary instructions without having to identify the precise place in the memory.

High-level languages

High-level languages most nearly relate to plain English. There are a number of these languages, each one having been devised for a particular use. The most commonly used for commercial activities is COBOL (COmmon Business Oriented Language). A single word or phrase in a high-level language generates a series of activities in the computer. For example the instruction to locate a particular piece of information may involve retrieving data, checking and comparing. This series of activities is generated by the command to "locate", which has been interpreted from the source program by the compiler into machine code instructions.

Some programming languages

Language name	*Meaning*	*Level*	*Use*
COBOL	COmmon Business Oriented Language	High	General business*
ALGOL	ALGOrithmic Language	High	Mathematical and scientific

Language name	*Meaning*	*Level*	*Use*
FORTRAN	FORmula TRANslation	High	Mathematical and scientific
BASIC	Beginners All-purpose Symbolic Instruction Code	High	General business* (especially on micro computers)
ATLAS	800 per cent bigger than FORTRAN. Contains 440 words which can be read by both humans and machines	High	Interface language enabling incompatible computers to inter-communicate
RPG	Report Program Generator	High	Accounting
PL1	Programming Language 1	High	Provides for both commercial and mathematical data
APL	A Programming Language	High	Lists of items which are ordered in some way and share some common characteristic/s
PASCAL		High	More complex programs on micro-processors*
PROLOG		High	Artificial Intelligence

* Can be used with microprocessors

Artificial Intelligence

The word "intelligence" suggests the power of thinking. Computers are now being developed which can *apparently* think. For example they can be programmed to play chess, recognise patterns and shapes—even faces, prove mathematical theorems, etc. This is known as Artificial Intelligence, or AI.

DATA PREPARATION

It is possible for us to read from and write on a variety of materials. We can scratch letters, figures and pictures on stone; we write on parchment, paper, chalkboards, whiteboards, transparencies, etc. If we wish to retain the information we write on something which can be kept permanently, e.g. paper. In the same way computers read information from and write new information on to various types of medium. The information is retained so that it can be referred to again and can be updated. The process of recording the information for processing is known as data preparation, data entry or data capture.

There are six media which are commonly used to feed information into the computer, receive information from the computer, and store it for reference or future updating. Some systems need updating at specified times, e.g. billing, payroll, personnel and training records. Other systems are constantly active, i.e. changes are occurring at random, e.g. airline and hotel reservations, payment to customer accounts, production schedules. The medium used will to some extent depend upon the volume of information being processed, stored and referred to regularly.

Types of medium

Punched card

Punched cards are manilla cards, providing eighty columns across and nine columns down. Figures are represented by a hole being punched in the appropriate space in the vertical column and letters are represented by a series of holes which are, in fact, numerical codes. Figure 66 shows the letters of the alphabet, figures, punctuation signs and symbols punched in accordance with the British Standard Code.

Cards are punched on a machine called a key punch. The operator has a batch of documents, the information on each one being keyed in on to a card. The information is usually printed at the top of the card as well. After the first keying in the cards are passed to a verifier who repeats the keying in process. This is to identify and correct any errors in the first processing.

Magnetic tape

Information is "written" in the form of magnetic dots. A 2,400ft reel of magnetic tape can hold 160 million bytes of information. A

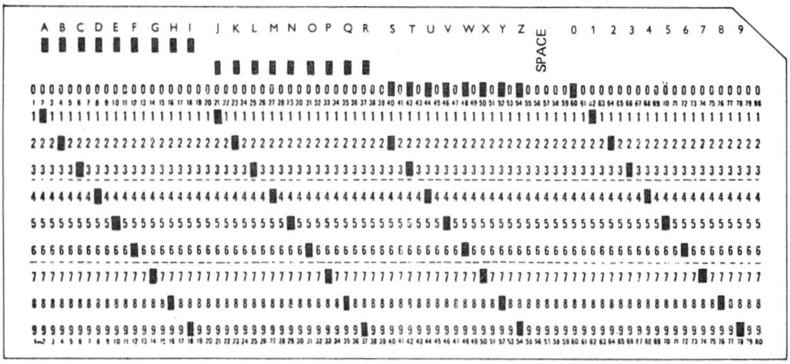

Fig. 66(a). *Alpha-numeric characters punched in accordance with British Standard Card Code.*

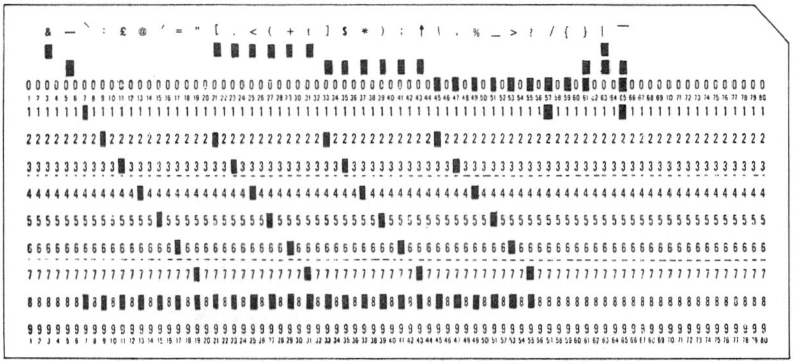

Fig. 66(b). *Special symbols in British Standard Card Code.*

file held on tape is divided into records. A record is a group of elements, called fields, relating to one item, e.g. a customer, a product. This is illustrated diagrammatically in Fig. 67. The information is stored serially, which means that the records follow in sequence which may be numerical, alphabetic or some other classification.

Magnetic diskette (floppy disk)
See Fig. 68.

Floppy disks are used in some micro computers, e.g. word processors. They are inserted into a disk drive in which the disk revolves at high speeds. Information is stored at random according to an arithmetic coding. When particular information is required,

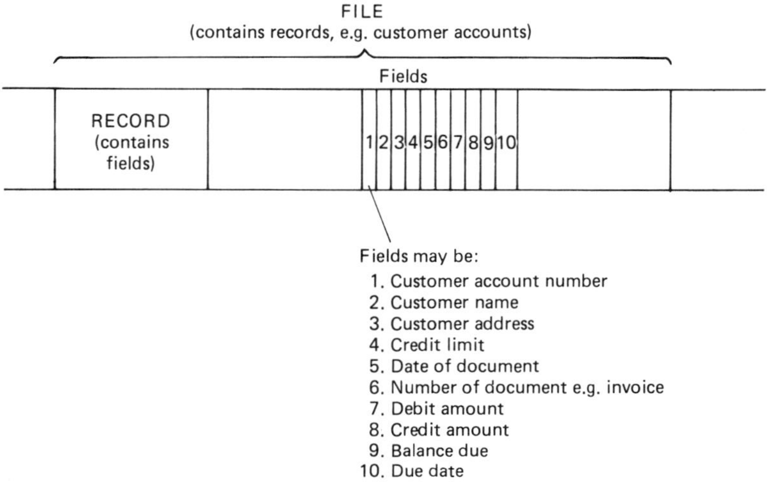

Fig. 67. *Format of information recorded on magnetic tape.*

Fig. 68. *Magnetic diskette.*
(Courtesy Vydek UK Ltd.)

the program "searches" for it—this is known as random access. The capacity of diskettes varies from about 50 pages to 250 pages. New diskettes are being developed which are smaller in size ($3\frac{1}{2}$ ins) but can hold up to 1 megabyte of information (approximately 400 pages).

Magnetic disk
See Fig. 69.

A magnetic disk is often referred to as a hard disk and can hold from 30 million to 600+ million bytes. The nearest equivalent in paper volume is probably about 24,000 A4 pages. This capacity is steadily being increased. A hard disk consists of a number of "plates" attached to a central spindle with a gap between each one. Each plate has "tracks" on both sides, called faces. Each face has its own read/write head for identifying and recording information. The top and bottom faces of the pack are not used. The number of plates varies from two, known as a disk cartridge, to twelve.

Fig. 69. *Magnetic disk.*
(Courtesy Vydek UK Ltd.)

Mass storage
A large store of information is known as a "database". A mass storage medium may be needed so that the whole database can be accessed. There are storage cartridges which hold from 35 billion to 472 billion bytes of information. The future mass storage medium is likely to be the optical disk operated with lasers.

INPUT

Input to computers may be either by indirect entry or direct entry. It is usually necessary to have some kind of interface equipment when indirect entry methods are used. That is to say there has to be a machine which interprets the input and transforms it into another form suitable for transmission to the computer.

Punched cards are normally produced on a key punch. The cards are passed through a card reader which scans the holes with a light. The information is interpreted and transferred on to magnetic tape or disk for processing by the computer. Punched cards can also be produced on a typewriter, accounting machine or cash register. The marks are converted into holes by a mark sensor. It should be said that the use of punched cards is gradually being discontinued in many organisations.

Kimball tags are another form of punched card (*see* Fig. 70). They are currently used mainly by retailers on clothes. The tags are processed in the same way as punched cards.

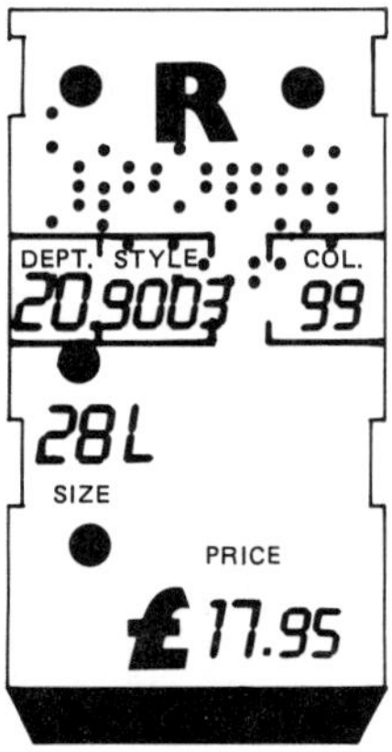

Fig. 70. *Kimball tag.*

Key-to-tape/Key-to-disk is replacing punched card input to a large extent. As the data is keyed in it is recorded directly on to magnetic tape or disk. This cuts out the second process of interpreting and transferring data from punched cards on to tape/disk. When the information has been keyed in by one operator it is verified by another operator in the same way as with punched cards. The data is then ready for processing.

Magnetic Ink Character Recognition is a method of input used primarily by banks. The characters at the bottom of cheques are printed in magnetic ink (*see* Fig. 71). When the cheques are processed the handwritten information is keyed in, and is printed in magnetic ink so that all the relevant information can be transferred by a magnetic ink character reader on to disk. Paying-in/credit transfer vouchers are processed in the same way.

⑈892870⑈ 20⑉6045⑆ 00787655⑈

Fig. 71. *Magnetic ink characters as printed on cheques.*

Optical Character Recognition is a means of input by which pre-printed material can be recorded on diskette, tape or disk by optical scanning. Until a few years ago optical scanners were capable of "reading" only text printed in special characters known as OCR characters. The latest scanners are able to "read" a range of type faces and pitches. Optical character readers are still not one hundred per cent accurate but they do provide a means of recording information on to magnetic medium quickly. The information can then be retrieved on screen, checked and amended if necessary.

Bar codes are now found on many products. They are also used on components and parts in stores, in libraries and in retailers such as Argos shops. The bar code (*see* Fig. 72) is scanned by either a laser or optical scanner. The laser scanner is under a glass panel over which the bar code is passed. An optical scanner is usually in the form of a "pen" which is held in the hand and passed across the code. Laser scanners are very accurate. The thick and thin lines represent numerical codes which are interpreted and the information is transmitted to a storage medium or terminal. A typical tally roll printout from a supermarket checkout terminal is illustrated at Fig. 73. Bar codes may also be recorded on a magnetic strip which is "read" by a hand-held magnetic scanner.

5 000218 001023

Fig. 72. *Bar code on, for example, grocery packaging. The code is scanned from right to left either optically by a light pen, or by a laser beam.*

F/HOUSE LOAF	.22
MEAT	.60½
JAC/MALLOWS	.21
GREEN GROC	.32
MEAT	.50½
MARS BAR	.12
BOURNVILLE	.19½
CRUNCHIE BAR	.12
BOUNTY	.12
GREEN GROC	.25
GREEN GROC	.10
GREEN GROC	.36½
GROCERY	.04½
GREEN GROC	.15½
TOTAL	3.33
CSH TEND	5.00
CHANGE DUE	1.67

16/10/79 12:46 0486/ 6

HAVE A NICE DAY

Fig. 73. *Tally roll printout showing details of items purchased.*

Badges or plastic cards have a magnetic strip on which information is recorded. These are used for access control to prevent unauthorised entry into security areas. The card is slotted into a device attached to doors. The device "reads" the code and either accepts it, activating a switch which allows the door to be opened, or does not react. Bank cards and certain credit cards operate in a similar way. Their use will be discussed in Chapter Ten.

Electronic writing pad such as Micropad or Telepad allows information to be input by normal handwriting with a ballpoint pen or pencil. A pre-printed form is laid on an electronic pad. As letters, etc., are written the shape of the pressure is sensed, converted into a code which is then transmitted to the computer or on to tape or disk for later processing.

Voice recognition is being developed but has not yet reached the stage of common usage. Input direct from the spoken word is possible but there are still problems to be overcome. For example the voice of someone with a cold, or drunk, would not be recognised, assuming that the computer had recorded the voice when it was normal.

There are many variations of the method of input. Those discussed are the ones most commonly used in business.

Video terminals
These normally consist of a keyboard and a visual display unit (VDU). The normal typewriter QWERTY keyboard is the most commonly used but the Maltron keyboard, which is said to be ergonomically superior and faster to operate, is gaining popularity. The information "keyed in" is reproduced on the screen for checking and is then transmitted.

Video terminals may be "on line", i.e. in direct communication with the computer which is updating its files on tape or disk as the information is keyed in. Alternatively the information may be held in a buffer store until keying in of part or all the data is complete (depending on the capacity of the buffer store). The data is then "filed" from the buffer store on to the magnetic tape or disk.

Many video terminals are two-way, i.e. send data to the computer and receive data from it on the visual display screen in answer to requests for information. These terminals are known as "interactive".

Light pens
These are used to touch a spot on the front of a cathode ray tube to select an item from several displayed on a screen. This method of input is used primarily for educational and research work, and for design by, for example, architects.

OUTPUT

When information has been processed in the central processing unit the new data will be stored on one of the storage media, e.g. tape or disk. It will also frequently be produced in a human readable form. There is a variety of peripheral devices which can do this.

Visual output
Output that can be read can be produced on printers, microfilm and interactive terminals.

Printout

There are five different types of printer used for producing data.

(*a*) *Serial printers* usually print with a daisywheel and produce the text or figures character by character. These printers are relatively slow, speeds varying from about 2,000 characters to 3,000 characters a minute. That means a fairly full A4 page in about 20 seconds, on average.

(*b*) *Line printers* operate with either a drum or a chain. They print at speeds ranging from 300 to 2,400 lines a minute. The drum type printer has 132 characters across it with either 64 or 128 characters round. The more characters there are on the drum the faster it can print. Figure 74 illustrates the way a drum printer works. The chain operated printer has the advantage of being easily interchangeable, so that different print styles can be used as required. Individual slugs in the chain can be changed, e.g. a £ sign can be replaced by a $ sign. It operates on the basis of a chain revolving around two sprockets (*see* Fig. 75).

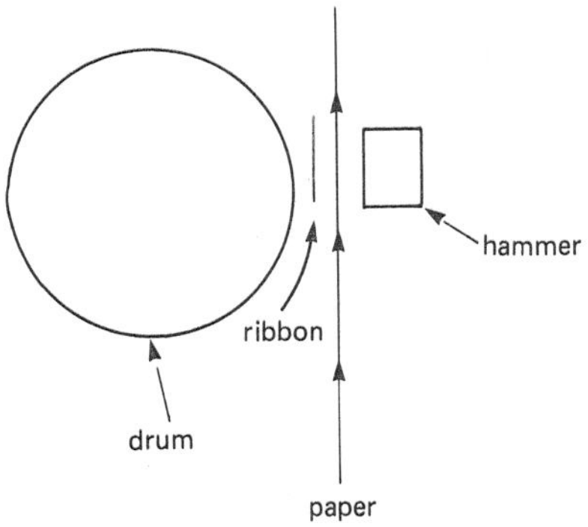

Fig. 74. *Drum line printer. The drum revolves and as the character required comes into position for printing the appropriate hammer (there are 132) hits the back of the paper causing an impression to be made by the ribbon.*

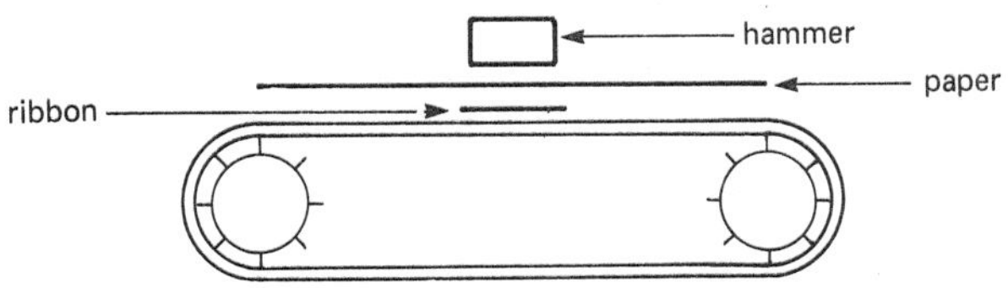

Fig. 75. *Chain line printer. The chain revolves around sprockets. As the required character reaches the printing position the hammer behind the paper strikes the paper in the same way as the drum printer.*

(*c*) *Laser printers* are faster, being capable of producing up to thirty-six A4-size letters a minute. It can be incorporated into an "intelligent" copier which can receive data direct from a computer, merge it with a standard letter and print out the result. Each document is an original.

(*d*) *Ink jet printers* are faster again. A special ink has to be used because it has to be wet enough to spray, yet quite dry the moment it reaches the paper. It works on the basis of magnetic fields, in the same way as xerographic copiers. Information on the tape or disk is recognised and magnetised. The magnetised area attracts the ink from the jet.

(*e*) *Electronic printers*, of which there are currently very few in the United Kingdom, reproduce hard copy from their own disks. The file on the computer tape is read on to the printer disk in page format. The printer belt receives the image of page 1 and prints it. This process is repeated for page 2 and so on, throughout the document. The printing of the document in this way can be repeated as many times as required, each copy being an original. It is produced in collated form ready for fastening or binding. The electronic printer produces two A4 size pages per second, or 120 pages a minute. Thus ten copies of a sixty-page report can be produced in 5 minutes, all ready for distribution.

Traction feeds are used with printers to feed the paper into the machine in the form of continuous stationery. The paper has sprocket holes down each side. The holes fit on sprocket wheels on either side of the printer and as the wheels turn it draws the paper into the printing position. The printed sheets are fed out of the printer in "concertina" form and are later "burst", i.e. separated, on a special machine.

Hopper feeds are used when printout is required on individual sheets of paper, e.g. letterheads. The paper is stacked in the hopper feed which pushes one sheet at a time into the printing position.

Graph plotter

There are various types of graph plotter available. The basic principle of this type of output is that statistical information is keyed in and the output is shown on the VDU as a bar chart (horizontal or vertical), histogram or graph. Alternatively, output may be on a printer in the form of a graph. Both screen and printing may be in colours. Special software packages are necessary for graph plotting.

Computer originated microfilm (COM)

Instead of printing out information on paper, the computer can produce data from tape or disk directly on to microfilm. This form of output may be used when the information is to be distributed widely or when it is intended mainly for reference purposes at random, e.g. stock records. It is also used when the information is needed for storage rather than action.

Computer assisted image processing enables a terminal operator to retrieve information on a special image terminal (*see* Fig. 76) linked to an on-line data terminal. With interface equipment the image terminal can itself be on-line. Large documents such as insurance policies can be viewed on the image terminal screen. A printout can be obtained by simply pressing the "PRINT" button.

Fig. 76. *Kodak 1MT-150 Image Terminal.*
(Courtesy Kodak Ltd.)

Visual display units

These present information keyed in and information requested. It is a television style screen, usually green characters on a paler green background. There are also blue screens and black on white screens, the latter mainly used on some word processors. There is two-way communication between the terminal operator and the computer.

Console typewriter
This is used by the computer operator to control the programming of the computer and to carry out checks. The operator receives feedback from the computer.

SECURITY

Storage
The media on which data is stored must be kept secure as well as free from dust and dirt. Tapes and disks are stored on racks in cupboards, usually in locked rooms near the computer room, or off the computer room. These rooms must have fire extinguishing equipment and smoke detection devices.

To ensure that vital data is safe it is usual to make a copy of all tapes and disks. It is quite common for the duplicates to be stored at another location.

Three generation storage is usual. This means that files are kept until they have been updated three times, i.e. there are always three "generations"—grandfather, father, son. This is shown diagrammatically below in Fig. 77. This can be very important if problems arise during the day when a file is being updated for example. Disks can be corrupted in various ways and if the system "goes down" it can mean that the information being worked on is lost. Although the input may have to be repeated the back up ensures that the previous information is not lost.

Access control
Access to data held on files or in the database must be limited to those people who need to use the information. This is especially important where confidential information, e.g. personnel records, is concerned. It is also necessary to ensure that updating and destruction of files is carried out by only those people authorised to do so. Each person so authorised has a personal code, which may be a name, series of letters or a number. This identification is keyed in by the person concerned before information is "released" from the files.

SUMMARY

1. The hardware of a computer system consists of the central processing unit (CPU) and a variety of peripheral devices for input and output of information.

2. The central processing unit operates on two digits, 0 and 1. All input has to be converted from human readable form into binary

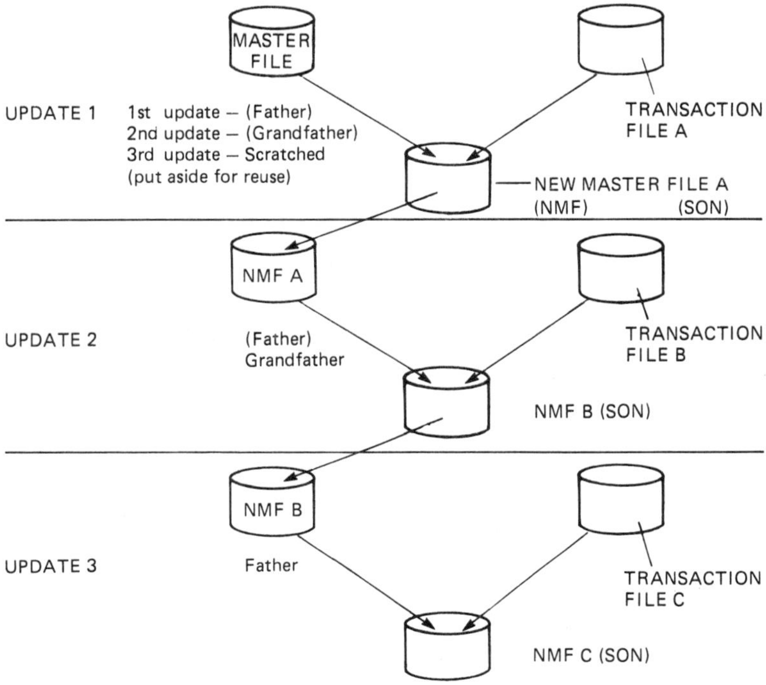

Fig. 77. *Three generation storage.*

arithmetic and output has to be converted from binary into human readable form. The CPU contains a compiler and/or assembler to do this.

3. A program is a series of instructions which "tell" the computer what to do. A program is written in a special language depending on the type of work it is controlling.

4. A computer programming language may be low-level or high-level. Low-level languages usually consist of symbols and abbreviations which are converted by the assembler in the CPU to binary form. High-level languages generate a series of activities by one instruction or statement. The compiler in the CPU converts this kind of instruction into machine readable form, i.e. binary.

5. A program may be written in narrative form and is usually prepared diagrammatically as a flow chart. This enables the programmer to see that the sequence of activities is logical and to identify alternatives and possible problem areas.

6. There is a variety of methods for preparing data for input to the

computer. Some of the media, e.g. punched tape, cannot be "over-written", i.e. used again, when previous information is out of date. Magnetic media, e.g. tape, can be used many times. The kind of media used depends on the quantity of information to be stored or accessed.

7. Security of information is vital. Precautions must be taken to ensure that access to data is available to authorised people only. The safety of stored information is usually secured by "three generation storage" and protection against fire hazards.

SELF-ASSESSMENT QUESTIONS

Answer all questions as quickly as possible. Do not turn back to the Chapter until you have completed the test.

1. What is a computer system?

2. Name the components of the central processing unit and state the purpose of each component.

3. Briefly define the following:
(*a*) input and output peripheral;
(*b*) high-level language;
(*c*) compiler;
(*d*) assembler;
(*e*) machine readable language.

4. What is a bit?

5. Briefly explain:
(*a*) COM;
(*b*) graph plotter.

6. How many types of instruction can a computer accept? What are they?

7. What is meant by the term "a 256K computer"?

8. What is a flow chart?

9. Name three high-level program languages used for different purposes.

10. How is data entered on a punched card?

11. Name four types of magnetic media giving a guide to the amount of information which can be stored on each.

12. What do the abbreviations MICR and OCR represent?

13. In supermarkets many commodities are now marked with a block of black and white stripes printed on the wrapping. What is this block of stripes and how is it used?

14. What is an interactive terminal?

15. Explain the following:
(*a*) key-to-disk;

(*b*) video terminal;
(*c*) line printer;
(*d*) three generation storage;
(*e*) access control;
(*f*) interface equipment;
(*g*) badge code reader;
(*h*) hopper feed;
(*i*) ATLAS;
(*j*) byte.

ASSIGNMENTS

Assignment 1

There are 20 employees at Bright Nuts and Bolts Ltd. The age range is from 18 to 65 years. On 1st January each year all employees receive a salary increment. Those aged 18–20 years receive 5 per cent, 21–25 years 8 per cent, 26 years and over 10 per cent.

Write a narrative program for the computer to update the salaries of all employees on 1st January next year. Prepare a flow chart to ensure that all details have been included.

Assignment 2

If you are working in an organisation which has a computer installation, or if your tutor can arrange for you to visit an installation, write notes on the system. Your notes should include details of how the data is received and processed for entry into the computer, the peripheral devices, information about the CPU, methods of output and security arrangements. Include appropriate illustrations (photographs, drawings, diagrams, forms).

CHAPTER TEN

Using a Computer System

> CHAPTER OBJECTIVES
>
> After studying this chapter you should be able to:
> * identify the applications of electronic data processing to:
>   (*a*) routine business systems, and
>   (*b*) management and other non-routine systems and techniques;
> * explain the procedures involved in computerising an existing manual or automatic system;
> * recognise the importance of input standards to the efficient functioning of a computerised system.

DEFINITION AND PURPOSE

What is meant by the application of a computer system? Quite simply it is the purpose for which the computer is used, e.g. keeping records of stock. There are routine applications, and non-routine and specialist applications. Routine applications are those which any organisation would normally wish to load on to the computer.

Having installed a computer system it is most important to use it cost effectively. It is also essential to ensure that the electronic system is as efficient, or if possible more efficient, than the existing manual or mechanical system. At first sight it may seem that these criteria are the responsibility of the computer department staff. This is true but they are not solely responsible. The effective application of a computer system depends on each person who is concerned at any point from the completion of the first document or giving of the first instruction, through to the person or people who use the output in whatever form it may be.

THE PEOPLE INVOLVED

The data which computers process has to come from somewhere, so there must be people at the input end of the system. Someone needs the data which is produced as a result of the processing, so there must be people at the output end of the system. The computer itself has to be instructed to carry out the various types of processing, so there have to be people to design the systems, write the programs and operate the machines. Let us look first at the work involved and the computer staff.

Computer functions and staff

There are three main *functions* in the computer department, namely *systems analysis*, *programming* and *operations*. Depending on the size of the organisation there may be several staff working within each function or there may be very few staff and their work crosses functional boundaries. Computer departments can vary in size from two people to several hundred.

The computer department in many organisations is an integral part of the management services function. This is because the normal management services activities are often closely linked to computer activities.

In the organisation chart shown in Fig. 78 the structure is based

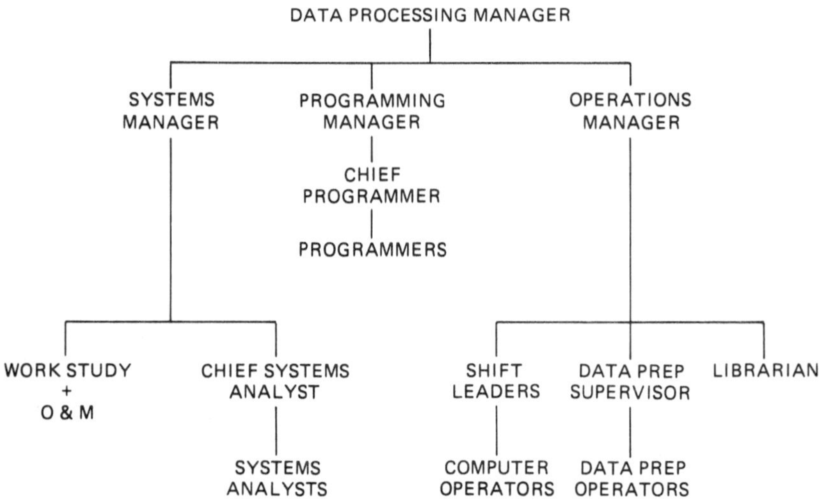

Fig. 78. *Computer department organisation based on functions.*

on functions. You will see that work study and O and M (Organisation and Methods, which is discussed in Chapter Thirteen) are part of the systems function. An alternative organisation structure, based on project development, usually more appropriate to a large DP department, is shown at Fig. 79.

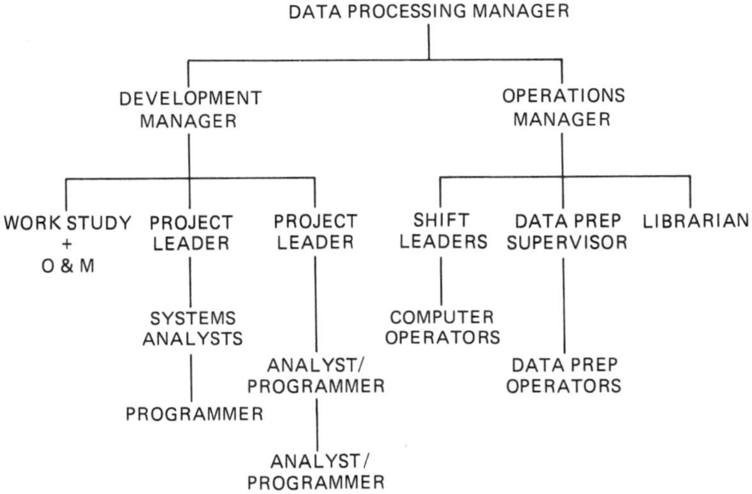

Fig. 79. *Computer department organisation based on project development.*

Computer (or DP) manager

The computer manager is in over all control of the department. His role is to ensure that an efficient and cost effective service is provided for the organisation. This means close liaison with senior management, strict control of projects for taking on new systems applications and monitoring of performance to ensure that faults are dealt with promptly.

Systems analysts

The systems analyst takes a broad view and looks at the over all system from input, through the computer processing, to the output. He is concerned with the planning and implementation of changeover from manual or automatic systems to computerised systems. There are also *systems designers* who undertake the actual design of the computer system after the system requirements have been investigated by the analysts.

The systems analyst may have responsibility for a wide variety of activities. These usually include investigating and recording existing systems, reporting on possible alternative systems, controlling the introduction of new systems and checking results. Each project or task the systems analyst undertakes is usually carried out in phases.

1. A feasibility study is carried out to find out whether a prospective user would benefit by having a computer or computerised system. The systems analyst needs to investigate current methods

by examining existing procedures and interviewing users. He records the activities (frequencies, volume, who does them) and incorporates this information in a *feasibility report*. He also devises possible methods of using a computer to carry out the work and includes details in the report with a recommendation as to the best one to be adopted. Time schedules, costs and benefits to the user will also form part of the report.

2. If the feasibility report is accepted and a policy decision is made to change the system, the analyst prepares a more detailed *system specification*. This provides a basis for final agreement with the user and gives instructions to the programmer who will write the appropriate program/s.

The system specification usually includes:

layouts for input forms and/or screen displays,
structure of files and records,
format for output reports—printout, screen display,
procedures for file loading and conversion,
training needs,
time schedules for the various activities.

3. While the program is being written, the analyst liaises with user and operations departments to ensure that staff are briefed on new procedures. Computer report formats must be explained to all staff who will use them.

4. When the program has been written the analyst checks that it has been tested to prove it will work satisfactorily. He examines test data runs and, ideally, compares output from a *parallel run* on the computer with identical data processed through the old system.

5. The systems analyst takes part in a review of the new system to ensure that the users and the computer department staff are happy with it. If any changes are necessary, he must see that they are made and proved satisfactory.

6. The systems analyst does not relinquish responsibility for the new system until the head of the user department signs a *User Certificate* stating that the system is operating to the required standard.

Programmers

The programmer writes the program for a particular system based on the requirements outlined by the systems analyst. He also validates the programs by monitoring test runs and debugging, i.e. correcting faults, before the system goes into operation. Security and control of data also lie within the programmer's areas of responsibility.

Operations staff
Operations staff may include data control clerks, operators, library clerks. Data control clerks log and check input as it is received for processing. They check output and ensure correct distribution.

Operators control the day-to-day running of the operational systems. They deal with the loading of programs onto the computer, ensuring that schedules are maintained and that output is produced in accordance with schedules. There are many activities for which operators are responsible concerning the running of the computer and its environment.

Library clerks are responsible for filing printout, and keeping records of disks and tapes used and storing them.

Operations manager
The operations manager is the main link between the computer department and the user department/s.

Input originators
The information which is fed into the computer system can be derived from many sources. The original source may be a document completed by a member of the public, e.g. a census form or an income tax assessment form. It may be a document completed by a member of the organisation staff, e.g. meter readers. In this case the source document, as it is called, can be completed in a particular way because the originator can be trained. The data may come out of a person's head, being keyed in on a typewriter, telex or video terminal.

Because the computer will simply process the information as it receives it, following program instructions, it is vital that the input be one hundred per cent accurate. It is possible to build checks into a program so that if, for example, an account number has been incorrectly written by having one figure too many or too few or a transposed figure, the program would reject it and produce an error report. There must always be verification of the input. In the case of punched cards this is done by punching twice so that differences will be highlighted and checked. The visual display unit attached to a keyboard, cash register, etc., or the hard copy (paper copy) produced on typewriters, telex machines, etc., provides checking facilities.

The person or people responsible for completion of documents and for feeding information into the system have a vital role to play in ensuring accurate output. There is a term used in computer departments—GIGO. This stands for "Garbage In, Garbage Out"!

Output users

The people who use the output must know before the system is set up exactly what information they require and the form in which they require it, depending on the purpose for which it is to be used. They must examine carefully the relative importance of the various details. It is sometimes necessary to compromise on certain requirements in order to achieve greater efficiency in the system as a whole.

Users must be trained to use the output medium so that they can identify information they need without difficulty. Usually it is possible to give users the information they have always had from the manual or mechanical systems, frequently with additional details. Very often however the computer format is quite different from the format used previously, which can be very confusing to the uninitiated. The phases of a computer project and the people involved in each phase are shown diagrammatically in Fig. 80.

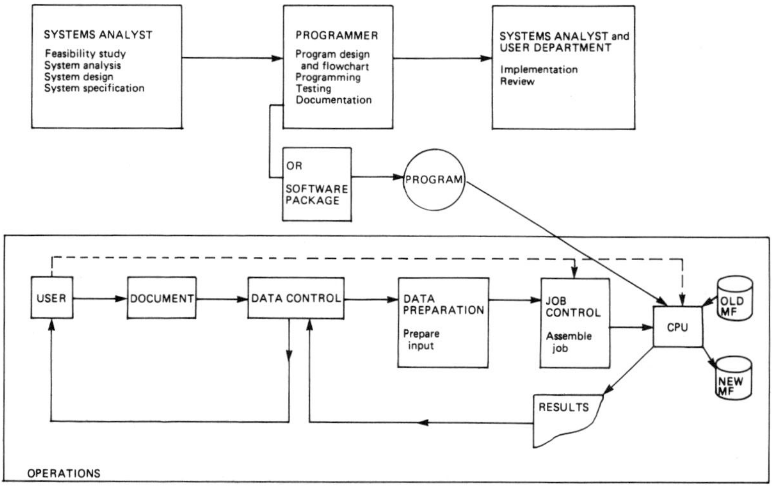

Fig. 80. *Phases of a computer project showing the people and activities involved.*

SETTING UP A COMPUTER SYSTEM

As computer capacity increases it is becoming possible to computerise more and more systems. The process of computerising a system follows a pattern of stages. These are:

(*a*) feasibility study;
(*b*) detailed system analysis and design;

(*c*) system definition;
(*d*) program specification;
(*e*) implementation;
(*f*) review.

Feasibility study

A most important part of the installation of a computer is the previous examination of office systems and data processing (perhaps previously performed by accounting machines), and the assessment of the possibility and the advisability of installing a computer. It should be understood that the result of the feasibility study may be that the system should *not* be computerised.

A computer manufacturer will carry out this study as part of an advisory service to business, but as the sale of an expensive machine is involved the assessment of needs may not be wholly impartial. It is essential that those who know the business, the line of trade and the requirements of management are involved in the study.

While internal staff with many years of experience could produce a report on data processing requirements, they would not necessarily have computer expertise on the capabilities of machines, or the detailed requirements of programming, etc., and in fact many businesses do not even have experts in office systems. Anyone involved in the feasibility study who is not *au fait* with computers should attend a computer appreciation course as part of his or her involvement.

It is usual for a feasibility team to consist of representatives from the accounts department, line managers from the departments most affected by the proposed changeover and the work study and/or O and M office. Representatives of, say, two computer manufacturers may be asked to join the team which will jointly investigate the business information and data processing systems and make a report to management on the possibility and advisability of installing a computer. This may take anything from six months to several years, depending on the scope of the system being investigated. The thoroughness of the investigation will affect the success of the end result.

The main activities involved in a feasibility study are outlined in the work of a systems analyst on page 211.

At the end of the feasibility study a *feasibility report* is produced. The contents of this report may include:

(*a*) terms of reference;

(*b*) an outline of the current system;
(*c*) information flow—alternative routeings;
(*d*) the outline of the proposed system;
(*e*) cost involved—equipment, running costs, staff, etc.;
(*f*) savings to be made—equipment, staff, finance, etc.;
(*g*) benefit to be gained—accuracy, control, more information, faster availability of information, etc.

A specimen block diagram showing the main features of a computerised system for handling customers' orders is shown in Fig. 81. This kind of diagram is frequently included in a feasibility report.

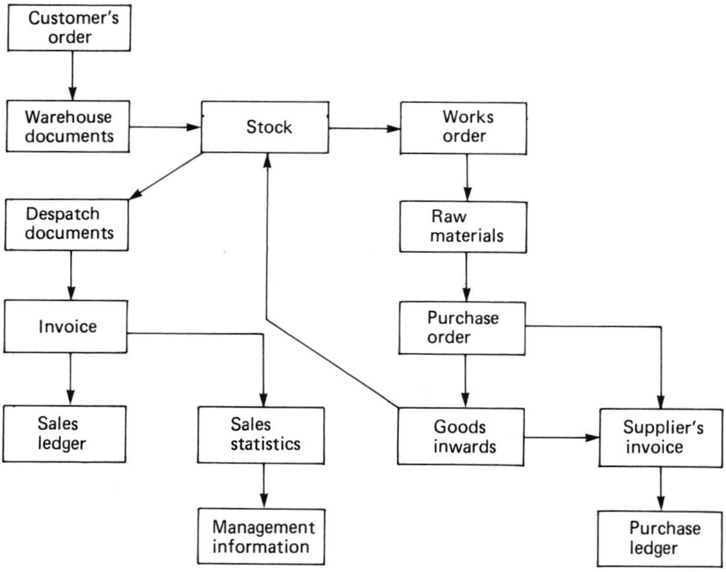

Fig. 81. *Specimen block diagram in a feasibility report.*

Detailed system analysis and design

At this stage the systems analyst or analysts will liaise with the chief programmer and the operations manager within the computer department and with the managers of the user and related departments. The tasks involved in this stage are:

(*a*) to determine detailed requirements;
(*b*) to establish the origin of the source data;
(*c*) to define the procedures;
(*d*) to establish the control and security requirements, cost

limitations, capacity of the computer memory and peripherals available;

(*e*) to define the computer system—programs and files, etc.;

(*f*) to design the input documents;

(*g*) to design the reports, for formats, i.e. printout or Computer Originated Microfilm or displays on visual display units/video terminals;

(*h*) to agree with the users.

System definition (system specification)

The system definition is the manual which sets out in detail how the system will operate from the point of the source data to the point of output. Typically the manual may contain the following information:

(*a*) objectives of the system—the data it will produce for what purpose;

(*b*) narrative outline—an explanation of the proposed system;

(*c*) procedures:

(*i*) clerical (normally concerned with input),

(*ii*) control of input, storage and output,

(*iii*) operation;

(*d*) system flow chart;

(*e*) program descriptions—an outline of the program;

(*f*) file descriptions—the information which will be held;

(*g*) input specifications—forms, keyboard instructions;

(*h*) output specifications:

(*i*) report (printout) formats,

(*ii*) VDU screen formats;

(*i*) system test data—for validation and control when the system is operational.

Program specification

The program specification is the document which provides the detail from which the programmer can work to produce the instructions for the computer. Typically a program specification may contain the following information:

(*a*) the purpose of the program;

(*b*) description of the process—a broad outline of the logic;

(*c*) block diagram—shows the main items in the system and the main items in the program;

(*d*) detailed flow chart—tells the programmer exactly what is wanted;

(*e*) file descriptions—precise details to be held on file;

(*f*) input specifications;
(*g*) output specifications;
(*h*) test data;
(*i*) test results.

Implementation

The implementation of a system involves all the people who have worked on the preceding stages.

User department

The staff in the user department/s must be trained. This involves:

(*a*) an explanation of the system;
(*b*) training in the use of new equipment, e.g. visual display units and keyboards;
(*c*) completion of source documents or other input;
(*d*) use of output—format and extraction of information;
(*e*) lines of communication between the various departments and sections involved in the system.

Computer operation staff

The operation staff have to be introduced to the new system. They need to know:

(*a*) the details of the system;
(*b*) work schedules;
(*c*) file allocation and control.

Data preparation staff

The staff who are responsible for data entry or data preparation by batch processing need to be introduced to the new input documents.

Control section

The staff who control the systems need to be given:

(*a*) an explanation of the system;
(*b*) an appreciation of the user input and output documents;
(*c*) the lines of communication.

A new system is always test run so that faults can be corrected. This is known as debugging. When the systems analyst, programmer and operations manager are satisfied that the program is working efficiently they will "go live", i.e. start running the system alongside the manual or mechanical system. It is essential to maintain the existing system in parallel until the user department is quite certain that the computer system is providing the service required. This includes the information required, in the form it is required, at the time it is required. There may have to be modifications to the program before the system is satisfactory. When the user department is satisfied that all is well a *User Certificate* is signed by the Head of the Department.

Review

It is advisable that any system, manual, mechanical or electronic, should be reviewed from time to time to ensure that it is not only working efficiently, but that it is cost effective. The computer manager builds into the departmental work plans time for reviewing systems with the user departments. The frequency of the review depends on the systems, their complexity and usage. A reasonable average is probably every two years or so.

COSTS

The cost of buying a computer may be reducing steadily but it is still expensive equipment. There are also other costs involved in running computers. A brief outline is given below.

(*a*) *Input*— Staff time
Equipment (rental or depreciation)
Accommodation

(*b*) *Output*— Stationery or microfilm
Equipment for form bursting and/or decollating (rental or depreciation)
Staff time

(*c*) *Media*— Provision for backing store (three generations)
Supplies—disks, tapes, etc.

(*d*) *Computer*— Equipment—rental or depreciation, power for running, maintenance
Air conditioning—depreciation, power for running, maintenance
Staff—management and supervision
systems analysis, programming, operating
input/output control

(*e*) *Transmission*— Equipment—rental or depreciation
Telephone lines—rental

PROCESSING

There are various methods of processing data and information. These include direct job entry, remote job entry, batch processing and front-end processing.

Direct job entry means that the information is being fed into the computer from a peripheral device linked to the computer.

Remote job entry means that information is being fed into the computer from a remote location, e.g. a video terminal linked by a telephone line.

Front-end processing means that data is accepted, processed and stored by a computer, usually a mini or micro, and is then transmitted to a mainframe computer for updating of master files. The mini computer serves as interim storage.

Batch processing means that data is stored up into batches either until there is a specific quantity or covering a specific period. It can then be processed in one operation. For example, a day's stock issues and receipts may be recorded manually on forms. The forms are then sent to the computer department in a batch where the stock record files held on computer are updated in one processing. Bank transactions are dealt with in the same way. The day's transactions at the branches are processed overnight at the bank's computer centre so that each day the branch can tell a client the state of his account as at close of business the previous day.

TRANSMISSION

In order to transmit data from a terminal to a computer and vice versa, and from computer to computer, it is necessary to have a suitable telephone line or lines. These may be private circuits or switched (public) circuits. Public circuits may be leased so that the lessor has sole use of the line. Alternatively the user may have "dial-up" facilities which means that when the use of a line is required a "call" is made from say a terminal to the mainframe.

To transmit data along a telephone line it is necessary to change, or encode, the input at the terminal into electrical impulses which can travel down the line. The electrical impulses must then be changed into computer acceptable form at the other end. The reverse process has to be carried out when data is transmitted from the computer to the terminal. For this purpose *modems* are linked into the telephone lines at either end. Modem is an abbreviation for the two words modulator and demodulator. A system of terminals with modems is illustrated at Fig. 82. Various other configurations are in common use.

When "dial-up" facilities are used the modem is in the form of an acoustic coupler. The subscriber dials the number which gains access to the computer, places the handset of the telephone on the coupler and either keys in the data to be transmitted or transmits direct from pre-recorded diskette or tape.

A Private Datel Exchange may be required to control the incoming and outgoing "calls" from mainframe to terminal and vice versa. This may be operator controlled or automatic and is normally installed on private networks.

When a number of terminals are linked into a CPU which processes a variety of data, the transmission lines are routed through a multiplexer which services each line in turn, byte by byte, and interrupts the CPU to place each byte in the memory.

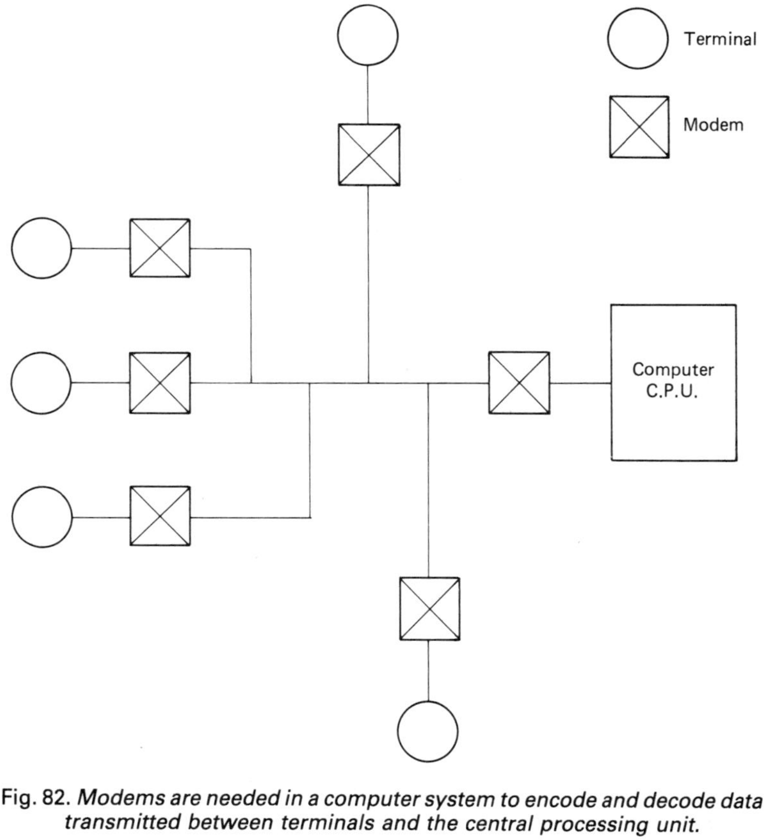

Fig. 82. *Modems are needed in a computer system to encode and decode data transmitted between terminals and the central processing unit.*

COMPUTER BUREAUX

There are many computer bureaux which provide computer facilities for clients. Small clients may send input documents for complete processing. Organisations may have terminals linked to a bureau mainframe for input and/or updating information. Many organisations send prepared data for processing, particularly if they use a bureau to supplement their own computer capacity. Some organisations use their own computer for specialist applications and have standard applications such as payroll covered by a bureau.

APPLICATIONS

There are three major categories of computer system applications, namely standard or routine applications, communications applications and non-standard, management or specialist applications. The way in which a computer system is applied in any organisation depends on the type of organisation, the capacity of the CPU, the cost of each application and the effectiveness of computerisation in each particular instance. It is possible to computerise virtually any system but it is not necessarily appropriate to do so for reasons of cost effectiveness and the priority of certain applications for the use of available capacity. We discussed the capacity of the CPU memory in Chapter Nine. The limitation of applications is often because additional applications would overload the CPU. The cost effectiveness of computerising a system has to be weighed against the cost of additional computer equipment.

Standard applications

When an organisation installs a computer or uses a computer bureau it is most likely to use it first for such applications as:

(*a*) order processing;
(*b*) sales billing/invoicing;
(*c*) credit control;
(*d*) stock records and stock control;
(*e*) production control;
(*f*) payroll;
(*g*) ledgers—sales, purchases, nominal;
(*h*) pensions;
(*i*) personnel and training records.

For these applications it is possible to buy a *software* package from a computer software supplier. The user can either modify his system to fit the package or modify the package to fit his requirements. The former procedure is normally more satisfactory unless there is a compelling reason for maintaining a particular procedure. Many software houses will now prepare "bespoke packages", i.e. packages modified or designed for the specific requirements of a client's system. Although software packages are still fairly expensive it is much cheaper to buy an "off-the-hook" program than prepare a new one. It also has the advantage of having been very well tested.

These programs may combine a range of procedures. For example, information concerning stock issues and receipts automatically updates the stock inventory. It may also provide a printout indicating items which have reached re-order level. A program for customer ledger accounts would also produce a printout showing overdue accounts and may produce the letters to clients as well. When sales orders are keyed in the program might include extracting prices from database, calculating VAT, updating stock records, producing production instructions and billing. All the documents, including job cards, labels, etc., required for the completion of an order (*see* Chapter Five) may be produced by the computer.

Commercial organisations such as insurance companies, brokers, banks and travel agents are now using computer systems to handle their routine work. Most bank branches have a terminal installed so that clients' balances can be called for from the bank's computer centre.

Communication applications

The application of computers to communications has increased rapidly in the last few years. Some of the applications are outlined briefly below.

Telecommunications

The integration of telecommunications and computer systems is known as *convergence*. It may include an electronic telephone system, telex, electronic mailing, facsimile transmission and datel.

Electronic telephone switchboards are the push button type. The system provides many facilities for the extension users, some of which are mentioned in Chapter Eight.

Telex can be computerised in various ways. The punched tape used for transmitting the message can be produced on a typewriter, memory typewriter or word processor. The latter two machines allow standard messages to be held in the memory or on diskette for use when needed.

Telexpads are terminals which allow messages to be handwritten with a ballpoint pen or pencil. The writing is "sensed" from the pressure as on the Micropad (*see* page 200). The advantage is that the intermediate typing by the secretary and/or telex operator is eliminated.

Automatic dialling facilities are available which enable the operator to dial an abbreviated "address code". The full telex number is then dialled by the equipment. "Store and forward" facilities allow messages to be transmitted to a mini-computer where they are stored until the required telex number is free. When a telex line is engaged or not available for some reason the system holds the message in a queue and keeps dialling until the connection is made.

Names and addresses used regularly can be stored and retrieved to "merge" with messages when required. When the same message is to go to a number of addressees the system repeats the message as many times as necessary until all the addresses have been dealt with.

A further development is a video telex terminal which allows the operator to key in the message, check it on the screen for accuracy, "file" it on disk and instruct the computer to transmit the message.

British Telecom have a new range of computerised telex terminals. The Puma is a keyboard which produces a punched tape and/or hard copy. Its memory store can hold up to 2,500 words and will not lose the contents of its memory in the event of temporary disconnection from mains. Puma can be instructed to make calls and transmit messages while unattended. If you call certain numbers frequently you can have up to 25 numbers stored. To use them only 2 digits are keyed in—calling is by typing the numbers required instead of dialling. Text editing—insert, correct, delete—can be carried out on any messages in the memory.

Cheetah is a telex terminal with a visual display unit. It has all the facilities of Puma but its memory is 16K or 32K, providing greater memory storage capacity. Messages are received and transmitted automatically, even while other messages are being prepared. A message can be held in the memory until a pre-set time when it will be transmitted. If connection cannot be made it will keep trying approximately every two minutes. Incoming messages are held until the printer is free. Single character codes can be used for up to 16 telex numbers. (*See* Fig. 57 in Chapter Eight.)

"Cardsure"

A new-style telephone service developed by British Telecom to cut the fraudulent use of plastic payment cards came into use early in 1983. The new telephones, known as transaction telephones (*see*

Fig. 83), enable the validity of cards to be checked at high speed through Telecom's data network—for instance, in the case of American Express, to Phoenix, Arizona and back within seconds.

Customers will know that if they have reported a card lost the likelihood of fraudulent use is greatly reduced. They will also spend less time waiting while sales assistants telephone in to check credit limits and validity, as at present.

When a customer presents a plastic card at the point-of-sale the assistant "wipes" or slides the card through a slot in the transaction telephone. The information on the card's magnetic strip is read and the telephone automatically connects a call through British Telecom's data network to the card company's computer. Valid transactions will be authorised by the computer and within seconds an appropriate response will appear on the transaction telephone's liquid crystal display.

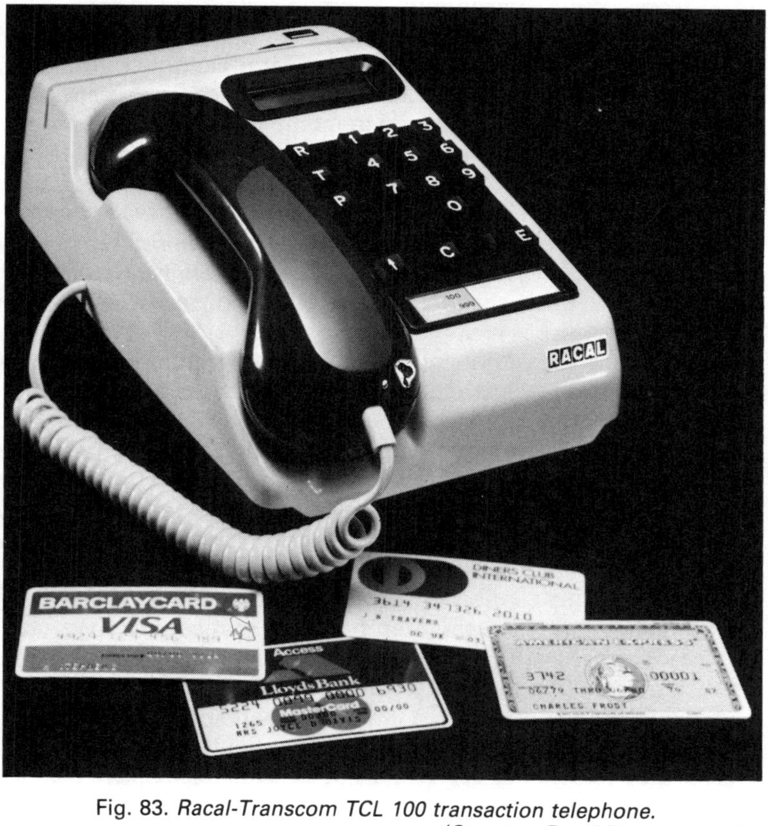

Fig. 83. *Racal-Transcom TCL 100 transaction telephone.*
(Courtesy Racal-Transcom Ltd.)

At present only Barclaycard and American Express cards are being checked but the equipment is suitable for most credit cards now used and it is expected that the use of "Cardsure" will become general within a short time.

Electronic mailing is the transmission of information direct from one point to another, e.g. a terminal in one location to a terminal in another location. This screen-to-screen transmission has led to the term "paperless office" being used. Information is keyed in on a video terminal, transmitted to the CPU with instructions to transmit to a particular terminal or series of terminals. By using a special code it is possible to inform the users of the addressee terminals that a message is waiting. The terminal operator can file the information received in the same way that any other information on screen is filed. It may be necessary to print out for distribution, e.g. to managers. Electronic mailing is now being used between word processors. With appropriate communications software and/or interface equipment a word processor can transmit to other word processors. British Telecom are to provide a Teletex transmission facility which will enable non-compatible machines to communicate with each other. There are likely to be major developments in this area.

Facsimile transmission, or FAX, is another name for the facility provided by a facsimile copier (*see* page 161), but generally refers to machines which use digital transmission as opposed to normal telephone lines. Digital transmission is faster because the receiver can "skip" the white sections of the paper. Average transmission time for an A4 sheet is about 45 seconds.

Facsimile transceivers incorporate "electronic handshake" which ensures that the copy has been received, "automatic answer" which indicates to the sending machine that transmission can proceed to an unattended machine (as with telex), line quality check to ensure that the copy can be transmitted accurately, and selection of lower transmission speeds to ensure compatibility with other machines. The machines can be programmed to transmit a series of documents without the attention of an operator.

Datel is a British Telecom facility by which data is transmitted over the telephone network from remote terminals to a CPU. The service operates at different speeds. The slower speeds are more costly but more accurate. Datel 2412 and 4824 are commonly used on the public network, but the current highest speed of 9,600bps is frequently used on private lines where the quality of transmission is higher. An additional service, PPS, is available which enables terminals operating at different speeds to communicate.

There are also International Datel services to 24 countries. These operate at 200, 600, 1,200 and 2,400 bits per second. It is also possible to lease private circuits for transmission of data between a subscriber's premises in different countries.

Viewdata

Viewdata is operated by British Telecom in the UK under the registered name of "Prestel". It operates over a telephone line coupled to a television screen called a Prestel receiver. The subscriber "dials" for information by pressing a key on the keypad attached to the receiver. A wide range of information is held on the Prestel computer files, to which the index is held on the system itself. The information is provided by a large number of Information Providers (known as IPs) ranging from small specialist firms to large international organisations. Information, which is provided for local areas as well as nationally, includes news and weather, TV and radio guide, sport, holidays, travel, hobbies, facts and figures, market place, buying advice, jobs and careers, Stock Exchange and Commodities, company and market information, manufacturing industry guide, service industry guide, reference information, government information, calculations and messages.

An Information Provider can have a Viewdata Editing Keyboard which allows him to up-date the information he has provided whenever required. This enables an organisation to ensure that information is right up-to-date all the time. It can also be a useful internal communications medium. For example, salesmen can key in their orders to head office at the end of a day via a viewdata terminal in their homes. They can call up on screen outstanding orders being processed in order to see the progress on each one. There are many other applications which are gradually being extended.

The cost of the Prestel service comprises the cost of the terminal, telephone calls at local charge rate, a very small British Telecom usage charge and an information charge, which depends on the type of information and/or the user involved.

Prestel may be connected to direct exchange lines, plans 1A, 4, 105, 107, PABX with recall plan 4 and 1A.

Two other similar services, Ceefax and Oracle, are provided by the British Broadcasting Corporation and the Independent Television Companies' Association respectively. The information available on these teletext services is limited to a maximum of 800 pages per channel and is one-way, i.e. receiving, only. Prestel, however, has virtually unlimited information capacity and it is possible for users to send messages or respond to the computer.

Prestel and teletext services are now being provided by individual companies for their customers. Registered users (customers) can obtain information about products/services and key in their orders via a keyboard terminal direct to the company's computer system. The orders are recorded, credit clearance obtained and documentation produced as a result of input from the customers. A holiday tour operator provides this service to travel agents by showing current holiday availability. There are endless possibilities.

Word processing

Word processors come in three forms. A stand alone system has a keyboard, VDU, printer and CPU with one or more disk drives. Diskettes, or floppy disks, are the medium used for storing information. A shared logic system consists of several terminals, some video with disk drives and some printers, linked into one CPU. A distributed logic system means that the terminals are linked to a mainframe. They may be on line so that material can be stored and retrieved as required from the disks on the computer. Alternatively information may be keyed in and stored in a buffer store for transmission to the CPU and filing on disk later. Distributed logic systems may allow both word and data to be processed on the same terminal.

Word processors operate either by being programmed or by menu selection. The former type means that the program telling the machine to "behave" as a word processor is held on diskette. When the machine is switched on the program diskette is inserted into the disk drive and the program is taken into the CPU memory. The program disk is then removed from the drive and the working disks are inserted as required. The operator then gives commands which are interpreted and carried out by the machine.

With menu selection the operator is provided with a list of functions on the screen. The function required is selected and the appropriate command is given in accordance with the instruction indicated on the list. Word processing software for use on computer terminals and microprocessors frequently operates in this way. This is often referred to as "user friendly" as the operator is guided through the procedures rather than having to remember them.

Word processing facilities vary from one machine to another but the following are common.

(*a*) Text editing means that text stored on diskette can be retrieved and amended by deleting or inserting words/lines/sentences/paragraphs/pages, transferring sections of text from one place to another in a document, locating and changing particular words throughout the text of a document, and paginating.

(*b*) Personalised standard letters are produced by merging the standard letter with a mailing list, selecting those names and addresses required. The standard letter may contain "variables", e.g. amounts of money in letters requesting payment of overdue accounts.

(*c*) The ease with which text can be amended allows for updating of all kinds of records including stock records, personnel and training records, financial records and accounts, in-house telephone directories, mailing lists, etc.

(*d*) Legal documents commonly consist of a series of paragraphs which may be selected from a wide range of standard paragraphs. Standard paragraphs are recorded on disk and the appropriate ones are selected for each particular document and printed out.

A stand alone word processor capable of the activities outlined above and many others is illustrated at Fig. 84.

Typesetting

Computer typesetting is now a standard application. Two programs are used, one for composition and one for the actual setting. When the text has been recorded on tape the composition and typesetting programs automatically divide the material into columns with justified (i.e. even) right-hand margin, ensure that linked text or data

Fig. 84. *Stand alone word processor.*
(Courtesy Philips Business Systems.)

is not split from one line/page to another, make up pages with page headings if required, paginate, select the founts, i.e. style, and size of print required for the various types of headings and the text. The pages of text to be printed are finally produced on positive film or bromide paper from which offset plates can be made for printing. The process of typesetting is in two parts as illustrated in Fig. 85.

Interface equipment now exists to produce "camera ready" copy, as outlined above, from text stored on word processor diskettes. This means that the original keying in of the text does not have to be repeated.

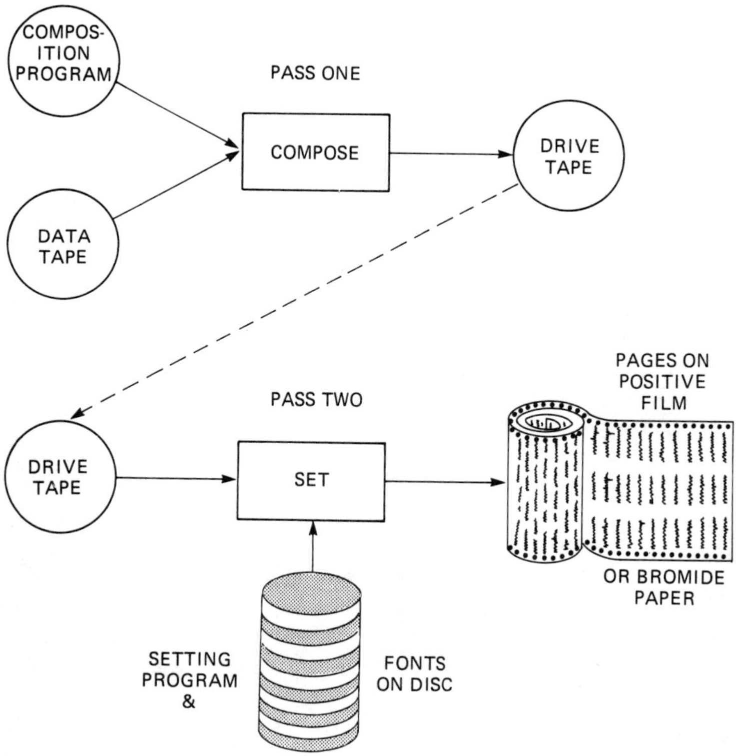

Fig. 85. *The process of computer typesetting.*

Copying

Material to be reproduced is held on disk with instructions for the printing format. This material is copied from the disk onto a tape or disk on the copier. Each page to be reproduced is imaged onto the copying mechanism which produces an original copy. The next page is processed in the same way and so on throughout the document. This process can be repeated as many times as required, thus producing original copies collated and ready for fastening or binding. For more details *see* page 203.

Mailing

Mailing lists held on magnetic tape or disk can be used to produce envelopes or labels, to "merge" with standard letters to produce "personalised" letters and to keep information such as might be kept on an index card, e.g. account number. The lists can be sorted into a variety of sequences for different purposes, e.g. alphabetical, by geographical location, in numerical order by say account numbers. It is also possible to select certain sections of the list for different purposes.

Real-time order processing

Terminal operators can key in the details of orders, the information being transmitted to the CPU, which then updates the stock records and produces the necessary documentation. Real-time means that the CPU is reacting to the input virtually instantly, subject to operating availability. Delay, if any, will be fractional.

Access control

There are various methods of controlling entry to locations. Plastic cards or badge codes may be used. A card is inserted into a device at a door. The signal is transmitted to the computer which searches to find identification. If it exists the computer sends a signal which activates a switch to unlock the door.

Electronic keypads are frequently sited to control access within an organisation or within a department. Only people who are authorised to enter a particular area are told the code number which has to be keyed in on the keypad. This code number activates a switch which releases the door lock. It is usual to change the code from time to time for security. The system can be reprogrammed to accept the new code.

Voice recognition is another means of location entry control. Every human voice is different and once registered by the owner no one else can impersonate the voice and expect to "get away with it". The computer will react only to those voices recorded on its files. This method of access control is not yet commonly used.

Microfilm

Computer output is not always required in paper form or on video screens but it may still be necessary to store the information in a human readable form. A cheap way of doing this is to produce processed information directly from the computer onto microfilm, usually in the form of microfiche (*see* page 105). This is known as COM, Computer Originated Microfilm.

Talking terminals
In the distributors of a large car manufacturing company a storeman can dial directly into the manufacturer's computer memory banks and key-in enquiries about the availability of a particular part. The pre-recorded spoken answer includes availability, changed part numbers and the latest price. The storeman can then place the order, the computer monitoring the information keyed in to ensure that no detail needed to execute the order is omitted. If there is an omission the computer indicates the requirement.

Voice response
Computers can react to voice instructions, e.g. a salesman's orders given over the telephone, producing the required documentation, etc.

Digital voice computers
Digital voice computers are still being developed. The speech is quite recognisable though intonation tends to be distorted as the speech is by syllables and in a monotone. Voice computers are probably most likely to be used for educational and research purposes.

Financial transactions

A computerised system of transferring funds internationally is provided by SWIFT, Society for World Wide Inter-Bank Financial Telecommunications, which has its main offices in Brussels and Amsterdam. This system enables financial transactions to be conducted between banks in different countries very rapidly.

The client abroad instructs his bank to make a payment to a supplier. The bank enters the transaction on its computer with appropriate instructions. The client's account is debited and within a short time, perhaps half an hour (depending on transmission availability), the transaction is recorded on the computer in Britain. The supplier is duly informed of the payment, thus eliminating the need for documentary credit to secure payment for goods supplied. On production of a bill of lading the supplier's account is credited, thus ensuring supply of the consignment to the customer.

In 1982 the software for SWIFT was updated and modified to

eliminate various types of errors. Many banks are now operating SWIFT II. The number of countries where this facility is available is steadily increasing.

The Banks Automated Clearing System, BACS, is a system whereby the clearing banks are able to clear cheques with each other via computers. At the end of a day's trading each of the clearing banks has to determine how much money it owes to or is owed by each of the other banks when the day's cheques have been debited to the drawers and credited to the payees. Each of the banks is linked into BACS enabling the necessary calculations to be made automatically.

Management applications

A major contribution that computers have made to management is the provision of a wider range of information, more quickly and more accurately than was possible before. There are many types of information which a manager or group may need in order to make a decision or series of decisions. Some examples of the kind of activity which can be aided by information produced by computer are:

(*a*) manpower planning;
(*b*) sales forecasting;
(*c*) discounted cash flow;
(*d*) analysis of data—sales, costs, etc.;
(*e*) network analysis;
(*f*) sensitivity analysis;
(*g*) operational research;
(*h*) mathematical models, which are means of setting up an experimental system without upsetting the on-going operational system, and testing it to make sure that it will do what is wanted before putting it into operation.

A data base or data bank (*see* Chapter Nine) is used to provide relevant information for decision-making. The type of information and the format in which it is required to be presented vary greatly from one organisation to another, and from one department to another. Some simple examples of information which might be readily available are specifications of any kind; training courses—their content, objectives, for whom intended; stock items; travel information; mailing lists of customers; statistics of all kinds; trends; and costs. It has to be stressed that the data base must be completely up to date and the information must be easily and quickly retrievable if it is to be of value to management. For this reason input and output tend to be video based nowadays.

The strategic planning which is essential in achieving long-range corporate objectives will be a major application in the foreseeable future. The interrelationship and interaction of the many and varied factors involved will be analysed and evaluated much more quickly, objectively and thoroughly by computer than by the human mind. In addition, monitoring and reviewing of operations and results should be more effective, so that modifications to strategic plans ought to be easier to make as a result.

INTEGRATED SYSTEMS

Systems which interlink individual systems are known as integrated systems. The bar codes used at supermarket checkouts for example set up a chain reaction updating stock records, checking re-order levels, generating orders if necessary, updating sales statistics, transmitting the price to the checkout.

Integrated systems are essential as a tool to provide information for management. This month's sales figures are of little value unless related to forecasts, production, previous year's figures, etc.

Manpower planning can be done only by relating to personnel records, production forecasts, project development, etc.

It is to the development of management information systems (MIS) that systems analysts, designers and programmers are now devoting much of their time in many organisations.

MICROPROCESSORS

A great deal has been written and spoken about the "microchip revolution". The microchip has brought the computer into the home and into the office so as to make computerisation an everyday possibility for relatively trivial operations.

The microchip has printed on it many thousands of circuits which means that powerful machines can be made quite cheaply. Indeed it is possible to buy a computer for a few hundred pounds which will carry out most of the standard applications. Often word processing can be carried out on such a machine.

Memory

The memory capacity of a microcomputer is usually 32K, 64K or 128K bytes. Currently a number of manufacturers are making great efforts to produce memories with 16-bit words. Upgrading is possible by adding more memory chips. These memories are of two main kinds—ROM or RAM.

ROM—Read-Only Memory means that the program held in the

memory cannot be over-written. The *interpreter*, the resident program which converts the source program statements into machine code, cannot be changed. The contents of ROM remain constantly in the memory even when the machine is switched off. There are variations of Read-Only Memory which do allow the user to program the memory himself.

A special chip called a PROM programmer allows the user to write his own programs into memory. PROM stands for Programmable Read-Only Memory.

EPROM is yet another variation. It stands for Erasable Programmable Read-Only Memory which means that when a program is recorded it remains constant in the memory but can be changed by being obliterated so that a new program can be written on the memory chip.

RAM stands for Random Access Memory which holds application programs, data being processed and the results of the processing, e.g. a section of an updated stock list, or a page of an internal telephone directory.

Microcomputers normally use cassettes (tape) or diskettes as the medium for storing data. In the same way that the tapes and disks used on mainframe computers allow serial and random access, so do cassettes and diskettes.

Microcomputers normally consist of an input keyboard, cassette or diskette drives, central processing unit containing the memory, VDU and printer.

Software

Software packages can be bought for standard applications such as sales/purchase/nominal ledger, stock control, payroll, word processing. Many such packages operate on the menu selection basis described earlier in the Chapter. Wordstar and its subsidiary packages for various functions is commonly used for word processing.

Alternatively the user can write his own programs. BASIC is the language commonly used on microcomputers. It takes time to master the techniques required to write a program—the "logic" has to be learned as well as the words used in the instruction statements.

Uses

Apart from being used by small businesses for general office systems such as accounting and word processing, microcomputers are used in larger organisations as "dedicated" machines. This means that a machine is installed in a particular department to be used for a specific purpose, e.g. stock list up-dating, personnel records.

A major extension of the use of micros is as terminals to a mainframe computer. They may be used as buffer stores, holding information which is transmitted in batches to the mainframe for up-dating of files. Frequently they are used as front-end processors doing a certain amount of processing and then transmitting at off-peak times to up-date the main files.

A micro may be on line to a mainframe for retrieval only. For example a customer order may be received. The mainframe would be accessed to retrieve the details required, the order would be keyed in on the micro and would be transmitted later, possibly overnight. This reduces costs and avoids overloading the transmission lines and mainframe memory.

SOME MICROCHIP APPLICATIONS

Microwriter

Originally called a pocket typewriter, the Microwriter enables text to be keyed in wherever one happens to be. Letters and figures are coded, i.e. one or more keys are pressed simultaneously to represent a particular letter or figure, as there are only five keys on the machine. It takes only about one hour to learn the coding system. The Microwriter can then be plugged into a television screen on which the text is displayed. It can be edited as required and then printed out on a printer.

Typecorder

An interesting development by one word processor manufacturer is a machine called a Typecorder. This is a dictating machine-cum-typewriter. The user can dictate in the usual way, recording on a cassette, or he can key in information which is recorded on the same cassette.

There is a range of equipment which enables the information keyed in to be processed. It can

produce punched paper tape for telex transmission,
use an acoustic coupler to transmit to a computer,
link up to a disk unit so that when the information has been transferred from cassette to disk it can be retrieved on a word processor screen,
use a typewriter actuator unit which types out the text automatically on any standard electric typewriter.

Turn round time on production of reports, etc., is greatly reduced as they need only to be edited.

"Mind reader"

This is a machine designed for executives to record their appointments. Each day the screen indicates the appointments for that day. Some machines also provide a "bleep" which reminds the executive to look at the screen as an appointment is due.

SUMMARY

1. Computer staff include systems analysts, systems designers, programmers and operations staff.
2. Computer departments may be organised on the basis of three sections, viz. systems, programming and operations, or on the basis of project development and operations.
3. Data preparation, or data entry, is one of the most important functions of a computer department from the point of view of accuracy because the computer processes whatever information it is given. The producer of the source document also has a major responsibility to ensure the accuracy of the data given.
4. The installation of a computer system involves six stages which can take years to complete. All staff who are likely to be affected in any way, at any stage, should be included in the discussions and/or training programme.
5. When a feasibility study is undertaken the result may be a decision *not* to change a particular system.
6. All computer applied systems should be reviewed regularly to ensure that they remain efficient and cost-effective.
7. There are various methods of processing data, including batch processing, direct job entry and remote job entry.
8. Software packages are commonly used by individual organisations and computer bureaux for standard computer applications.
9. There is a wide range of communications systems which can be linked into a computer system. This integration is known as "convergence". The three main advantages are increased speed of operation, steadily increasing range of facilities and greater control.
10. Once a database of appropriate information has been established, many management techniques can be improved.
11. Microprocessors have virtually unlimited applications, hence the term "microchip revolution".
12. The efficiency of any computer system can only be as good as the accuracy of the input.

SELF-ASSESSMENT QUESTIONS

Answer all questions as quickly as possible. Do not turn back to the Chapter until you have completed the test.

1. Briefly describe the duties of the following:
(*a*) a systems analyst;
(*b*) a programmer;
(*c*) an operations manager.
2. Draw an organisation chart to show a typical data processing department organised on the basis of project development.
3. What is the role of a data processing manager?
4. What is an "input source document"?
5. Why is it vitally important that source data be one hundred per cent accurate?
6. When a manual or mechanical system is computerised training is an essential part of the project. Who may have to be trained?
7. (*a*) Name the six stages involved in setting up a computer system.
(*b*) Explain three of the stages, saying who is involved and what is done.
8. It is essential to have the co-operation of staff involved in the changeover to a computerised system. How would you ensure that this co-operation was forthcoming?
9. You are asked to prepare a budget for the running costs of a computer department. What items would you include?
10. Explain the following terms:
(*a*) batch processing;
(*b*) remote job entry;
(*c*) "dial up" facilities;
(*d*) modem;
(*e*) data transmission.
11. It is possible to computerise virtually any system. Give two major reasons why many office systems are not computerised, even in organisations which have computer facilities.
12. Name five standard systems which are commonly among the first to be put on computer when an organisation installs a computer.
13. (*a*) What is a software package?
(*b*) State two advantages of using a software package for, say, a payroll.
14. What is the term used to indicate the integration of communications systems with computer systems?
15. Explain the following:
(*a*) viewdata;

(*b*) electronic mailing;
(*c*) typesetting.

16. Word processors may be "stand alone" systems, "shared logic" systems or "distributed logic" systems. What is meant by "stand alone", "shared logic" and "distributed logic"?

17. What is meant by the term "text editing" when it is applied to word processing?

18. Give five examples of types of work which may be carried out on a word processor. Explain the advantages of using a word processor instead of a typewriter.

19. Explain the following terms:
(*a*) access control (i.e. controlling access to a location);
(*b*) convergence;
(*c*) voice recognition;
(*d*) SWIFT (Society for World Wide Inter-Bank Financial Telecommunications);
(*e*) database.

20. What is a microchip?

ASSIGNMENTS

Assignment 1

Working individually find out what administrative activities of any kind have been, or can be, carried out, by some form of computer application. Try to find non-standard applications. Use as many sources as possible, i.e. books, computer publications, office equipment publications, e.g. *Index*, *Business Equipment Digest*, and personal contacts.

Assignment 2

Working in groups of three or four discuss the various applications you have found and their advantages/disadvantages under the following headings:
(*a*) saving of manpower;
(*b*) cost saving;
(*c*) faster operation;
(*d*) greater accuracy;
(*e*) more information.

Bear in mind that there has to be information input which must be absolutely accurate.

Consider in what type and/or size of organisation, or in what circumstances, each application would be feasible, i.e. result in more cost effective and/or more efficient performance.

Assignment 3

Choose the three or four (depending on the number of students in the group) applications most suitable for either a small, medium or large organisation. Each member of the group is to write a report on one of the applications (a different application to be reported on by each member) explaining its purpose and advantages.

CHAPTER ELEVEN

Work Planning

> CHAPTER OBJECTIVES
>
> After studying this chapter you should be able to:
> * work methodically;
> * apply the basic principles of work planning to your own work;
> * use work planning methods appropriate to given situations;
> * use work planning charts;
> * co-operate in fulfilling plans related to organisation, co-ordination and control of work;
> * operate follow-up procedures.

DEFINITION AND PURPOSE

What is work planning? Work planning is based on a series of principles which can be applied in different ways to suit different circumstances. It is a means of ensuring that work is done in accordance with the work plan of the department/organisation. It establishes the way in which work is to be done in order to meet pre-determined objectives of the individual and group.

Work planning must be done in order to:

(*a*) establish priorities;
(*b*) ensure that priorities are dealt with as priorities;
(*c*) ensure that deadlines are met;
(*d*) ensure that individual tasks are co-ordinated either within that individual's duties or within the activities of a group;
(*e*) facilitate re-scheduling of individual and group work when organisational/departmental plans are changed or emergencies arise.

PRINCIPLES OF PLANNING WORK

There are many ways of planning work but they are all based on the same fundamental principles. Planning should always be based on the longest unit of time which is applicable to a job or a particular task. There are three "ranges" of planning, viz. long term, medium term and short term. The length of each "term" depends on the type of organisation or job, the circumstances at the time when planning is done, and the future prospects or intentions. For example in the aircraft industry five years is relatively short term, while a company making umbrellas would regard five years as almost long term.

Within an organisation or department plans are devised to meet specific objectives. Similarly the individual must plan to meet his specific objectives or targets. These will have been derived from the departmental objectives. Long-range plans are of necessity fairly general. Medium-range plans have more detail in terms of financial requirements, development of objectives and actions that will have to be taken to implement strategic plans prepared by the board of directors. Short-term plans are the day-to-day plans of precisely who is going to do what, when, where and how.

At the individual level the longest reasonable unit of time is ascertained, say a year, and the items which occur regularly once or twice a year are then noted, preferably on a year-plan chart such as the one illustrated in Fig. 86. This plan is merely a reminder system for what is to happen.

The next unit of time might be a month. Again certain activities take place regularly every month, and these are jotted in on a month-plan chart. In addition you look at the activities indicated in the relevant month on the year-plan chart and insert them in the appropriate place in the month-plan chart. At the same time you look ahead to future months to see what ought to be started, e.g. preparations for a meeting. A month-plan chart is illustrated at Fig. 87.

The next unit would be a week, which is worked on in exactly the same way. Finally there is the day. The tasks listed on the day chart should be divided into three categories—"must do", "should do" and "could do". The important thing to remember is that the "should do" jobs which are not done today will become the "must do" jobs tomorrow or the next day. The aim is to keep "must do" tasks to a minimum so that there is time to cope with emergencies and crises when they arise—as they inevitably do.

Using this simple system of charts these basic principles can be applied to a wide range of duties, providing the person's duties are not too many or complex. There are many other methods of applying them. Some of these methods are explained in the Chapter.

Cyclical planning

Many organisations have a five year plan. Every year, or in some cases every six months, this plan is reviewed and updated. More detail is sketched in three and four years ahead, while the next two years are outlined in fairly fine detail. Departmental managers are informed of the detailed plans so that they can in turn adjust their objectives, plan their work and that of their staff. In this way

YEAR: 19--			
JANUARY	FEBRUARY	MARCH	APRIL
MAY	JUNE	JULY	AUGUST
SEPTEMBER	OCTOBER	NOVEMBER	DECEMBER

Fig. 86. *Year plan chart.*

MONTH:
W. beg.
W. beg.
W. beg.
W. beg.
W. beg.
Notes

Fig. 87. *Month plan chart.*

planning becomes an on-going process, plans being constantly reviewed, adapted to changed circumstances, and modified to meet unforeseen eventualities.

WORKING METHODICALLY

Work planning can be effective at any level only if the workers themselves are well organised. We all know the people who work "in a muddle". How does the well-organised person work?

(*a*) He has a tidy desk while working. That is not to say that it may not be covered in papers and files, but they are there because they are needed, not because they have not been put away!

(*b*) He has tidy drawers, shelves and cupboards, with items frequently used in a position where they are easily accessible. Stationery and "tools" are in specific places so that they are kept in good condition, as well as being easy to pick up.

(*c*) He works on one task at a time. "Hopping" from one task to another means that each task eventually takes a lot longer than necessary.

(*d*) He takes action on each piece of paper he picks up. He does not keep "picking up and putting down".

(*e*) He organises his work into batches so that all of one type of work is done at the same time.

(*f*) He has a routine procedure for such things as checking and ordering stationery requirements, so that he does not find himself having to rush to the stationery store because he has run out of a particular item. This is especially important when rush jobs come along.

(*g*) He replaces each file in the cabinet, or places it in the out tray for collection, when he has finished with it so that it can be found again immediately when required.

(*h*) He writes everything—*everything*—down so that he can never forget. Writing materials are always to hand.

(*i*) He tackles the large and/or difficult tasks early in the day while he is fresh. It is a mistake to work on the small "bits and pieces" first because one gets tired and they always take longer than expected, with the result that the large tasks have to be put off yet again.

(*j*) He does not put off unpleasant tasks, or tasks which he is not sure how to tackle. Unpleasant tasks become seemingly worse the longer they are put off. If he is unsure of how to get going, he asks.

(*k*) He does daily tasks daily. In rare cases it may be necessary to leave a routine task until tomorrow when an emergency arises, but if it becomes a habit "tomorrow" never comes. A typical example is filing, which grows from a small pile into a mountain. It is then a mammoth task to cope with it.

(*l*) He has a time of day for each routine daily task. The time is not sacrosanct, but it does help self-discipline. Similarly he has a particular day for each routine weekly task and monthly tasks are allocated an appropriate date for action.

(*m*) He develops the ability to estimate reasonably accurately the time a task will take so that he can indicate to his superior a realistic deadline.

(*n*) He uses checklists (*see* below).

(*o*) He tries to find out from his superior what work is expected in the next week or so in order to plan his work, bearing in mind large tasks which may be coming in. He also anticipates likely work.

(*p*) He operates a follow-up system which saves him having to remember what information should be coming in, and also avoids "chasing" by a superior when he forgets!

(*q*) He prepares handing-over notes for his routine tasks. The notes are reviewed regularly so that they are up-to-date when he is unavoidably absent or preparing to go on holiday. Checklists and action sheets, explained later in the Chapter, ensure that the stage at which individual tasks stand is easily identified by anyone else.

This list is not comprehensive. Points mentioned are quite basic but, if followed, they do ensure that the individual is in a position to plan his work. Perhaps the most important aspect of working methodically is to keep calm under pressure. Panic gets everyone concerned nowhere very fast.

METHODS OF PLANNING WORK

The principles of work planning explained earlier in the Chapter can be applied in many ways. We shall now discuss simple and effective applications which can be used or adapted to suit the individual, the group and the organisation. What works well for one person may be totally unsuitable for another because of differences in the types of work, responsibilities, relationships, etc.

Checklist

A checklist is one of the simplest means of ensuring that nothing is overlooked. It is a list of items or activities.

Preparing a checklist

(*a*) Write a list of the tasks which have to be performed. This should be done in any order in the first instance. The list can then be rewritten in priority order, most urgent details first. Alternatively the urgent items can be highlighted, e.g. by having a red dot inserted beside them, or circling.

(*b*) Each item is written on a slip of paper or card as it comes to mind. The cards are then sorted into priority order and written as a list. This is appropriate when a lot of details are involved. The important thing is to jot down the items as they occur to you so that they are not forgotten.

Use of checklists

A simple checklist as explained in (*a*) above can be used for requisition lists, e.g. for shopping, stationery requirements, points to discuss at an interview, or for listing activities to be carried out, say for a day or a week.

A more detailed checklist may be used itemising all the details which must be covered in a larger undertaking, e.g. organising a meeting/conference, arranging interviews, making travel arrangements, preparing material for the printer.

Example

An example of a checklist for organising a mail shot is shown as Fig. 88. The activities have been sorted into various stages of planning, preparation and follow up. This list can be adapted for small meetings, for board meetings, or for meetings where visual aids will be used. In the latter case additional items concerned with hiring and transporting equipment will have to be inserted.

As each activity is completed it is ticked off in the right hand margin. This means that anyone can see at any time what has been done, and what has to be done. This is particularly useful in case of sickness or when handing over for holiday periods.

Activity scheduling

Activity scheduling is the sorting of activities into the order in which they must be undertaken. It must be borne in mind that some items have to be completed before others can be dealt with. In some cases two or more activities are so closely interrelated that they must be dealt with simultaneously. When arranging a meeting, for example, the availability of a room for the meeting and the availability of the people may not always synchronise. Therefore the two activities must be worked on together until a suitable date and time can be found.

How activities are scheduled

From the prepared checklist you identify the key items, i.e. the items on which other activities depend; for example, you cannot prepare a purchase order in some organisations without a departmental requisition for goods. Therefore getting the requisition approved is a key item because nothing can happen without it.

When activity scheduling is used
Activity scheduling can be used for any task which involves a number of activities which have to be undertaken in sequence.

CHECKLIST FOR A MAIL SHOT

		Check
1	Open file	....
2	Obtain names and addresses for mailing list and key in on word processor	....
	OR	
	Review and up-date mailing list	....
3	Decide if labels are to be used or envelopes addressed directly	....
4	Check number of envelopes/labels required	....
5	Check stocks of envelopes and order if necessary	....
6	Check stocks of labels and order if necessary	....
7	Receive envelopes	....
8	Receive labels	....
9	Run off envelopes	....
	OR	
	Run off labels	....
10	Draft letter	....
11	Get draft letter approved	....
12	Amend letter approved	....
13	Print letters merging mailing list	....
14	Sign letters	....
15	Fold and insert letters into envelopes, seal, stick on label if necessary	....
16	Frank envelopes	....
17	Arrange for collection of bulk mailing by Post Office mail van	....
	OR	
	Arrange delivery of bulk mailing to Post Office	....
18	Bundle filled envelopes into 50s or 100s	....

Fig. 88. *Checklist for a mail shot. By checking off each activity completed an up-to-date record is available for anyone to take over if required.*

Time scheduling
A time schedule sets out the items of a checklist in the order in which they have to be undertaken (activity scheduling) and indicates the time required for each item.

Making a time schedule

First the time required to perform each activity is determined. This must be done in relation to the activity schedule which indicates what items are dependent on each other and on people. For example it may be necessary to get approval from a senior manager for some particular document or expenditure. If it is known that this particular person is somewhat elusive allowance must be made for this in the time schedule.

The total time required to complete any particular task, e.g. a mail shot, can be determined by adding together the various times taken for each activity. However some activities can take place simultaneously, which reduces the total time (*see* the example below).

Example

The main activities involved in a mail shot of 500 letters in a small office might be the following

Draft letter Approval of draft	7 hours
Reproduction of letter on word processor using existing mailing list	9 hours
Preparation of labels	1 hour
Signing of letters (allow time for signing in batches)	3 hours
Sticking labels on envelopes	2 hours
Folding and insertion of letters into envelopes Sealing of envelopes	3 hours
Franking	1 hour

In this example the preparation of the labels can be started immediately while the letter is being drafted. Similarly the labels can be stuck on the envelopes immediately afterwards. This coordination can be shown clearly on a bar chart (*see* page 252).

When time scheduling is used

A time schedule must be worked out in order to know the time needed to complete all the activities involved in a task. It enables you to set deadlines.

Action sheet

An action sheet is compiled from the activity and time schedules. It indicates the number of days/weeks/months before an event that each activity must be undertaken.

How an action sheet is compiled
A period of time before the final event at which each activity must be undertaken is determined by relating the amount of time required for each activity and its relationship with other activities. In the mail shot example an action sheet might look like this.

Activity no.	*Activity*	*No. of days before*
1.	Draft letter	4 days
2.	Approval of letter	4 days
3.	Reproduction of letter	3 days
4.	Signing of letter	1 day
5.	Preparation of labels	1 day
6.	Sticking labels on envelopes	1 day
7.	Folding and inserting letters in envelopes	same day
8.	Sealing envelopes	same day
9.	Franking envelopes	same day

The number of days before the event are the latest times. In time scheduling we said the labels could be prepared while the letter was being drafted which might cut down the overall time by a day. An action sheet sets out the maximum time that is required. This means that five clear working days ought to be allowed to complete the entire task.

Finally dates would be added to the action sheet. If the mail shot were to be sent out on Monday 4 July the action sheet would now look as in Fig. 89.

When an action sheet is used
An action sheet is invaluable for any undertaking involving activities which are carried out over a period of time, whether that period of time be a week or a year. In some cases, e.g. organising a conference, it could be two or three years.

Bar charts

A bar chart indicates the time to be taken for each activity and shows the time relationship between one activity and another.

Activity no.	Activity	No. of days before	Date	Action	
				Begun	Complete
1.	Draft letter	4 days	28.6		
2.	Approval of letter	4 days	28.6		
3.	Reproduction of letter	3 days	29.6		
4.	Signing of letter	1 day	1.7		
5.	Preparation of labels	1 day	1.7		
6.	Sticking labels on envelopes	1 day	1.7		
7.	Folding and inserting letters in envelopes	same day	4.7		
8.	Sealing envelopes	same day	4.7		
9.	Franking envelopes	same day	4.7		
10.	Mailing		4.7		

Fig. 89. *Final action sheet for a simple mail shot.*

How a bar chart is prepared
The activities are listed on the chart, usually on the left hand side. Across the top of the chart is a time scale. The times when each activity will begin and end are joined by a line. *See* Fig. 90.

When a bar chart is used
A bar chart is particularly useful when you want to see at a glance the time schedule for a series of activities. It also enables you to keep control of progress because a daily check can be kept on deadlines.

Diary
There are many types of diary, ranging from a small pocket booklet, which has a small space allocated for each day of the week on one page, to an A4 size page-a-day desk diary. There are "planner" diaries which provide a "spread" for six months or twelve months. There are appointment diaries for various professional purposes such as for doctors, dentists, hairdressers. Specimens of diary formats are illustrated in Fig. 91 (*a*), (*b*) and (*c*).

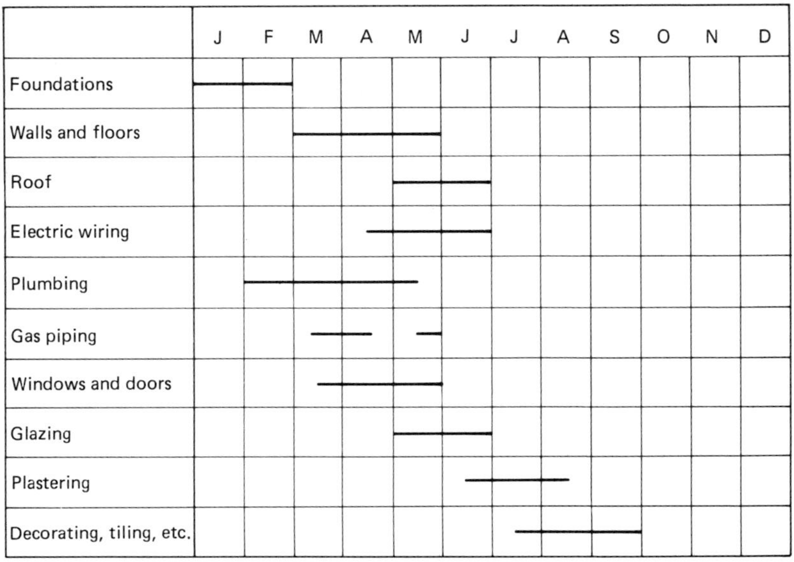

Fig. 90. *Bar chart: time schedule for building.*

How a diary is used
Appointments are entered against the appropriate time (if times are printed in the diary) on the appropriate date. It is very important to check that the correct month is being used. Many an appointment has not been kept because it was entered on the correct date under the wrong month. Many diaries have a section for notes, either for each day or for each week. It is useful to use daily note sections for a checklist of priority jobs, telephone calls to be made, etc. Some people keep two diaries—one for appointments and one for work scheduling.

Arranging appointments

When making an appointment the following information is needed.

(*a*) The name and designation of the person you are to see.
(*b*) The exact name and address of the organisation.
(*c*) The telephone number of the organisation and the extension number of the person you are to see.
(*d*) The topic to be discussed.
(*e*) The time, date and expected duration of the meeting.
(*f*) The location of the meeting.
(*g*) Directions to the organisation, including the entrance if there are more than one.

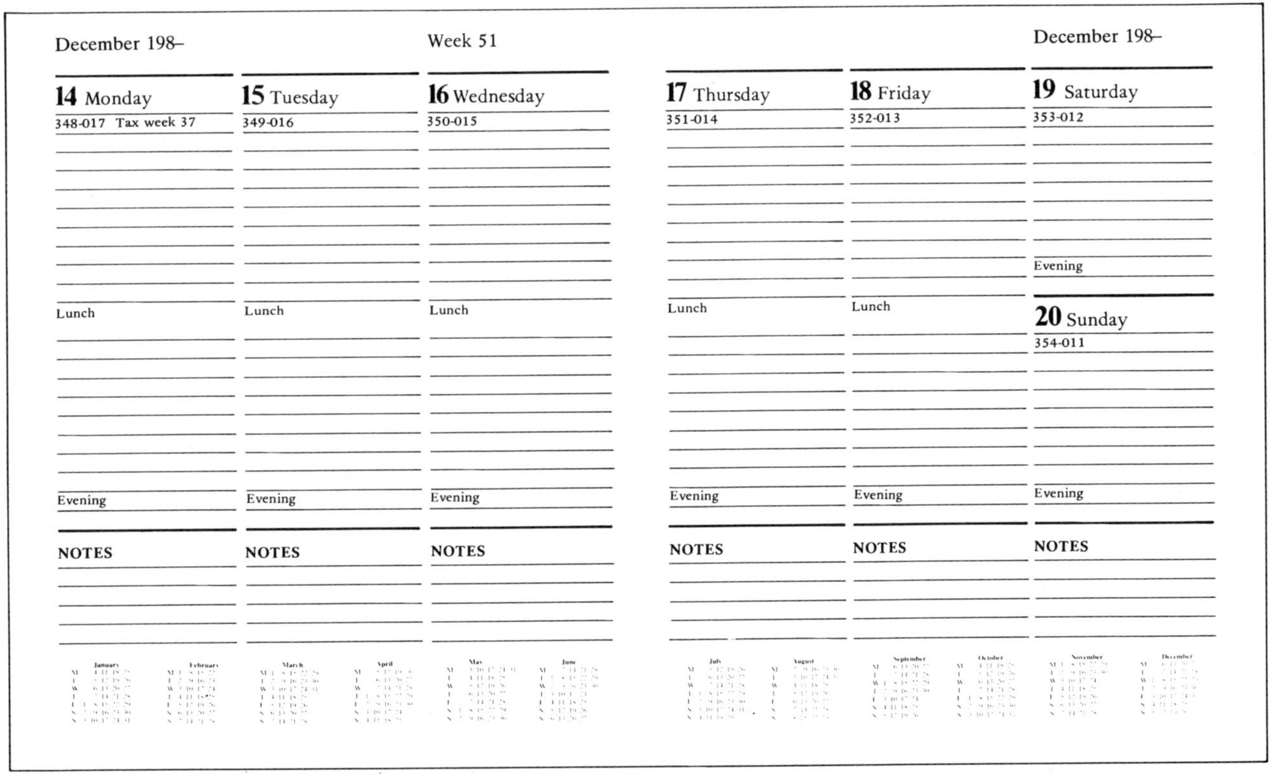

Fig. 91(a). *"Week at a glance" diary format with space for notes each day.*

November 198–		Morning	Afternoon	November 198– Evening
Sun	1			
Mon	2			
Tues	3			
Wed	4			
Thurs	5			
Fri	6			
Sat	7			
Sun	8			
Mon	9			
Tues	10			
Wed	11			
Thurs	12			
Fri	13			
Sat	14			
Sun	15			
Mon	16			
Tues	17			
Wed	18			
Thurs	19			
Fri	20			
Sat	21			
Sun	22			
Mon	23			
Tues	24			
Wed	25			
Thurs	26			
Fri	27			
Sat	28			
Sun	29			
Mon	30			

Fig. 91(b). *Monthly planner or appointment pocket diary.*

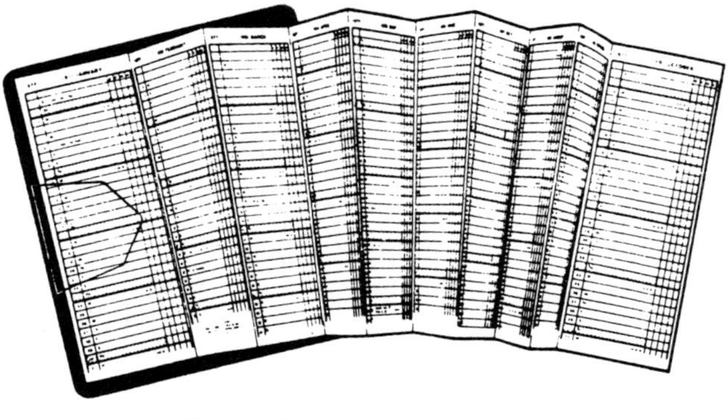

Fig. 91(c). *Fold out year planner.*

(*h*) Car park facilities.
(*i*) Security and reception procedures.

If you are making an appointment for someone to come and see you it is helpful to send a map giving clear directions if the person has never visited you before, particularly if the location is difficult to find.

Arranging meetings

If you have to arrange a meeting of several people there can be difficulties because it is rare indeed that everyone is free at the same time or that a room is available when the people are free. It is useful to establish who the key people for the meeting are, i.e. the people who must be present. One way to sort out possible times is to prepare a chart listing the names of the people concerned and showing the times when the room is available. Such a chart is illustrated in Fig. 92.

	TUESDAY		WEDNESDAY		THURSDAY	
	AM	PM	AM	PM	AM	PM
MR A						
MR B						
MR C						
MR D						

Fig. 92. *Simple chart to help establish the availability of people for a meeting.*

This chart enables you to see at a glance when all, or the majority of, the people are available at the same time.

Bring-forward systems

Bring-forward systems are variously called "bring-up", "diarying" or "follow-up" systems. A bring-forward system is a series of procedures which enables you to put away documents until they are needed and bring them out for action at the exact time when they are required. It may be operated in a diary, on cards or in file folders.

How a bring-forward system operates

Anything which is to be done at a later date, whether it is action on a letter, making a telephone call, discussing a problem, is noted. The "bring-forward" date is decided. The note may be made in a diary on the appropriate date. A letter may be marked with the "bring-forward" date and filed in a "bring-forward" file (*see* below). A note may be made, dated and filed. A "bring-forward" file may be a concertina file which has pockets, one for each day of the month, and an extra pocket at the back. Each piece of paper is filed in the appropriate pocket if it is to be brought forward in the current month. Items for next month and beyond are filed in the pocket at the back.

Alternatively you can have a file folder for each month and a file folder for each day of the month. The folder system works in the same way as a concertina file except that papers for months following the current month are filed in the appropriate monthly folder. At the beginning of each month the papers are sorted into the daily folders. Diary files are illustrated in Fig. 93.

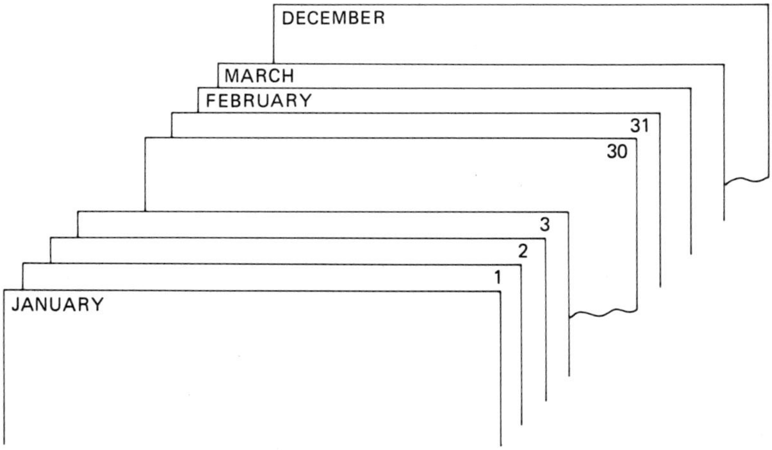

Fig. 93. *Diary files, also known as "bring-forward" and "bring-up" files.*

Another method, particularly useful when files are to be brought forward, is for the user to attach a prepared slip to the front of the file when returning it to the central registry. The filing clerk detaches the slip and files it in a card index system in "bring-forward" date order. The file is returned to its correct storage place. Each day the filing clerk takes out the slips for the day, retrieves the files required, attaches the slips to the appropriate files and sends them to the people who wanted them. The "bring-forward" slip is illustrated in Fig. 94.

Please bring forward

file no.________________________

on________________________

Signed:________________________

Fig. 94. *A "bring-forward" slip which ensures that files are retrieved for action when required.*

When a "bring-forward" system is used
A "bring-forward" system is needed in every office. Anything that needs action at a later date should be processed through a "bring-forward" system. The choice of system depends on the amount of material you need to action at a later date. In most offices a concertina file is adequate, but in certain types of work a larger system is necessary.

Work-requisition forms
A requisition form is a document which indicates work to be done. It should contain all the details required to complete the task. Such forms are usually self explanatory but need to be carefully designed (*see* Chapter Thirteen) to ensure that they are easy to complete and provide space for all necessary information. A specimen requisition form for copying is illustrated in Fig. 95.

When requisition forms are used
It is useful to have such forms in any situation where individuals or a section/department are providing a service. Examples are printing departments, a typist or secretary serving several managers, libraries.

Plan charts/boards
There are many types of planning charts and boards produced by well-known manufacturers for a wide range of uses. Common examples are charts for staff holiday rotas, year-plan charts showing events/meetings, visits, courses, etc. Manufactured charts and boards range from the simple "write-on" type laminated paper to magnetic boards on which strips and symbols can be arranged and

To: **Print Room Supervisor** Date ______

From: Name ______ Extn. No. ______

Department ______

Title of Document ______

No. of copies ______

No. of pages ______ Reverse print* ______

Size of original ______

Reduce* ______ to size ______

Colour of paper ______

Collate* ______ Staple* ______

Collect* ______ by ______ am/pm

Deliver* ______ on ______

Authorised ______

*Tick if required

PRINT ROOM USE ONLY

Job Code ______

Completed ______ Checked ______

Fig. 95. *Requisition form giving instructions for copying.*

others made from more sophisticated types of material. A typical planning board is illustrated in Fig. 96. Such boards can also be used to indicate the progress of activities.

CO-ORDINATION

A fundamental ingredient of work planning is effective communication. It is essential that each person knows exactly what is expected of him, what he is to do, how he is to do it, and when and where he is to do it. Changes of plan must be notified to all concerned. Everyone who is affected by the implementation of a work plan, or changes in it, must be kept informed.

Co-ordination has to be planned. Suitable reporting procedures

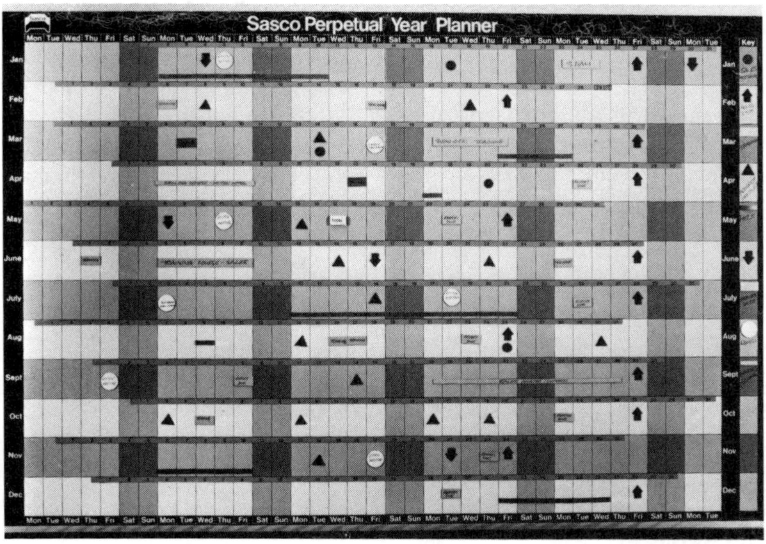

Fig. 96. *Work planning on a magnetic board. The various shapes represent different activities.*

(Courtesy Twinlock UK Ltd.)

must be devised and one person must be made responsible for ensuring that the overall plan is kept on schedule. If any hitch occurs the reporting procedures must be such that the person in charge is aware of the hitch *immediately* so that action can be taken to rectify the matter or modify the work plan of other people if necessary.

Regular meetings to report progress and to keep all members of a section/department/team informed should be a feature of all work planning. This can be organised at individual level on an informal basis where only two or three people are involved, but it should be organised on a more formal basis, i.e. a properly chaired meeting, when a larger number of people are involved.

SUMMARY

1. Work planning is essential to ensure that priorities are established, deadlines are met and pressure is avoided as far as possible.
2. Work is planned in units of time starting from the longest, which is often a year. As planning reaches the shorter units it becomes progressively more detailed.

3. The worker must be a well-organised person and must develop a methodical approach to work.

4. Methods of planning work include checklists, activity scheduling, time scheduling, action sheets, bar charts, diary, bring-forward systems, work-requisition forms, plan charts and boards.

5. When more than one person is involved in a particular task or project there must be co-ordination of activities to ensure that all are completed on time so that other related activities can be carried out.

SELF-ASSESSMENT QUESTIONS

Answer all questions as quickly as possible. Do not turn back to the Chapter until you have completed this test.

1. Give examples of five office activities which can be organised in "batches".
2. List twenty ways in which an office worker can work "methodically".
3. What is meant by "cyclical planning"?
4. Planning from the longest unit of time down through progressively smaller units of time is often referred to as "forward planning". Explain how this method of planning works.
5. Some people argue that they do not need to plan their work formally because "it is all in my head". List five advantages of planning "on paper".
6. Describe two methods of preparing a checklist.
7. Suggest five purposes for which a year plan chart might be used.
8. Below is a list of activities involved in the production of a report with the time each is expected to take. Prepare a bar chart showing when each activity will be done. How many days will be needed to complete the job?

	No. of days
Manager dictates draft of report, on five tapes, approximately one tape per day	5
Tapes keyed-in on word processor	5
Manager edits draft	2
Manager requests drawing office to prepare diagrams	1
Preparation of diagrams	3
Edited draft photocopied and sent to two other people for review	4
Final edit by manager	2

	No. of days
Amendments on word processor Preparation of index Print out master	3
Paste in diagrams	1
Photocopy, collate and bind	2

9. When making an appointment to visit another organisation for the first time what information should you give the other person? What information should the other person give you?

10. You have to arrange a meeting of ten people. It is essential that seven of them attend themselves. The other three may send representatives. State in sequence the steps you would take to arrange the meeting.

11. (*a*) What is a "bring-forward" system?
(*b*) Why is it essential to have a "bring-forward" system?
(*c*) Explain two methods of operating a "bring-forward" system.

12. What is the purpose of a work requisition form? Give three instances of the use of such a form.

13. "Suitable reporting procedures must be devised to ensure co-ordination of activities." Explain this statement.

ASSIGNMENT

Working in groups of two or three choose an event or task to plan. Here are some suggestions:

a conference;
an induction course;
preparation and production of a printed document, e.g. a conference programme;
changing over from individual typing of various standard letters on a typewriter to production on a word processor;
making arrangements for a business trip overseas;
arranging for a party of schoolchildren to be shown round your organisation, with refreshments at some stage.

Plan by working through the following stages.

(*a*) Prepare a checklist.
(*b*) Schedule and number the activities in sequence.
(*c*) Estimate the time required for each activity.
(*d*) Prepare an action sheet.
(*e*) Decide the deadline and prepare a chart with date headings (months and days) indicating the number of the activity in the appropriate date space.

CHAPTER TWELVE

Work Measurement

CHAPTER OBJECTIVES

After studying this chapter you should be able to:

* describe the most commonly used means of measuring output in an office;
* explain productivity;
* describe the methods used to monitor individual productivity;
* recognise and use work monitoring documents.

DEFINITION AND PURPOSE

What is work measurement? It is a system of measuring the work of an individual or a group of people (a section or a department) against pre-determined standards of time and accuracy (or quality).

Why is it done? It is essential to control the standard of work done, both quantity and quality. Work completed is commonly referred to as *output*. There is no point in having fast output which is inaccurate: at the same time it is very expensive to have perfect work if it takes a person a very long time to do it perfectly. Everyone is human and people are bound to make mistakes occasionally. The question of whether mistakes are acceptable has to be decided. If it is agreed that it would be too expensive to get 100 per cent accuracy, an error tolerance, i.e. the number of errors allowable, must be established. This means that not only must output, i.e. the quantity of work completed, be measured but also productivity, i.e. the quality in relation to the quantity.

TYPES OF MEASURABLE OFFICE WORK

It is not possible to measure precisely every individual activity which is carried on in an office, but it has been estimated that an average of up to two-thirds of all office work can be measured. Tasks which are easy to measure include ledger posting, preparation of invoices and statements, envelope addressing, envelope franking, filing, typing letters/invoices, reprographic operations and most operations involving the use of a machine.

Non-standard activities such as making and receiving telephone calls, receiving visitors, dealing with queries cannot be "measured" against a standard, but they can be measured in terms of the amount of time spent on them. This can be very useful when one wishes to find out how an individual allocates or spends his time over a period, e.g. a week or a month.

METHODS OF MEASURING WORK

Methods of work measurement vary from imprecise to very precise. But before output can be measured for control purposes standards must first be set.

Setting standards for output

Standards against which output can be measured can be set in various ways. These include:

(*a*) obtaining estimates from supervisors;
(*b*) obtaining estimates from subordinates;
(*c*) obtaining diary sheets completed by individual staff members;
(*d*) activity sampling;
(*e*) personal observation, making time recordings repeated over a period of time.

Estimates from supervisors
These estimates may be reasonable in the case of repetitive work, provided the supervisor is experienced. This method is not suitable, however, when the subordinates' duties are varied because the supervisor is unlikely to be aware of the time spent on each duty. In such a case a subordinate may well resent having a standard set by a supervisor.

Estimates from subordinates
These estimates may not be reliable because it is difficult to be completely objective about timing your own work, particularly if you know that you will be held to your output standard. On the other hand, a person ought to be able to assess better than anyone else the implications of an individual task or series of tasks which he or she performs regularly. Problems arise with the non-measurable activities such as interruptions by the supervisor, telephone calls, etc.

Diary sheets
These are a more precise method of determining time spent on each task or activity. Diary sheets are completed either daily or weekly by each individual member of staff, daily sheets being more precise.

The information from each daily sheet is summarised on a weekly sheet and average times are determined for particular types of task. In some cases it may be necessary to have specimens of the work done for comparative purposes. For example letters or invoices may vary in content and thus in the time taken to complete.

Diary sheets are particularly suitable for recording non-measurable work. A specimen completed sheet is illustrated in Fig. 97. Such sheets are summarised weekly either for each individual or for a group of people. The completed weekly summary sheet illustrated in Fig. 98 highlights the variable amounts of time spent by different people on each of the activities.

Another use of diary sheets is to establish the usage of machines. This may be useful in determining idle time of a machine or establishing the necessity for a certain type of machine. For example if a secretary demands a word processor but spends only five per cent of her time on typewriting duties, i.e. less than two hours per week, the extra expense could not be justified on the grounds of fatigue. It might be justified on the grounds of appearance of the documents, but that is not relevant to work measurement.

Activity sampling

This means that work is observed at different times of the day, perhaps several times a day, on different days. At each inspection the kinds of work being done by each member of staff are recorded so that an estimate of the volume of each kind of work can eventually be established reasonably accurately.

Personal observation

This is similar to activity sampling but is applied to particular activities. The main disadvantage of any observation technique is that individual workers may react unfavourably either by making a special effort while being observed or by being less efficient because they are worried about being watched. It is always necessary to observe a good number of individuals to ensure that realistic standards are set, particularly if the standard is for a group.

Relaxation allowance

When setting standards for clerical work a relaxation allowance (R.A.) of 15 per cent is added to the measured times. No one can work "flat out" all the time. This allowance takes into account natural breaks in concentration, fatigue and variations in the individual's optimum working capacity at various times of the day. Everyone has "peak" and "off peak" periods of concentration and productivity through the day and even through the week.

Time Off: ....

Overtime: ....

Boss Away: ....

DAILY LOG OF UNMEASURED WORK

Name Bertha

Department ....

Date ....

Time grid (A.M.): 9 — 0 5 10 15 20 25 30 35 40 45 50 55 | 10 — 0 5 10 15 20 25 30 35 40 45 50 55 | 11 — 0 5 10 15 20 25 30 35 40 45 50 55 | 12 — 0 5 10 15 20 25 30 35 40 45 50 55

A.M.		TOTAL
Taking Dictation (inc. walk to & from)	(1)	30
Unmeasured Typing	(2)	
Amendments to Stencils	(3)	
Check by Call-over with another typist	(4)	
Collating & Stapling Reports	(5)	
	(6)	
Opening, Sorting & Despatching Mail	(7)	
Filing	(8)	10
Messages & Errands	(9)	
Work connected with Survey	(10)	
Sickness absence return	(11)	10
Telephone enquiries	(12)	25
Queries	(13)	20
Travelling expenses	(14)	
Despatching teleprinter message	(15)	
Checking film report	(16)	
Diary entries	(17)	5
	(18)	
	(19)	
Waiting Time (no work available)	(20)	40

No. of Envelopes typed ~~||||~~ ~~||||~~ ~~||||~~ ~~||||~~

No. of Phone calls ....

No. of Emidiscs loaded & unloaded ....

loaded & unloaded ....

Notes: Horizontal lines should be drawn as work is done to show how time has been spent.

No lines of less than five minutes should be entered. All jobs should be rounded off to the nearest full five minutes.

Number of envelopes, phone calls, etc. to be recorded in five barred gate fashion against the appropriate description. (~~||||~~)

Fig. 97. *Daily diary sheet for recording secretarial work which cannot be measured (morning only).*

SUMMARY OF UNMEASURED WORK

NAME	Taking Dictation (inc. walk to & from)	Unmeasured Typing	Amendments (Stencils, Orders, etc.)	Check by Call-over	Collating & Stapling Reports	Other Work associated with Typing	Filing	Messages and Errands	Queries & Discussion	Looking for Papers, Files etc.	Photocopying	Miscellaneous	Secretarial Duties	Clerical Duties	TOTAL	Waiting Time (no work available)
	1	2	3	4	5	6	7	8	9	10	11	12	13	14		15
TOTAL																

Fig. 98. *Weekly summary sheet for unmeasured work.*

Measuring output

Having set standards it is necessary to have methods of checking to ensure that standards are reached. Diary sheets, activity sampling and personal observation can be used for measuring output as well as for setting standards. There are additional methods of measuring work. They are:

(*a*) inspection and counting of tasks completed;
(*b*) pre-determined method time study (PMTS);
(*c*) British work-measurement data foundation system.

Inspection and counting of tasks completed

This is time-consuming and often resented by subordinates. It is simpler to check outstanding work held by each individual. The supervisor needs to keep a record of when (date and time) the work was handed out. Realistic deadlines should have been agreed by the supervisor and the subordinate. This is not a precise method of measuring work done.

Pre-determined method time study (PMTS)

This involves the analysis of each task into individual activities, which are in turn analysed into very precise elements. The performance of each element is timed with a stop-watch so that a total time is achieved for each activity and for the whole task.

Example

Task: recording an entry on a card.

Activities:

(*a*) Retrieve card from cabinet.
(*b*) Enter information on card.
(*c*) Check entry.
(*d*) Return card to correct place in cabinet.

Elements in Activity (*a*):
(Assume cabinet accessible to clerk when sitting.)

(*i*) Turn to cabinet.
(*ii*) Move hand to drawer.
(*iii*) Pull drawer open.
(*iv*) Identify section required.
(*v*) Identify card required.
(*vi*) Move hand to extract card.
(*vii*) Take hold of card.
(*viii*) Extract card.
(*ix*) Move hand to place card on desk.
(*x*) Move hand to drawer.
(*xi*) Push in drawer.

Each element is then timed; in some cases the element may be measured in thousandths of a second. In this particular activity there are elements which may be variable, particularly elements (*iv*) and (*v*). It would be possible to establish an average time for these elements out of a large number of timings.

The British Management Data Foundation system

This is an extension of PMTS in that precise times have been established for activities involved in specific tasks such as operating various machines and clerical operations. The standard relaxation allowance of 15 per cent is built into the times.

The time specifications established by the Foundation can be bought and used for establishing standards within an organisation. Information about the system can be obtained from the Foundation's registered address: 1 Cecil Court, London Road, Enfield, Middlesex EN2 6DD.

MEASURING TYPEWRITING

There are three main ways of measuring typewriting. The simplest method is by the number of lines. When measuring letters, the number of lines in the body of the letter are counted (a measure in 1/6 inch divisions is used as there are six lines to the inch on most standard manual and electric typewriters) and 10 per cent is added for addresses, etc. The average amount of work expected of a competent typist is sixty lines an hour on elite type (twelve letters to the inch) or seventy-two lines an hour on pica type (ten letters to the inch).

Two other methods of measurement are the square inch grid and "treasury unit". In both cases a transparent printed overlay is placed over the body of the letter or the page of the report and the amount of work done is read off.

There are various factors which may affect typewriting/word processing production, including:

(*a*) the complexity and accuracy required, e.g. legal or accounts documents, technical work;
(*b*) the amount of tabulation, i.e. work set out in columns, especially figures;
(*c*) the number of copies required—collation of carbon packs or copying takes time;
(*d*) the legibility of the draft;
(*e*) the standard of dictation;
(*f*) the number of times the typist has to refer to other sources, e.g. files, for information;
(*g*) interruptions, e.g. telephone calls.

MEASURING WORD PROCESSING

It is difficult to measure word processing output realistically because much of the work may be up-dating and amending text, printing hundreds (even thousands) of standard letters, producing letters from standard paragraphs stored on disk, etc. Thus it is impossible to demand a certain number of lines or pages of typescript.

Experienced operators become quite accurate at estimating how long a job will take to complete, provided they know the standard of input and the likely problems. A log of work received, turn round times and details of the work, e.g. number of pages, whether original keying in or up-dating, will build up an over all outline of productivity. Such an ongoing record will ensure that if turn round time increases the amount of work passing through can be checked against previous weeks or months. Machine down time must be recorded and taken into account, as well as time spent duplicating disks, referring back to authors, etc.

As far as is known no specific work measurement technique has been devised for word processing or, indeed, for random computer input. The work of data preparation operators is measured by key strokes which are recorded by the computer. This is easy to do as the work is purely keying in of original data.

TIME SCHEDULING

Time scheduling means fitting the task into a given time rather than allocating time in accordance with the amount of work to be done. For example, wages cannot normally be started before a certain time on a certain date and must be prepared and ready to be out by a certain time on a certain date. Thus no matter how much work is involved the job must be done within those fixed time points. It may mean bringing in extra staff, having staff work overtime, installing machines or some other solution.

Time scheduling can be controlled by the use of charts which show the time allocated for a particular job. The actual time taken is recorded on the chart for comparison. It enables the supervisor to see at a glance when a particular task is falling behind schedule.

Handing out work in batches with a deadline for completion is another method of control. All batches must be of equal quantity. This type of control is adequate for straightforward typing, records, filing.

INDIVIDUAL PRODUCTIVITY

People can produce only what they are given to do. It is essential therefore that when an individual's daily output is measured it is first established that a full day's work has been given. A survey of typewriting output carried out by the author established an individual productivity of two words a minute over a day. The typist had long periods of the day with nothing to do, but in terms of cost of production this proved very expensive.

Individual productivity must be related to cost, not only of the individual employee's time but all the other costs involved in running an office. If it costs £50 a day to accommodate, equip and pay a typist who produces five letters a day, each letter has cost £10, in addition to the variable costs such as dictation time, stationery, internal mailing services and postage. If the typist can produce twenty letters a day this cost is reduced to £2.50 per letter plus variable costs.

METHODS OF CONTROLLING QUALITY

At the beginning of the Chapter we said that people are human, therefore mistakes will be made. Nevertheless, nearly all mistakes cost money. A typing error in a letter means re-typing. This means that productivity decreases and unit overhead cost (the overhead cost on each letter) increases. An arithmetic mistake in a document may mean the organisation loses an amount of money to which it is entitled, or a customer complains which involves telephone calls and/or correspondence. It also impairs the image of the organisation. Therefore work measurement must include methods of controlling quality as well as measuring quantity. There are three main methods. These are:

(*a*) 100 per cent checking;
(*b*) random sampling;
(*c*) partial checking.

One hundred per cent checking

This should be done for only the most important work, e.g. statistics for the board of directors, material being sent to the printer, reading printer's proofs. It is a very expensive method of checking since it is virtually doing the work a second time.

Random sampling

This means checking samples of work at random, but on frequent occasions. The frequency and amount of checking would depend on the experience of the staff doing the work and the importance of the work itself.

Partial checking

This is the most commonly used method of checking work in an office. Only the most important part of the work is checked, or the activities of tasks which are most frequently inaccurate.

CAUSES OF ERRORS

When checking reveals errors it is essential to identify the cause, otherwise the same errors will continue to occur. Most errors can be reduced to a minimum, even if not eliminated completely. Errors may be attributed to the worker him or herself, to management or to the working conditions.

Fault of the worker

Too hasty work (causing, perhaps, transposition of figures).
Lack of method in working (due to bad training).
Lack of theoretical knowledge.
Inexperience.
Bad writing (schooling may be to blame).
Tiredness (perhaps due to domestic cause, or to office conditions).
Gossiping (lack of supervision).

Fault of management

Defective training (either initial or follow-up training).
Bad selection of staff.
Insufficient and vague instructions.
No grouping of activities to provide specialisation for employees.
Lack of control.
Bad organisation (perhaps unsuitable for the purpose of the office).
Bad morale ("couldn't care less" attitude).
System too complicated (work simplification needed).
Forms badly designed and worded.

Poor working conditions

Bad lighting (especially where filing cabinets are housed).
Unsuitable colour of paper used for office forms.
Temperature not controlled, inadequate ventilation.
Too much noise which impinges on concentration.
Unsuitable furniture which results in unnecessary fatigue.
Unsuitable decor.

It is often found that the number of errors increases with the size of the task. An error rate of 0.5 per cent in a particular task may reach as much as 10 per cent in a task barely double the size. Thus the error rate increases twenty times, reducing productivity by 9.5 per cent.

Incentive schemes for accuracy are often effective in reducing errors, sometimes by as much as 65 per cent. Such schemes are usually effective only if they are first carefully worked out and agreed with the staff concerned.

ERROR TOLERANCE

If it is decided that a certain number of errors must be accepted it is usual to set a level of error tolerance. It is impossible to state a general level for any particular type of job because it will depend on the individual circumstances of each organisation, and indeed of each department/section within the organisation, as to what is acceptable. As a general guideline the question of cost is usually one of the main deciding factors. Will it cost more to check all items on an invoice between £1 and £4.99 than would be saved by correcting the errors? If so check only items of £5 and over. The cost of checking increases more and more the nearer one gets to 100 per cent accuracy requirements.

It is useful to decide beforehand whenever possible what level of checking is required. Draft reports are going to be read and edited by the author. It may be sensible to tell the typist not to proof read. She can thus produce more. A letter that is to be signed should be totally accurate. Therefore double checking by the typist may be necessary. In the case of legal documents checking by two people is essential. The result of an error could be disastrous and create a great deal more work. In such a situation it is cheaper to check than risk the cost of an error.

SUMMARY

1. Work measurement is used to control the quantity and quality of work done by employees.

2. Up to two-thirds of all office work can be measured.

3. Non-measurable work can be recorded so that the amount of time spent on it in relation to the requirements of the job and to measurable tasks can be determined.

4. Standards must be set for volume of output, i.e. amount of work that can be realistically expected in a given time.

5. All work measurement times should include relaxation allowance (normally 15 per cent).

6. The productivity of each individual takes into account volume and accuracy of work completed in relation to the cost of production, bearing in mind that overhead costs decrease as accuracy, as well as quantity, increases. Inaccurate work increases overhead costs as well as variable costs.

7. In certain types of work a level of error tolerance can be established, generally based on the cost of checking compared with the loss incurred by having inaccuracies.

8. The cause/causes of errors should always be established and whenever practicable remedied.

SELF-ASSESSMENT QUESTIONS

Answer all questions as quickly as possible. Do not turn back to the Chapter until you have completed this test.

1. Suggest at least five tasks (in addition to those mentioned on page 262) which could be measured easily.
2. Suggest at least five activities (in addition to those mentioned on page 262) which cannot be "measured" against a pre-set standard but can be recorded for purposes of determining time spent on them.
3. Why might it be important to know how long an individual or a group of people spend on non-measurable activities?
4. What is the principal difference between activity sampling and personal observation when setting standards?
5. What are the disadvantages of obtaining estimates from supervisors and from subordinates when setting work measurement standards?
6. What is the main difference between measuring output and measuring the productivity of individual workers?
7. What do the letters PMTS stand for? Explain this method of work measurement.
8. State five factors which affect the productivity of a typist or word processor operator.
9. Describe briefly the three methods of checking the quality of output.
10. Errors may arise from three main sources. Name the sources and state five possible causes of error from each source.
11. Why is it not possible to insist on 100 per cent accuracy in all work?
12. Suggest five types of work where total accuracy is essential.

ASSIGNMENTS

Assignment 1

Working in pairs set time standards for a routine office task. Following the procedures outlined on page 267, each pair work together first to analyse the task into activities, and then to analyse the activities into elements.

One person from each pair should then perform the elements while the other person times with a stop-watch. If a stop-watch is not available use a watch with a second hand and time several elements together. The times taken to perform each element must be carefully recorded. The process should then be repeated by switching roles.

When everyone in the group has taken a turn in performing the task and recording the time taken the group should state the times taken to perform each element, or series of elements, and an average time can be worked out. Major differences, i.e. very slow or very fast times, should be discussed.

Assignment 2

If you are working in an office prepare a daily diary sheet (*see* Fig. 97) listing the tasks which you perform in the course of your day's work. Make a copy for each day of the week. Keep a record of the time you spend on each task throughout the day and do this every day for a week. At the end of the week prepare a summary sheet (*see* Fig. 98) and insert the total times spent on each activity throughout the week.

Study the summary and ask yourself whether the times are what you would have expected. If they are not, try to establish why they are different. Then discuss the implications of the amount of time spent on each particular task with your tutor, colleagues or supervisor.

CHAPTER THIRTEEN

Organisation and Methods

> CHAPTER OBJECTIVES
>
> After studying this chapter you should be able to:
> * explain the function of organisation and methods;
> * recognise the importance of organisation and methods in administration;
> * apply basic principles of organisation and methods to routine systems and procedures in the office;
> * identify shortcomings in systems and procedures leading to loss of output and suggest remedies.

DEFINITION AND PURPOSE

What is organisation and methods, or O and M as it is commonly called (in America it is referred to as "work simplification")? The function of O and M is to establish the best form of organisation, the best system/s and the best procedures for carrying out a particular task or series of tasks, by an individual, section or department, taking into account human, financial and time constraints. O and M has been described as "an attitude of mind". It is true that at the individual level it requires a methodical approach.

The principal objective of O and M is to eliminate waste—of time, human energy, equipment, supplies, space, expertise—and thus money. If this objective is achieved it will normally enable the ultimate objective to be achieved, viz. increased productivity. A further very important objective may be to improve job satisfaction of individual staff.

ELIMINATING WASTE

There are many causes of waste. A few are suggested here.

(*a*) Inaccurate work which wastes time, supplies, equipment/machine time, supervisors'/managers' time.

(*b*) Duplication of tasks, often the result of inadequate or non-existent co-ordination (*see* Chapter Eleven).

(*c*) Inadequate or unreliable support services from secretarial and clerical staff, perhaps the result of poor communications, lack of training, lack of interest in the work/organisation or insufficient staff.

(*d*) Badly organised work flow involving unnecessary "travelling" of documents.

(*e*) Badly designed organisation structure which means that there is overlapping of some duties and gaps between others. There may also be insufficient attention paid to keeping job descriptions and specifications up to date.

The golden rule in eliminating waste is simplicity. Generally the simpler the system the less likelihood there is of resources being wasted.

THE O AND M DEPARTMENT

Most large organisations and governments have a management services department whose function is to provide advice to all departments, either when requested to do so by departmental managers, when instructed to do so by senior management (perhaps because objectives are not being met in a particular department), or as part of a regular "audit" of departmental performance. The O and M staff usually form a section within the management services department. In smaller organisations which are not big enough to have a management services department there may be just one O and M officer. Groups of companies often have one management services department for the whole group, with O and M staff in the individual companies.

If there are a number of O and M staff they will be headed by an O and M manager. The O and M officers may be specialists in certain areas such as computers, form design, time and motion study.

THE O AND M SURVEY

When a department or section is considered to be lacking in efficiency, either by the departmental manager or by someone more senior, it is usual to ask an O and M officer (or group of officers if the department is large) to carry out a survey and make recommendations for improvements. There are normally five stages to a survey. These are set out below.

Define objectives

The O and M staff and the departmental manager together agree the objective/s of the survey. This is confirmed in writing.

Plan survey

The survey is planned, i.e. it is decided what is to be investigated, by whom, by what methods, when and over what period of time. When the O and M staff have decided this they will discuss their plan with the departmental manager and then with the staff of the department concerned. This meeting is essential because staff must be assured that their jobs are not at risk, that there is no intention of criticising individual job performance, and, indeed, that the final result should result in greater job satisfaction for everyone.

Collect information

The information is collected by the O and M staff. Facts may be collected:

(*a*) from existing records;
(*b*) by personal observation;
(*c*) by discussion with people doing the jobs and their supervisors/managers;
(*d*) by questionnaire;
(*e*) by having staff complete record sheets specially prepared for the survey.

Analyse information

The facts collected are analysed. This involves using Rudyard Kipling's six honest serving men. The questions may include the following.

(*a*) *What* is done, and what is the unit of work?
(*b*) *Why* is it done? (This may give answers connected with other office routines.)
(*c*) *When* is it done? The question of time-tables, frequency of operation and cycles of time has to be considered.
(*d*) *Where* is it done? Is it necessary for it to be done where it is, or could it be done better elsewhere?
(*e*) *Who* does it? This involves the study of the relationship of staff and the work.
(*f*) *How* is it done, and how many are concerned in it? This involves a mastery of procedures, equipment, office machines and so on.

Recommendations

Recommendations, known as a proposal, are prepared and submitted to the departmental manager and possibly more senior managers. The contents of the proposal are normally discussed with managers and staff concerned during the survey.

WORK CHARTS

When an O and M survey is undertaken it very often involves

charting procedures and systems. There are several kinds of charts which are used by O and M officers for this purpose. Although it is often necessary to prepare a narrative analysis first, a chart has the advantage of showing at a glance what happens within a system. It may highlight a fault in the system more easily than discussion or description.

Two charts in common use are flow process charts and procedure flow charts.

Flow process chart

The flow process chart shows what happens to a particular document. Symbols are used to show what is happening at each stage. These symbols are shown in Fig. 99.

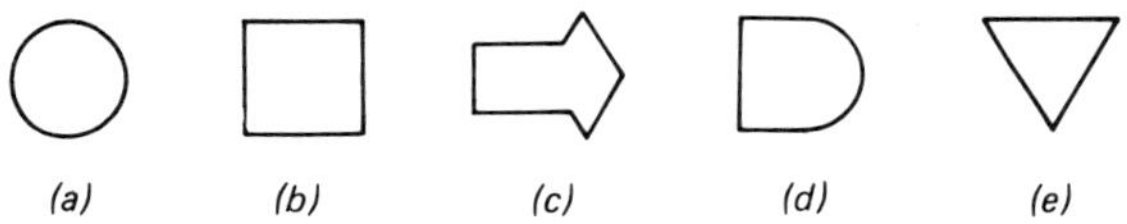

Fig. 99. *Flow process chart symbols:* (a) *operation, i.e. action is being taken;* (b) *inspection;* (c) *transport, or movement from one place to another;* (d) *delay, usually awaiting action;* (e) *storage.*

It can be seen from Fig. 100 that this chart can also be used to measure the distance the document travels—again this may highlight unnecessary movements or delays.

Procedure flow chart

A procedure (or forms) flow chart shows the flow of work from one work station to another, or between departments. It is often used to show the movements of various copies of a document or series of documents when, for example, an order is executed. Figure 101 shows a typical procedure flow chart of this type.

STAFF REACTION TO O AND M

The O and M officer does not always have an easy task. He or she has to be very tactful, persuasive and reassuring to the people whose work he/she investigates. Staff tend to put up defences giving a wide variety of reasons why an O and M survey is a waste of time. Here are a few selected at random.

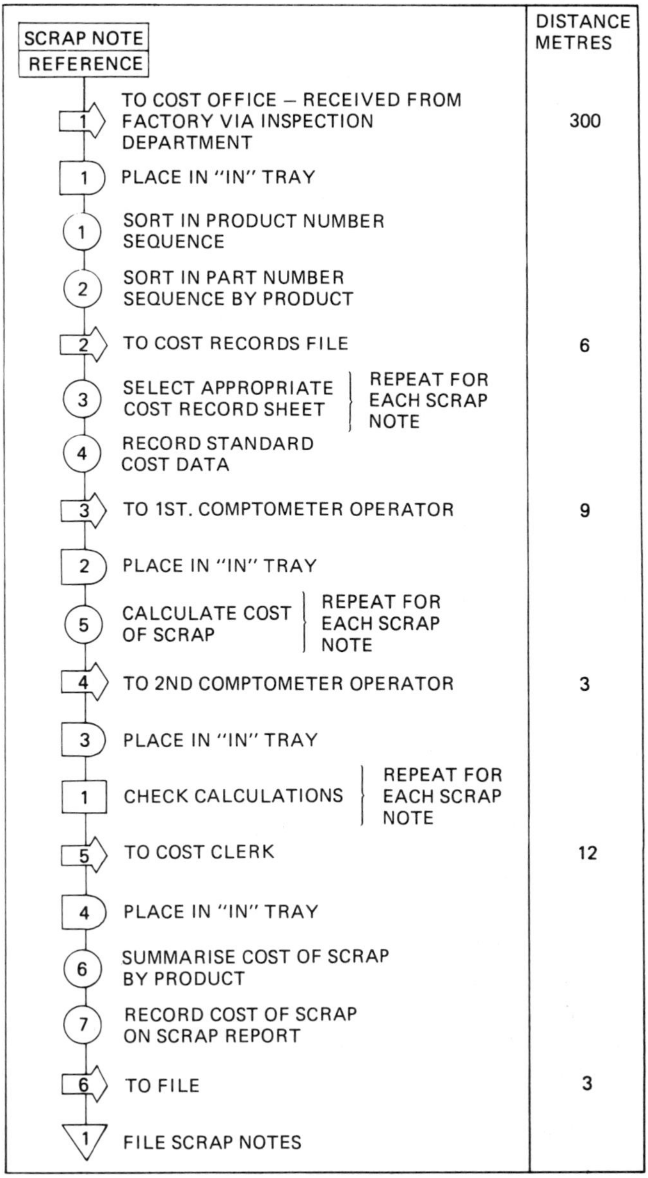

Fig. 100. *Flow process chart.*

(*a*) "Our department is different."
(*b*) "There is no time to do it in any other way."
(*c*) "We have always done it this way and it is all right."
(*d*) "We have tried it before."
(*e*) "That wouldn't work."

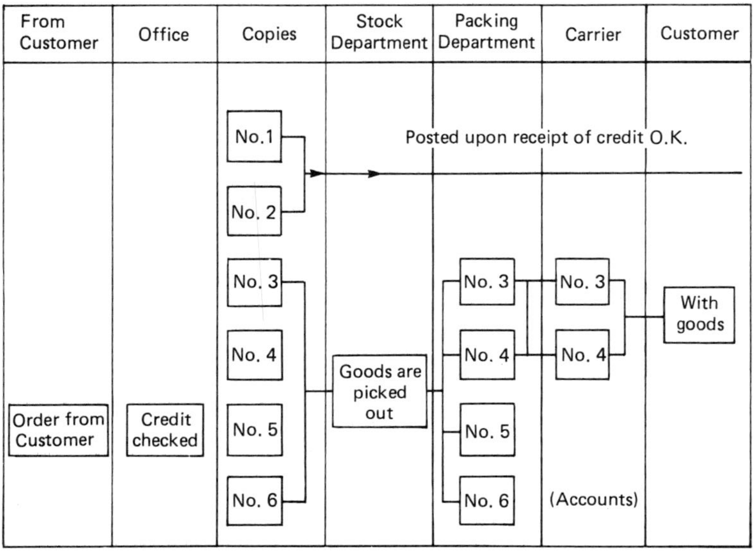

Fig. 101. *Procedure flow chart showing the history of a customer's order.*

METHODS OF INVESTIGATION

The methods of measuring work discussed in Chapter Twelve are used by O and M officers to establish the efficiency, or otherwise, of systems and procedures. In addition they will:

(*a*) analyse organisation charts;
(*b*) scrutinise job descriptions and specifications;
(*c*) scrutinise procedure manuals;
(*d*) collect and scrutinise forms;
(*e*) check control systems;
(*f*) use time and motion study.

TIME AND MOTION STUDY

Time and motion study is related to work measurement but

normally precedes the setting of standards, i.e. the amount of work that should be done in a given time. It is the method by which the most effective way of performing a task is identified. This usually means finding the simplest, and therefore quickest, way.

Motion study is concerned with the way a task is performed; the speed of operation; the availability of equipment; the layout of equipment, machines, documents, etc.; the kind of seating needed. The movements of the worker are also studied—the actual stretch of the arms, which arm is used, finger movements, body movement, etc.

Having identified the least fatiguing way of doing things the elements of the task (*see* page 267) are then timed so that a realistic time standard can be set.

Time and motion study can normally be applied in its entirety only to standardised and mechanical tasks. Motion study can be applied to any task which involves movement and may be important in reducing fatigue as well as saving time.

RECOMMENDATIONS FOR ELIMINATING WASTE

Recommendations may involve major or minor changes. Possible suggestions include:

(*a*) reorganisation of staff duties;
(*b*) revision of job descriptions;
(*c*) preparation of procedure manuals (if non-existent) or revision of existing manuals;
(*d*) re-design of forms;
(*e*) better control systems;
(*f*) smoother path of work flow;
(*g*) installation of equipment/machines for routine tasks;
(*h*) computerisation of certain tasks;
(*i*) redeployment of staff;
(*j*) reduction of staff.

The last point is always contentious and is normally implemented on the basis of natural wastage. This means that as a member of staff leaves of his own volition his post will not be re-filled. However it may involve discussions with union representatives even if no existing employee is to be made redundant. This depends on agreements that have been made with the union on the question of manning levels, redeployment, etc.

IMPLEMENTATION OF SURVEY RECOMMENDATIONS

The most important aspects of implementation are:

(*a*) setting up "test runs" of new systems to ensure that the objectives of the changes will be met; and
(*b*) training the staff to carry out the new procedures.

Implementation of recommendations is normally organised by the departmental manager and supervisors. In some cases the O and M staff may help. They will certainly monitor the results of implementation to ensure that the changes work, that the objectives are achieved, and to rectify any faults which may occur in the new systems.

DESIGN OF FORMS

Every day we see examples of forms in the office and in our daily lives. Most people dislike filling in forms. One of the fundamental reasons for this dislike is that so many forms are difficult to understand and to complete. Some of the many faults which appear on forms are:

(*a*) insufficient horizontal space allowed for first names;
(*b*) inadequate space for an address;
(*c*) no lines provided where forms are to be handwritten;
(*d*) too much printed information, such as "publicity blurb", printed on the form;
(*e*) too many type founts used (two or three should be sufficient);
(*f*) lack of distinction between forms, e.g. credit notes and invoices;
(*g*) inadequate information on forms produced on some types of accounting machines (unless the balance agrees with the account in the buyer's ledger it may be necessary to write for further details);
(*h*) the space for a signature is placed too near the bottom edge of the paper;
(*i*) the name of the organisation should be clearly placed at the head of the form and not in small print at its foot;
(*j*) inadequate margins—at least 2.5cm should be allowed at the left-hand side of the form for filing purposes, and a similar amount of space at the top and bottom for forms which are to be inserted into a typewriter;
(*k*) the various sections of the form not properly separated so that it is difficult and confusing to complete and extract information from it.

Scrutiny of most forms will usually reveal the need for improvement.

When designing a form you must ask certain questions. The most basic of these are the following.

(*a*) Who will complete the form? This may determine the wording to be used.

(*b*) Where will the form be completed? It may be completed in the office in good conditions, or by a lorry driver in his cab.

(*c*) Who needs the information, for what purpose? This may determine the sequence of the information inserted or the way it is set out. If the form is to be used as a source document for computer input, the design of the form will be materially affected.

(*d*) If several people need the information is it necessary to have several copies or is the form to be processed in a sequence of procedures, thus necessitating only one form?

(*e*) Are several copies of the form needed? If so colour coding, i.e. a different colour for each copy, would probably be helpful.

(*f*) Is the document to be filed eventually? If so an adequate left-hand margin (a minimum of 1in/2.5cm) must be provided.

CONTROL OF FORMS

A form is a means of communication. It is a tool for carrying out the basic functions of receiving, recording, arranging and transmitting information. It is essential therefore that:

(*a*) forms should be well designed to fulfil their function; and

(*b*) forms should be reviewed regularly (say once a year) to ensure that they are still fulfilling their function efficiently.

Indeed a review of forms may constitute an important part of an O and M survey. Questions must be asked about each individual form as follows.

(*a*) Is this form still used?

(*b*) Is this form still suitable for its purpose?

(*c*) Is all the information included on this form still needed?

(*d*) Do the people who receive the form still need all the information?

(*e*) Would anyone who does not receive this form benefit by doing so?

(*f*) Could this form be amalgamated with any other form?

OFFICE APPLICATIONS OF O AND M

O and M should be generally applied by everyone who works in an adminstrative capacity. Examples of simple everyday applications are given below.

(*a*) When having forms printed space the lines to match typewriter line spacing. This saves the typist adjusting her line spacing when completing a form.

(*b*) When designing a letterhead see that the important details are easily identifiable.

(*c*) Have dots or "corners" printed on a letterhead to indicate the position for typing the name and address of the addressee for use with window envelopes.

(*d*) Use properly designed tables/desks for machines.

(*e*) Lay out furniture in an office to achieve smooth work flow when documents have to be processed by a number of people.

(*f*) Organise batch working, e.g. saving up documents for copying and making one trip to the copier instead of several.

(*g*) Use the internal telephone to settle queries rather than going to another office and perhaps finding that the person you want is not there.

(*h*) Place material such as files, reference books, which you use frequently, in a position where they can be referred to without getting up from your desk.

(*i*) Use the right tools for the job, e.g. prepare draft reports on a word processor (if this facility is available) rather than having it typed.

(*j*) Use direct filing classifications whenever possible to avoid the necessity for a cross-reference index.

SUMMARY

1. Organisation and methods is a means of eliminating waste and ensuring that resources are used to maximum effectiveness.

2. O and M staff normally work in an advisory capacity. They may be called in to a department to investigate the organisation structure, systems and procedures.

3. An O and M survey has five stages, viz.

(*a*) setting of objectives;
(*b*) planning of survey;
(*c*) collection of facts;
(*d*) analysis of facts;
(*e*) recommendations/proposal for improvement/s.

4. It is essential to explain fully to staff what is involved. Their co-operation is essential if a survey is to achieve its objectives.

5. O and M staff use various methods of collecting facts about systems and procedures (*see* page 280).

6. The implementation of recommendations is normally the responsibility of departmental staff but is closely monitored, and later reviewed, by the O and M staff.

7. The design of a form has an important bearing on efficiency. The pitfalls outlined on page 279 should be avoided.

8. Forms must be reviewed regularly so that their use is strictly controlled. This is necessary to ensure that they are providing the information needed, when and where it is needed, and in the format in which it is needed.

9. Everyone who works in an office should practise O and M. It involves primarily the cultivation of good working habits.

SELF-ASSESSMENT QUESTIONS

Answer all questions as quickly as possible. Do not turn back to the Chapter until you have completed this test.

1. "O and M is an attitude of mind." Bearing in mind the definition of Organisation and Methods given on page 275, give two examples of how you think this attitude of mind could affect efficiency in office tasks.

2. What are the three most common objectives of O and M investigations?

3. Suggest ten ways in which waste occurs in an office.

4. List the five stages of an O and M survey.

5. List and explain briefly five methods of collecting information when carrying out an O and M survey.

6. Many questions have to be asked when analysing information collected in an O and M survey. Decide what questions you might ask in connection with the processing of sales orders. The present system is that sales orders are opened in the mailroom, sent to stores to check that the goods ordered are available, sent to sales to record the order, sent to accounts to raise the documents, which are then distributed to sales and stores.

7. Why is it important that the staff of a department, where an O and M survey is to be carried out, should be fully informed?

8. Your organisation has a fleet of chauffeur-driven cars which may be used by staff for business purposes. The cars are under the control of the transport supervisor. Design a requisition form to be

completed by a staff member who wishes to use a car. The form will be used in the transport department for recording information needed for their records.

9. How are forms controlled? Why is it necessary to have a system of forms control?

10. Ten applications of O and M in the office are suggested on page 284. In discussion with colleagues suggest at least ten more applications.

ASSIGNMENTS

Assignment 1

Obtain a form from within your own organisation or from a public office. Study it and answer the following questions.

(*a*) Is it a good form?

(*b*) If it is a good form list the points in its favour.

(*c*) If it is not a good form identify the faults and redesign the form so as to eliminate or minimise them.

Note: Suitable forms for study include tax return, passport application, vehicle licence application, social security forms of various kinds.

Assignment 2

If you work in an office choose, in consultation with your supervisor, one fairly simple system on which to carry out an O and M survey. Follow the guidelines set out in the section "The O and M Survey" (page 276). Prepare a report on your survey stating your findings. If the present system is satisfactory say why you consider no action is necessary. If improvements could be made, set out your recommendations, which must be supported by a clear indication of what implementation of the recommendations would achieve in terms of eliminating waste/reducing costs.

CHAPTER FOURTEEN

The Office Environment

CHAPTER OBJECTIVES

After studying this chapter you should be able to:

* list the main factors involved in planning and designing an office;
* explain the relationship between physical conditions in an office and productivity;
* consider an existing office layout critically and suggest appropriate changes to meet the needs of people and their work;
* analyse the effects of the main aspects of relevant legislation on environmental factors;
* develop safe working habits.

DEFINITION AND PURPOSE

What is the office environment? You must at some time have walked into an office and have felt either "What a dreadful place to work in!" or "How nice to work here!". The factors which created your impression were many and varied but instinctively you gain an impression from the "look" of a place. To the onlooker the way an office is designed and planned also creates an impression of the organisation as a whole, its efficiency—or lack of it, its type and "class".

An office is planned and designed to give people the conditions in which they can enjoy working, to provide suitable facilities for the work that has to be done, and to create an appropriate image for the department and the organisation as a whole.

DESIGNING AN OFFICE

The design of an office should receive as much care as the design of a room in a house. There are three major considerations, viz. the people who are going to work in it, the work that has to be done in it and the corporate image. Offices are usually designed for the building as a whole, e.g. when an organisation or part of it moves, or when a building has major alterations or innovations. There are occasions when an individual office is designed for a specific purpose, e.g. when a computer is installed, a secretariat established or a word processing centre set up.

How does one set about designing an office? First some decisions have to be made.

(*a*) Are the walls to be painted or papered? (Paint is easier to keep clean and less expensive to renew.)
(*b*) Is the floor to be carpeted, covered with carpet tiles or some other material? (Noise must be taken into account because certain floor coverings absorb sound more effectively than others.)
(*c*) Are the windows to have blinds? (If there is direct sunlight into a room blinds are needed.)
(*d*) Are the windows to have curtains? (Again noise is a consideration: curtains absorb sound.)
(*e*) What type of furniture and machines will be needed—wood, metal, fibreglass—and what colours?

Carpets and curtains soften the appearance of a room and make it more like "home" and therefore more conducive to a relaxed working atmosphere. Another major factor which must be borne in mind when designing an office is safety, which is discussed later in the Chapter.

Colour schemes

When the answers to the questions have been determined, the next consideration is colours. People react to colours and it is important that people who will be working in the office are consulted. Colours should be cheerful but not garish. Some colours cause eye strain, while other colours, especially green, are restful. The colours of the walls, carpets, blinds, curtains and furniture should blend to create a pleasing whole—a total concept. Size is an important factor to consider in choosing colour schemes; warmer colours are usually needed for large rooms while small rooms need colours which create an illusion of space.

Types of furniture

If existing furniture is to be used the scheme must take into account its size, style and type. If new furniture is to be bought, the purpose for which it is needed must first be agreed. Desks should be the size required for the job that is to be done on them. There are many different types of desks and chairs to cater for the wide variety of work done and machines used in an office.

Seating is very important. Many people suffer from back trouble as a result of sitting all day on unsuitable chairs. The height of desks and tables is important. Writing surfaces which are too high or too low can cause physical pain and eye strain and consequently lower a person's productivity.

LEGAL REQUIREMENTS

Working conditions in offices are included in several Acts of Parliament. These are:

Employers' Liability (Compulsory Insurance) Act 1969;
Offices, Shops and Railway Premises Act 1963;
Health and Safety at Work, etc., Act 1974;
Fire Precautions Act 1971.

Under the Employers' Liability (Compulsory Insurance) Act 1969 employers must cover their employees against injury and disease resulting from their employment duties. The insurance cover must be provided by authorised insurers and the certificate of insurance must be displayed permanently. Certain inspectors of the Health and Safety Executive (*see* below) may visit employment premises to check insurance policies and certificates. Employers who do not meet the requirements of the Act are liable to fines.

The Offices, Shops and Railway Premises Act 1963 specifically outlines physical conditions including space (an average of 11.3 cubic metres of space per person, ignoring ceiling height above 3 metres, or an area of 40 square feet must be allowed for each employee); cleanliness; temperature; ventilation; lighting; the provison of sanitary conveniences, washing facilities, drinking water; dangerous machinery, lifting of excessive weights, first aid, fire precautions, accidents and notification of accidents. A number of regulations have been published concerning sanitary conveniences, washing facilities, etc. It is intended that there shall be Regulations concerning lighting and reduction of noise.

The Health and Safety at Work, etc., Act 1974 (HASAWA) supplements the Offices, Shops and Railway Premises Act and lays a responsibility on the employer to provide working conditions which are safe and free from health hazards, as far as is practicable. In addition the employer has an obligation to provide information, instruction, training and supervision to ensure that the employee is following safety practices and not endangering himself or his colleagues.

Health and safety policy is a national concern and is the responsibility of a Health and Safety Commission appointed by the Secretary of State for Employment. The Commission consists of representatives from employers' and employees' organisations, and local authorities. It appoints the Health and Safety Executive which is responsible for enforcing the various legal requirements and for providing an advisory service.

The Fire Precautions Act 1971 supplements the two Acts

outlined briefly above. Under the Provision of this Act a fire certificate must be obtained for certain classes of premises. Smaller premises, not covered by the Fire Precautions Act, are covered by the Fire Precautions (Non-Certificated Factory, Office, Shop and Railway Premises) Regulations 1976 which provide for fire precautions to be taken.

PHYSICAL CONDITIONS

We have said that people react to physical conditions. Sometimes the reaction is subconscious so that a person becomes fatigued but does not know why. This could be caused by inadequate lighting or ventilation, the wrong type of seating or some other inadequacy.

Lighting

The best light is daylight. In many offices daylight is not sufficient or is non-existent so that artificial lighting is essential. Some shading of light is desirable, to avoid glare. Lighting requirements vary according to the size of the office, the height of the ceiling, the number of people working in the office, the position of desks, machines, etc., the type of work being done. Inadequate lighting, too bright lighting, strong shadows all cause eye strain.

Heating

A temperature between a minimum of 16 °C and a maximum of 19 °C should be maintained. Most offices are heated from the beginning of October to the end of April. When people are too cold their energy is channelled into keeping warm, with a consequent reduction in output, while an overheated atmosphere induces lassitude in many people, with the same result.

Ventilation

Many offices are air-conditioned so that windows do not have to be opened. Air-conditioning systems either draw in fresh air from outside or re-cycle used air after cleaning and re-oxygenating. Some systems create substantial draughts which limit the positioning of furniture.

If there is no air conditioning there must be adequate ventilation. A stuffy atmosphere is caused by increased carbon dioxide which reduces people's capacity to think and act, thus reducing output.

Noise

Older types of brick buildings absorb noise to some extent, while the walls of modern office blocks built of steel and reinforced concrete tend to reflect it. This is the reason why many modern offices have sound-absorbing floor covering, curtains and screens. Noise distracts and fatigues, causing loss of concentration. The position of machines must be carefully considered when they are used in offices where people do various kinds of work. Soundproof hoods for telex machines and word processor printers help to some extent; soft telephone bells or "bleeps" reduce the level of noise. Wherever there is noise, ways of reducing it should be sought.

In offices where people do monotonous routine jobs it has been found that taped music helps them to concentrate. Some organisations play the music at certain hours of the day when the majority of people are at a low ebb of concentration.

Cleanliness

Offices are normally cleaned daily, either by individual cleaning ladies or by cleaning contractors. It is essential that regular checks are made to ensure that cleaning is done thoroughly because dirt collects in corners, behind cabinets and machines, on ledges, etc. It is also essential that each individual keeps his or her own desk drawers clean and tidy. It is useful to have a duster available and clean up after any "messy" job. Clean, tidy working conditions make for faster work.

PLANNING THE LAYOUT

Planning the arrangement of furniture and machines is an integral part of the design of the office. Before anything at all can happen the type of layout has to be decided.

Types of layout

Offices are either individual, for one person or a small group of people, say up to four, or open plan. The major advantage of open plan offices is the saving of space. The major disadvantage is lack of privacy and the ever-present distractions of noise and movement.

Originally open plan offices were arranged with the desks in rows. The occupants sat as in a classroom under the eye of the supervisor who sat facing them. This arrangement was found to be impersonal, usually quite noisy and impossible for work needing intense concentration.

Landscaped offices, introduced into Britain from Germany in the 1950s, overcame the impersonality of the open plan office by having desks grouped asymmetrically, with screens, usually sound absorbent, to provide privacy. Plants soften the harshness of space and artificial lighting and create a more relaxed atmosphere.

Landscaped offices are designed to reduce noise as much as possible by the use of acoustic ceiling tiles, sound absorbing floor covering, non-metal types of furniture and "bleep" telephones.

Every two years the Institute of Administrative Management offers an "Office of the Year Award" for the best designed office. Roche Products Limited were the winners one year for their Building 40 landscaped office (*see* Fig. 102).

Fig. 102. *A landscaped office. This office in Roche Products Limited Building 40 won an Office of the Year Award presented by the Institute of Administrative Management. Note the spaciousness achieved by careful placing of furniture. The "strutted" ceiling provides diffusion for the lighting. (Courtesy Roche Products Ltd. and Organised Office Designs Ltd.)*

Workflow

Much of the work done in the office consists of processing carried out by several people. Workflow is an important factor in the layout of an office because it is desirable to ensure minimum movement of people and documents. It is therefore important to determine who works on what in what sequence, or who needs to consult whom very frequently for what purpose, or who has to use the video terminal in the office most often—and so on.

Another aspect of workflow is the proximity of people who work together, e.g. a manager and his secretary. Many secretaries work for more than one manager nowadays and they may find themselves situated quite close to one manager and far away from the others, or far away from all of them. This can make liaison difficult. If the secretary takes shorthand she may have to spend quite a lot of time walking to each of her managers' desks and back to take notes. The arrangement may be unavoidable but people concerned must adapt their way of working to minimise the time wasted. As far as practicable the managers should have a specific time of day for dictating and this would be combined with other tasks, such as going through the mail with the secretary. The telephone must be used more frequently, and non-urgent messages should be recorded on a dictating machine: indeed audio-dictation may well reduce wastage of time substantially.

Supervision

Offices should be arranged so that supervision can be maintained unobtrusively. The old idea of being "under the boss's eye" is no longer acceptable. On the other hand people need to be able to refer to their supervisors quickly and informally. In landscaped offices the grouping can be arranged so as to make this possible.

REVIEWING AN EXISTING OFFICE LAYOUT

It is not often possible to "start from scratch" with the planning of an office unless a new one is being set up, but improvements can be made where an existing layout causes problems. Before anything is changed the following steps should be taken.

(*a*) Identify and write down existing problems.

(*b*) Obtain or prepare a floor plan. The standard scale is one quarter of an inch to the foot or 20mm to the metre.

(*c*) Indicate on the plan the movement of traffic via doors, staircases and lifts.

(*d*) Indicate electric plug points and telephone points on the plan; also lights and radiators.

(*e*) Make coloured cardboard templates to scale of all the furniture and equipment units to be arranged in the working area.

(*f*) Arrange the templates on the plan taking into account the flow of work, which can be indicated in pencil so that it can be erased easily.

(*g*) Outline the template on the plan (a plastic template can be bought for drawing furniture, etc., to scale).

(*h*) Refer to the notes of existing problems and check that they will be resolved by the proposed changes.

Everybody who might be involved in the change should be given opportunities to discuss their problems and see the proposed changes. They may identify difficulties which might arise. Curing the original problems to create new ones is not the object of the exercise!

PEOPLE AND PRODUCTIVITY IN AN OFFICE

We have said that people react to their environment. An office which is decorated and furnished in pleasantly blended shades and tones and which creates a restful yet cheerful atmosphere provides the right background for a happy and stimulating working environment. The thoughtful planning of an office layout so that people have near to them the machines and equipment they need, will enable them to work with the minimum of fatigue. Anyone who has to refer constantly to files should have those files in their vicinity, either in a mobile cabinet or, if large quantities are involved, in an electronic retrieval system within the desk. People who have to refer to other people frequently, face-to-face, should be situated as near each other as is practicable. People whose work involves a lot of paper, reference materials, charts, etc., should have a large enough desk. Provision should always be made for the work the person has to do, and not for his or her status.

There are many reasons why ideal conditions cannot always be provided for each individual worker, not least of which may be lack of money. However, it is often possible to improve facilities with little or no expenditure. For example, filing trays are expensive but are essential where work needs to be kept in separate batches. The tops of Xerox copy-paper boxes do not look as attractive as a properly designed plastic tray but they cost nothing (assuming you use Xerox copy-paper) and serve the same purpose.

In Chapter Twelve we said that productivity is the amount of work people do at an acceptable standard of accuracy. Both the quantity and quality of people's output is affected by the environment in which they work. Anything which reduces fatigue increases productivity. Anything which is designed to minimize movement both saves processing time and reduces fatigue. The design and layout of an office has to be considered from the point of view of:

(*a*) the objectives of the individuals and the group who work in the office;

(*b*) individual likes and dislikes, trying to find a consensus of likes (some compromise will certainly be necessary, particularly in a larger group); and

(*c*) generally accepted standards, e.g. colours which harmonise, etc.

One further very important consideration is health and safety.

The environment should be thought of as a total concept. Decorations, colour schemes, the layout, the type of furniture, the acoustic materials (carpets, curtains, screens), ventilation, type of heating, lighting, should all make a pleasing whole which creates a single warm and cheerful impression when one enters the room, however big or small it may be.

HAZARDS

There are some 15,000 accidents known to occur in offices every year. These are accidents which result in the people involved being absent from work for more than three days as a result of the accident. These accidents have to be reported to the Department of Health and Social Security. It is estimated that the number of accidents which do not have to be reported is around 30,000.

There are two main types of hazard—fire and safety. Below is a list of the causes of many accidents, all of which can be avoided.

Administration

Desks, chairs, etc., too near door.
Top-heavy filing cabinet.
Carpet tiles curling at corners.
Torn carpets/broken linoleum.
Carpet edges fraying.
Highly polished floors.
Wet floors.
Projecting floor-plug covers.
Items on top of cabinets.
Furniture in poor repair.
Unsafe/broken electric plugs.
Inadequate ashtrays.
Projecting door handles (catch clothing).
Unmarked plate glass doors.
Sharp corners of furniture.
Unlit stairs and corridors.
Crowding of furniture, equipment and people.

Machines

Trailing wires/cables.

Moving parts of machine, e.g. drum of duplicating machine (although there is a safety device on most new machines).

Carrying machines incorrectly.

Careless use of paper cutter.

Untrained operator using guillotine.

Machines not switched off before unplugging.

Machines not unplugged.

Kettles boiling dry.

Steam from kettles.

Typewriters, calculators, etc., too near back of desk.

Overheating of machines.

Frayed electric cables.

Plugs wrongly connected.

Not reporting faults.

Regulations

Lack of trained first-aiders.

Fire doors left open.

Failing to maintain fire extinguishers.

Lack of protective clothing.

Instructions for emergencies not prominently displayed.

Smoking in restricted areas.

Careless work habits

Lack of safety consciousness.

Opening more than one drawer of a filing cabinet at the same time.

Desk drawers left open.

Liquid spilt on floors (especially tiles).

Sticky things on floors.

Carrying items, e.g. chairs, in such way as to block vision.

Packages left on floor of transit areas, e.g. corridors.

Coat stand unevenly loaded.

Drinks knocked over.

Running along corridors, especially round corners.

Cleaning fluids near cigarettes.

Cigarette ends/matches in wastepaper baskets.

Cupboards stacked too full.

Standing on unsafe base, e.g. swivel chair, to reach high shelves.

Overloading plug point.

Overloading/overcrowding lift.

Careless opening of windows/standing too near open windows above ground floor.

Broken glass in wastepaper basket.

Knife/scissors/drawing pins covered by papers on desk or not properly stored in drawer.

Papers left on desk overnight.

Taps left on.

Drying wet clothes near open fire/heater.

Wrong equipment for the job.

Lifting objects incorrectly.

Carrying heavy weights.

Unsuitable clothing.

SAFETY

Safety representatives

Many organisations have a safety committee made up of safety representatives from each department or specific area. It is vitally important that you know who your safety representative is. You are entitled to report to him or her any unsafe practice or any hazard in your office or in places within the organisation where you are expected to go in the course of your duties. The representative must then take up these matters at the safety comittee meeting, at which management are represented.

Health and safety enforcement

Statutory regulations contained in the various Acts of Parliament relevant to commercial offices are enforced by local authority inspectors appointed by local authorities, as required by the Health and Safety at Work, etc., Act 1974. Offices and factories are inspected by factory inspectors appointed by the Health and Safety Executive, which was established under HASAWA. All inspectors have the right to enter premises at any reasonable time and ask questions of any employee, and may ask for a signed declaration from any employee. There are prescribed penalties for obstructing an inspector in carrying out his duties.

Any individual who thinks that he or she is being asked to undertake any duty in unsafe conditions has the right to report the matter to the local inspector or the Health and Safety Executive, and should refuse to take the risk.

SUMMARY

1. The design and layout of an office should ideally be carried out

as a complete exercise in order to achieve a total concept, i.e. a carefully integrated scheme.

2. An office should be designed with three main factors in mind, viz. the people who will be working in it, the work that has to be done in it and the corporate image.

3. Legal requirements of relevant Acts of Parliament, and fire and safety hazards must be taken into account when planning an office.

4. Physical conditions in an office which affect people working in it include lighting, heating, ventilation, noise and cleanliness.

5. The layout of furniture and machines should be based on the work involved in processing and the need for liaison between various members of staff.

6. Anything which reduces fatigue helps to increase productivity.

7. An employer is responsible for providing a safe working environment for his staff: employees are responsible for following safe working practices.

8. Any unsafe working practice or hazard (fire or safety) should be reported to the safety representative (if there is one) or to management (if there is no safety representative).

SELF-ASSESSMENT QUESTIONS

Answer all questions as quickly as possible. Do not turn back to the Chapter until you have completed this test.

1. What three major factors would guide you if you were asked to design an office?

2. What is meant by "total concept" as applied to the office environment?

3. Noise is a major distraction in an office. (*a*) List five ways in which noise may be created. (*b*) List five ways in which noise can be reduced to some extent at least.

4. List two colours which you think are: (*a*) restful; (*b*) cheerful; (*c*) dull.

5. If you were asked to order a desk and chair for your office what points would you consider when choosing them?

6. What amount of space must be allowed for each employee in an office?

7. State ten aspects of physical conditions in offices covered by the Offices, Shops and Railway Premises Act 1963. Write brief notes on five of them.

8. If an employee has an accident in an office who is responsible?

9. What responsibility does each employee have in respect of safety?

10. Would you prefer to work in: (*a*) an individual office of your own; (*b*) an individual office with two or three other employees; (*c*) a landscaped open plan office? Give reasons for your preference.

11. Discuss the reason why the working environment is important from the organisation's point of view.

12. List ten ways in which you, as an individual, can help to ensure that working conditions are free of safety hazards.

13. List ten ways in which fires may be started in an office, either during and/or outside working hours.

14. What action should you take if you consider there is a safety or fire hazard in your office?

15. If you were asked to be a member of a committee which had been established to advise management on the working environment in your organisation, would you accept or reject the invitation? Give reasons.

ASSIGNMENTS

Assignment 1

In groups of not less than three and not more than six, discuss ways in which each individual who works in an office can help to ensure that the working environment is as good as it can be. Bear in mind the various factors mentioned in the Chapter and prepare a list of "dos" and "don'ts" under headings. Assume that you would be working in an office with at least four other people.

Assignment 2

You are asked to design a new office in which six people will be working. They are:

2 secretaries;
1 word processor operator;
2 typists;
1 clerk.

The secretaries pass work to the other staff who return it to them when completed.

The following furniture and equipment will be needed:

5 desks, 47in × 27in (120cm × 69cm);
1 collating table, 54in × 30in (137cm × 76cm);
10 chairs, 19in × 16in (48cm × 41cm);
1 word processor, 63in × 29 in (160cm × 74cm);
1 copier with collator, 75in × 23in (192cm × 59cm);

3 lateral filing cabinets, 36in × 18in (92cm × 46cm);
1 mobile trolley beside word processor, 17in × 12in (43cm × 31cm);
1 side table, with shelves, near each secretary, 43in × 18in (109cm × 46cm).

The room available is sketched below.

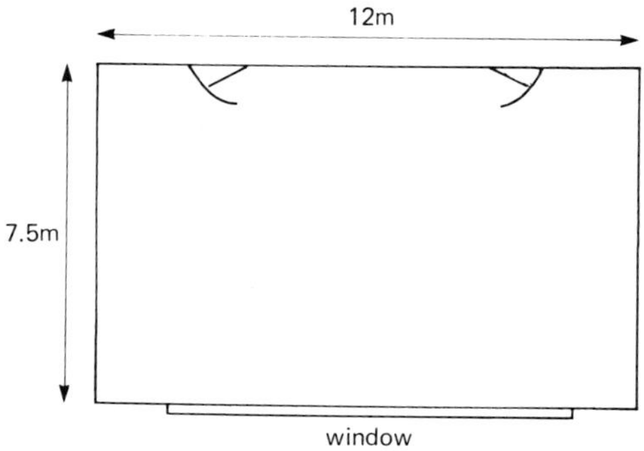

Each secretary does her own filing; the clerk has responsibility for departmental filing. All staff use the copier though it is primarily the responsibility of the clerk to copy and collate all large documents.
Working either individually or in small groups:

(*a*) prepare a plan of the office showing where the furniture and equipment will be installed;
(*b*) prepare a scheme for the decor—walls, carpet, curtains. The furniture is wood (medium oak), machinery mainly creams, fawns and browns.

CHAPTER FIFTEEN

The Individual and Office Work

CHAPTER OBJECTIVES

After studying this chapter you should be able to:
* state the individual needs of people at work;
* identify the personal qualities needed for leadership and for working as a member of a team;
* describe the influence of the working group on individual performance;
* explain the various ways in which people's attitude to work can be influenced.

DEFINITION AND PURPOSE

What do we mean by "people's needs"? Every individual has basic needs including food, shelter, warmth and clothing. A few, a very few people, are self-sufficient in every other respect once these basic needs have been provided. Most of us have many other "needs", both physical and mental. Since fulfilling these needs usually involves other people we talk of human relations, i.e. the way people get on together, work together, interact and motivate each other. Good human relations do not just happen. Everyone has to work hard to create the right relationships with individuals and with the groups of people of which they are a member.

COMMON NEEDS

Perhaps the most basic need of all is the "need to be needed". Everyone wants to feel that they matter to someone. Usually it is not enough to be needed by a husband or wife, by a parent, a child. Most people want to feel that they matter to someone within each environment, i.e. home, at work, in recreational groups, in the community as a whole. For some people it is enough to know that they are needed and that they meet that need by giving affection, by providing a service, e.g. caring for a child, going shopping for a neighbour. Everyone likes appreciation but some people need it as a stimulus. Indeed there are those who give service, e.g. voluntary social service, more for the "glory" than for the satisfaction of meeting a social need. Nevertheless in fulfilling their own need they are at the same time meeting someone else's need.

In the working environment people work for two major reasons, viz. to earn a living and to fulfil ambitions which may take the form of self-fulfilment.

Security

Because everyone has basic needs to meet in order to exist, each person must feel that these needs will always be met no matter what situation arises. Hence people's desire for a job, for "prospects"—salary increments, promotion—for the confidence which comes of knowing that they will receive sick pay if they are ill, unemployment benefit if they are unable to carry on working for any reason, redundancy pay if their job becomes extinct, a pension when they are no longer able to work. It can be argued that too much security is a bad thing because it makes people complacent. This may be true of some people but most people prefer to work and to have a job which provides a challenge to their capabilities. In any company where reorganisation is taking place, where redundancy is being discussed or where "moves" are afoot, there is always a feeling of insecurity among the employees. This is almost invariably reflected in lower output which results from lower morale.

Job satisfaction

It is often assumed that people's first consideration when seeking a job, or staying in a job, is salary level. In fact countless surveys indicate that this is not so. A minimum level of salary is essential to provide the necessities of life, but a high salary will not in itself attract many people. In some cases people are happy to undertake monotonous demanding work for a high salary in order to reap the benefits that the money can provide. Other people consider that they spend about a quarter of their lives at work so want to be able to enjoy it, which means being able to use their skills and knowledge effectively. Most people want "job satisfaction".

Which would you prefer—to earn £100 per week to operate an accounting machine or £90 to deal with queries. To a large extent your answer will depend on your character, on your personal skills and strengths. Both such employees are valuable to the organisation in which they work but the accounting machine operator appears to be the more productive, hence the higher salary. It would, of course, depend on the complexity of the problems to be solved as to what level of skills and knowledge would be required by the problem solver. In our example we have assumed fairly routine types of query. Provided the right person is found for each job both will have job satisfaction. Of course, the final choice would depend also on the financial commitments of the individuals concerned. A person who would really like the problem solving job from the point of view of job satisfaction may feel it essential to do the machine operating job because he needs the money.

THE INDIVIDUAL AND HIS NEEDS

Some years ago an American named Abraham H. Maslow undertook a major research project to establish why people work. His "hierarchy of needs" is now commonly quoted as the basis on which individual people build up their job satisfaction.

Above we mentioned three common needs, viz. basic physiological needs, security which enables a person to be free from anxiety about those needs, and belonging to groups which provide adequate relationships. There is another need which varies greatly from one individual to another and is reflected in a wide variety of ways. Maslow calls them "esteem needs". These include self-respect, achievement, competence, the recognition of themselves and their competence by peers, subordinates and superiors.

Finally there is the need for self-fulfilment. This is more than the need to be respected and esteemed. It is the desire to make the most of yourself, perhaps to please yourself, to please/help others, to satisfy other needs such as authority over others, i.e. power. In achieving self-fulfilment one may at the same time provide benefits for other people, e.g. a man who works very hard for promotion also benefits his employer. He may however be ruthless in his efforts to "get to the top", upsetting colleagues and subordinates on the way. This could damage the company. Such a person can create havoc in a department causing high labour turnover, which in turn creates insecurity in the work force and also costs money.

Needs generated by personal problems

Everyone has problems at one time or another. When we are young it may be boy- or girl-friends, ailing parents, sick children, lack of money to do the things we want to do. As we get older problems tend to be different but everyone has their problems and it is important that:

(*a*) we realise people other than ourselves have problems;

(*b*) we should try to leave personal problems behind us when we go to work; and

(*c*) there are many facilities, both at work and in the community, for discussing problems.

A discussion of a problem may not solve it but it does often help us to "put it in perspective". An outsider can usually be more objective and suggest ways in which we can come to terms with the situation and learn to "live with it".

There is a need for understanding. The person who is always "moaning" is perhaps seeking attention rather than suffering from a genuine cause for complaint. Perhaps greater appreciation of that person's work would help them to overcome a feeling of inferiority, which would make everyone happier. The bombastic person who "throws his weight around" probably has a feeling of insecurity. An understanding of a person's particular weaknesses does help one to work with them. That is not to say that anyone should stand outright discourtesy. It may be worth having a chat with such a person over a cup of tea. The fact that someone cares may be sufficient to make an individual improve his outlook.

Motivation

Most people are motivated in part by the necessity to earn a living. They are also motivated by the need to be liked, respected and for self-fulfilment. In terms of competence the desire to be liked can be counter-productive because it may inhibit a person from taking action which ought to be taken. The superior for whom popularity is important finds it extremely difficult to criticise his subordinates. Equally the desire for self-fulfilment may induce the manager to "drive" his subordinates hard, which may create respect rather than liking. If the manager takes the trouble to motivate his staff he can probably overcome this and be both respected and liked.

Most people need more than self-motivation. It is the responsibility of every employing organisation and every individual superior within the organisation to motivate the groups within it and the individuals within the groups.

FULFILLING PEOPLE'S NEEDS

If people are to give of their best, at home, at work, in society, they must be motivated to do so. There are basic motivators such as affection, the need for money, the desire to help. In the work situation there has to be more. Every employer must consider how he can get the best out of his employees—the best for the company that is. Of course this is selfish, but since the way to achieve the company's objectives is to help individuals achieve their personal objectives, everyone benefits.

Company policies

Employers have a duty to ensure that their employees are happy and can achieve job satisfaction. This means that there must be policies laid down and supported at Board level. One of the greatest causes of job dissatisfaction is company policy and administration.

Policy	*Effects*
Recruitment	Internal promotion provides career progression. External promotion provides new ideas. Higher level intake will mean higher salaries for new recruits so that the experience of existing employees must be reflected in their salaries to compensate. Combined with manpower planning, staff appraisal and training, proper recruitment ensures that each individual employee has an opportunity to make his best contribution to the organisation
Manpower planning	Ensures that the skills and knowledge of the present staff is reviewed regularly and the potential of individuals is identified
Staff appraisal	Gives everyone a chance to discuss strengths and weaknesses, ambitions, career progression, difficulties created, often unintentionally, by superiors. Identifies training needs
Training	Ensures that people are given the best opportunity to prove themselves and achieve their potential. The company training policy must be made public to all employees under the Employment and Training Act 1973
Safety	Ensures that everyone is aware of his or her obligations to work with consideration for fellow workers, report hazards and behave in a responsible manner. Under the Health and Safety at Work, etc., Act 1974 a company must have a safety policy made public to employees
Welfare	People feel their personal needs are considered and catered for. Flexitime might be an example
Consultation*	Involves people, in the sense of listening to their point of view, ideas and advice. Even if what they say is not accepted, provided the reason for non-acceptance is given, they feel they have a part to play

* To be discussed in more detail in the section on teamwork—*see* page 314.

Policy	*Effects*
Negotiation*	Usually undertaken with representatives of trade union members or staff associations, involves people in the final agreement on such things as pay and conditions of service. Usually requires compromise on both sides
Participation*	Gives individuals the right to make decisions either alone or in groups, e.g. in committees or at Board level, with responsibility for the effects of those decisions.

Statutory rights and obligations

Legislation concerning employment has been in existence since the Truck Act of 1831. Since that time more Acts of Parliament have been passed to ensure that employees get a fair deal and, to a lesser extent, that employers can expect fair dealings from employees. Most employers behave responsibly and fairly towards their employees, but it has not always been so, and there are a minority who would exploit their workers even today unless there were statutory constraints. The main features of the relevant Acts of Parliament are outlined very briefly.

Truck Acts (1831–1940)
Precise summary contained in the *Memorandum on the Truck Acts* published by HM Stationery Office in 1947. Prevented workers from being paid in kind and legalised certain deductions from wages.

Disabled Persons (Employment) Acts 1944 and 1958
To help disabled people secure employment or work on their own account. The Manpower Services Commission is responsible for maintaining a register of disabled persons—certain conditions are imposed before an individual can register. Employers are required to employ a quota of disabled people if the work force is more than twenty people except for merchant shipping and on oil rigs, which are exempt: the quota is currently 3 per cent.

Payment of Wages Act 1960
Legalises the payment of an employee's wages in certain specific ways, viz.

(*a*) if an employee requests in writing, and the employer does not refuse:

(*i*) by payment into the employee's bank account;
(*ii*) by cheque (legalised from 1 March 1963);
(*iii*) by postal order.

(*b*) payment can be made without request, when employees are absent through sickness or injury, by postal order but not by cheque.

The employer is allowed to make any deduction for payment in any of the specified ways.

Industrial Training Act 1963
(Amended by the Employment and Training Act 1973.)
Established the Training Services Agency (which became the Training Services Division under the later Act) and the Industrial Training Boards, the levy system by which employers were required to pay a percentage of their levyable payroll, i.e. employees who work for not less than 16 hours a week. Reimbursement for training provided was then claimed. The 1963 and 1973 Acts have been amended by the Industrial Training Act 1982 (*see* next page).

Offices, Shops & Railway Premises Act 1963
Lays down minimum requirements for working conditions (*see* page 289).

*Redundancy Payments Acts 1965 and 1969**
Amended by the Trade Union and Labour Relations Act 1974 and the Employment Protection Act 1975. Establishes the basis on which redundancy payments must be made to employees, depending on age, and the length of service with the employer.
A redundancy fund was established and is funded from employers' national insurance contributions. Employers are eligible for grants when they have made redundancy payments except for employees of normal retirement age or older.

Employers' Liability (Compulsory Insurance) Act 1969
Became law on 1 January 1972. Most employers must take out approved insurance policies with authorised insurers to cover their employees against bodily injury or disease resulting from their employment.

Equal Pay Act 1970 and Amendments 1984
Became law on 31 December 1973. Amended by the Employment Protection Act 1975 and the Sex Discrimination Act 1975. Men and

* Now incorporated into the Employment Protection (Consolidation) Act 1978 (*see* below).

women have the right to the same remuneration and conditions of service for similar work or for work which is of equal value under a job evaluation scheme. Similarly, with very few exceptions, all jobs must be open to both men and women. There are conditions regarding length of service, hours of work, etc., for women.

Complaints are dealt with first by the Advisory Conciliation and Arbitration Service, and if conciliation does not succeed it goes to an Industrial Tribunal.

Fire Precautions Act 1971

Requires a fire certificate to be obtained for certain types of premises used by employees in the course of their work. Further details are given on pages 289–90.

Contracts of Employment Act 1972

(Amended by the Trade Union and Labour Relations Act 1974 and the Employment Protection Act 1975, and now incorporated into the Employment Protection (Consolidation) Act 1978.)

All employees who work for 16 hours a week or more must be given a written contract of employment within thirteen weeks of starting work with an employer. Fifteen specific details must be included in the contract. Periods of notice of termination of employment are laid down depending on length of service.

Employment Agencies Act 1973

(Amended by the Employment Protection Act 1975.)

Employment agencies and businesses have to be registered and may charge fees to employers, not to people seeking jobs.

Employment and Training Act 1973

(Amended by the Industrial Training Act 1982.)

Established the Manpower Services Commission, the Training Services Division, and various other executive "arms" dealing with the many aspects of employment. The Training Services Division is responsible for the TOPS (Training Opportunities Scheme) courses, direct training services and the Industrial Training Boards. The 1982 Act gave the Secretary of State for Employment powers to abolish Industrial Training Boards. Of the original twenty-three Boards only seven remain. In some of the other sixteen industries voluntary bodies have been established under the auspices of the employers.

The 1973 Act changed the procedures for the payment of the levy and grant system enabling employers to obtain exemption from payment of the levy on the basis of the training carried out within the organisation, rather than paying the levy and then reclaiming for training done.

Health and Safety at Work, etc., Act 1974
Gives employers the responsibility to provide safe and healthy working conditions for employees, who in turn have a responsibility to follow safety regulations, and work with consideration for the safety of their colleagues.

Established the Health and Safety Commission which appoints the Health and Safety Executive, which enforces legal requirements and acts as an advisory body. (*See* pages 289 and 297.)

Rehabilitation of Offenders Act 1974
Sets a specific time following certain offences after which conviction becomes spent, i.e. can no longer provide grounds for termination of employment or any other discriminatory treatment. There are exceptions, e.g. teachers, doctors, police and prison officers, civil servants, certain people working in financial institutions.

Trade Union and Labour Relations Acts 1974 and 1976
Trade unions and employers' associations are given legal status to make contracts, to sue or be sued, and have an obligation to keep accounts which must be audited. These organisations cannot be sued for trade disputes which restrain trade. Employers' associations may register with the Registrar of Companies as corporate bodies: trade unions may not do so.

Social Security Pensions Act 1975, Social Security Acts 1975–80
Established national insurance contributions payable by insured people and employers, the various kinds of contributions, and conditions under which contributions are payable, including contracted out and non-contracted out (*see* page 59), and benefits.

Employment Protection Act 1975
Established the Advisory Conciliation and Arbitration Service which publishes Codes of Practice concerning specific areas of the Act. Codes of Practice issued so far include:

(*a*) disciplinary practice and procedures in employment;
(*b*) disclosure of information to trade unions for collective bargaining purposes;
(*c*) time off for trade union duties and activities;
(*d*) race relations.

A trade union wishing to be "recognised" by an employer for

negotiating purposes must follow certain procedures which must be accepted by the employer. If the employer does not agree the trade union can ask ACAS to intervene. Employers must disclose information to trade unions for the purpose of collective bargaining. Disclosure of information which would mean breaking confidence, be harmful to the employer's interest, or is illegal, e.g. national security, is exempt.

The employer must consult recognised trade union representatives concerning redundancy programmes at least 30 days before the programme takes effect if the number of people involved is between 10 and 99 and 90 days before if 100 or more employees are involved.

Protection of employees includes:

(*a*) guaranteed pay for up to five days for short time working or periods of laying off, subject to certain conditions;

(*b*) pay for up to 26 weeks for suspension for medical reasons resulting from employment;

(*c*) six weeks maternity pay for pregnant women and the right to return to the job within 29 weeks;

(*d*) the right to take part in trade union activities;

(*e*) reasonable time off during working hours for official trade union activities, duties as JPs or local councillors, or, when made redundant, seeking another job or undergoing training;

(*f*) the right of an employee to ask for written reasons for dismissal within 14 days of receiving termination of notice;

(*g*) fair and reasonable grounds for dismissal, which include misconduct, incompetence and redundancy. In the case of misconduct and incompetence the employee must be given a fair chance to improve his performance.

Sex Discrimination Act 1975

An employer may not discriminate against a man or a woman when recruiting, providing training or in conditions of service. Established Equal Opportunities Commission.

Race Relations Act 1976

Discrimination against a person by reason of his nationality, colour, race or creed is illegal in employment.

Employment Protection (Consolidation) Act 1978

Covers employment rights provided in the Redundancy Payments Acts 1965 and 1969, the Contracts of Employment Act 1972, the Trade Union and Labour Relations Acts 1974 and 1976, and the Employment Protection Act 1975.

Employment Act 1980

(Amended the Employment Protection (Consolidation) Act 1978.)

Allows trade unions to claim payment from Government towards expenditure incurred by them for holding ballots for specific approved purposes; allows the use of employers' premises to hold such ballots and the issues of Codes of Practice by the Secretary of State for Employment.

Moral rights and obligations

There are other rights and obligations which cannot be laid down by law, but which are important to the general working climate within an organisation. Everyone has a right to expect courtesy from fellow employees at all levels. Equally, each person should be courteous to fellow employees. Of course there are bound to be disagreements but it ought to be possible to respect another person's point of view and make one's own stance clear without being rude.

The employee who stands on his right to leave on the dot of the prescribed leaving time is entitled to do so. Equally when that employee wants to leave half an hour early for some personal purpose he must expect the employer to refuse to be flexible. "Give and take" is a much happier way of working, where this is practicable, so long as neither side expects to do all the taking.

An employee has a right to expect suitable equipment to be provided to do his job. The care of that equipment, by using it correctly, cleaning it and so on, is the employee's obligation.

These few examples indicate clearly that every right carries with it an obligation. There is no reason why "Mum" should make the beds for every member of the family since each sleeps in his or her own bed. If she does do so each member of the family can make their contribution to the household in another way. They have a moral obligation to do so. Similarly at work each person should contribute to the well-being of everyone in the organisation.

Understanding and dealing with fears

We have mentioned insecurity, a fear which can be engendered by situations over which one has no control, such as redundancy, and by personal lack of skill or knowledge which makes job performance inadequate. This feeling of insecurity can be brought about in many ways.

A current common factor is automation in the office. We hear phrases such as "the paperless office", "shorthand is a dead skill because it will be done by machines", "computers will take over all clerical procedures", "secretaries will be redundant because their work will no longer exist", and so on. It is true that many tasks which were done in the past (and still are done) by people are being and will be done by computerised machines. This is happening in the factory too. Let us be aware, though, that a machine, even a computerised machine, can do only what it is told to do. It cannot "think". Therefore the more we ask computers to do for us the more people will be needed to tell the computers what to do, and the more back-up will be needed to ensure that they do the job properly.

There is also the financial aspect to consider. Computers may get cheaper in relation to their capacity but they still cost a lot of money, and buying the computer is only the beginning. The software can be very expensive (*see* Chapter Ten). There are many jobs which still need the flexibility and adaptability, the creativeness and the "flair", of the human mind. Those jobs will remain. Sensible employers ensure that when automation is being considered the employees are involved so that the best possible use can be made of the machines. It is up to employees to ensure that the machines will work for them, not the other way round.

ATTITUDES TO WORK

How do you regard work? Is it something you do because it has to be done? Are there things you do because you enjoy doing them? Are there things you do because they enable you to achieve a pre-determined end result, i.e. an objective such as a qualification? Are there things you do which you hate doing but cannot live unless you do them? Of course there are all of these for all of us. In every job there is a certain amount of routine or drudgery, problems which frustrate, worry or anger, relationships which create difficulties. It is rare indeed to find a perfect job, but if the end result is the achievement of objectives, whatever they may be, it makes the parts we do not like easier to cope with.

Common attitudes

One constantly hears of "them and us" when employees talk about management. The managers are employees in the organisation and everyone's interests are the same, viz. to make the organisation viable in order to survive and develop. It must be said, however, that as people move up the ladder of status they tend to assume that enhanced status gives them the right to take liberties, e.g. being late and leaving early on occasions because they do a lot of overtime, taking long lunch hours, taking decisions, without consultation, which affect individuals, or not making the decisions which individuals need to make them feel secure.

There are common attitudes about groups of people, e.g. all young people are unreliable and selfish, all shop stewards are unreasonable, all politicians are dishonest, all old people are conservative and out of date, and so on. This stereotyping of people severely limits the possibilities of developing good relationships and working together for a common goal.

Desirable attitudes

We talk of the right attitudes, but what do we mean by "right" attitudes when we refer to employees? Employers are human and have needs, in the same way as their employees. In any case, those whom we refer to as "employers" are, in the larger organisations at least, managers who are themselves employees. It is important that people enjoy their work and are happy or content. As we discussed earlier in the Chapter, individual contentment can be achieved in a variety of ways covering the work force as a whole and on an individual basis. As a result of good policy, providing job satisfaction and caring for people as individuals we hope that each person will:

(*a*) give a fair day's work for a fair day's pay;

(*b*) be willing to contribute to the success of the organisation by striving to meet realistic objectives;

(*c*) be willing to think for him or herself and contribute ideas for improvement, innovation and the solving of problems;

(*d*) be flexible and willing to accept necessary changes providing they are introduced after consultation;

(*e*) be keen to develop his or her own potential for the good of the department and the organisation as a whole as well as for him or herself;

(*f*) realise the importance of good conduct, e.g. punctuality;

(*g*) realise the importance of working economically, i.e. keeping costs down.

Overcoming resistance to change

Perhaps one of the most difficult attitudes to overcome is the resistance to change. People are comfortable with what they know, even when they grumble about it. The unknown, be it a new procedure, a new system, a new colleague/subordinate/superior, creates a certain anxiety for many people. There may be the fear, especially in older people, that they will be unable to meet the demands made on them by the change.

There are three possible ways of dealing with such resistance.

(*a*) It can be accepted, things being left as they are; resulting in stagnation which will ultimately result in a company being overtaken by its competitors.

(*b*) It can be ignored and the changes be introduced by "edict". The result is almost certain to be a disgruntled, even openly hostile, attitude from employees. The people who accept the change will be divided from those who do not. In any case, people strongly object to being "steam-rollered" into doing something that they do not understand, or for which they see no necessity.

(*c*) The third possibility is to prepare the proposals for change carefully, ensuring that they are practicable. Then brief immediate subordinates (changes can be needed on a company basis, at departmental level, or for individuals) on the reasons why the changes are necessary, what the proposals for change are, and seek views and ideas. In some cases it may be better to simply explain the reasons why changes must be made and seek the co-operation of the staff in providing ideas. If they have made suggestions or contributed to the final decision they are likely to be co-operative when the changes are implemented.

Generating and maintaining desirable attitudes

The ways in which the "right" attitudes can be generated include:

(*a*) treat people as individuals;

(*b*) have good company policies geared to the needs of employees;

(*c*) encourage self-development;

(*d*) get individuals and groups of people involved when changes are to be made;

(*e*) use consultation as a management tool;

(*f*) set good examples to subordinates at all levels;

(*g*) provide the right environment;

(*h*) encourage people to use initiative and be innovative in their work when appropriate;

(*i*) set realistic objectives and ensure that everyone knows what they are and what part he/she has to play in the achievement of them;

(*j*) provide good leadership.

TEAMWORK

"There is no such thing as a bad crew, only a bad captain." Leadership is vital but the leader must also be a member of the team.

Thus everyone is working towards the achievement of predetermined objectives for the benefit of the organisation, not for an individual who happens to be more senior.

Building a team

A team does not just come together. It has to be built and nurtured. There are some prescribed methods though obviously the personality of the leader is of great importance.

(*a*) Set objectives, discuss them with the people involved and reach agreement on them.
(*b*) Ensure that everyone who is affected in any way by the final decision is informed.
(*c*) Make use of people's individual strengths. Maximise their benefit to the team as a whole.
(*d*) A leader should develop the qualities needed to create and nurture a team.
(*e*) Ensure that each person realises his responsibility to the other members of the team, i.e. their interdependence.
(*f*) Make clear to the team what kind of decision making processes are to be used in different circumstances.
(*g*) Ensure that everyone has all the information needed to do his job, to be "in the picture", to generate enthusiasm. This means ensuring that communications are given top priority.
(*h*) Ensure that each member of the team knows exactly what level of responsibility and authority he or she has.

DECISION MAKING

Normally people are given authority related to the level of responsibility they have. In meeting responsibilities decisions have to be made.

The decision-making process

The process of decision making involves:

(*a*) deciding exactly what the decision is intended to achieve, e.g. solving a problem;
(*b*) obtaining information, facts, views;
(*c*) analysing that information to assess whether it is complete, what it means in terms of the objectives to be reached or the problem to be solved;
(*d*) thinking of all the possibilities which these facts provide, e.g. different courses of action;

(*e*) assessing the implications of each possible course of action on people, on resources, on the team as a whole, on the organisation;
(*f*) coming to a conclusion as to the best decision.

Working through this process does not ensure that a decision will always be right, but it does ensure that thought is given to as many aspects as possible.

Decision-making methods

Decisions can be reached by one person alone or by a group of people working together. In the latter case personal relationships are important if the discussions are to be short and effective. When a person has authority to make decisions concerning subordinates and their work he can use that authority in a number of different ways.

(*a*) The superior makes the decision and imposes it.
(*b*) The superior makes the decision and then persuades his subordinates to accept it.
(*c*) The superior makes suggestions and asks for questions.
(*d*) The superior makes suggestions and asks for views and other ideas, which may change the decision.
(*e*) The superior explains the problem and invites suggestions for its solution from which he makes a final decision.
(*f*) The superior explains the problem, the constraints which confine any solution, e.g. finance, space, time, and then asks the team to make the decisions.
(*g*) The superior asks the team to define the problem, which may require investigation before it can be defined, and find the solution.

It is vital that each member of the team knows what method is being used in each case and that every member of the team is aware of the extent, or limits, of responsibility and authority within which the group is working.

CONFLICT AT WORK

In most organisations each person is required to work with other people in the same working area, and/or on the same job. Every person is an individual. Each has his own personality, likes and dislikes, attitudes, strengths and weaknesses. It is this very individuality which gives people the ability to do particular things well, to establish relationships, to show flair, to develop qualities needed for leadership and so on. This individuality also provides the biggest challenge because some of it at least has to be overcome in the course of establishing relationships and working within a group.

Given that human nature is what it is, some conflict is inevitable. Provided we recognise this fact and deal with it in a positive way it can be turned into an advantage. To achieve this each person has to devote time, thought and energy to using conflict constructively.

Conflict

What is conflict? When we enter an office, or indeed the reception area of an organisation, we get a "feeling". There is an "atmosphere" to which people are sensitive, some more than others. That atmosphere can be positive, giving feelings of happiness, camaraderie, energy, enthusiasm, purpose and achievement. In this positive atmosphere there is usually empathy between individuals and one's immediate reaction is a feeling of interest and even excitement.

A negative atmosphere is sometimes recognisable by outward signs such as a brusque manner on the telephone or from people, a casual attitude, "sloppy" movement of people, untidiness and lack of cleanliness. Negative reactions to questions—"No, I don't know"—also indicate lack of initiative and drive, but a negative atmosphere may not be openly manifested. Again one sometimes gets a "feeling" which results in comments such as "I don't like the place. I don't know why; there is nothing I can put my finger on". There is a certain falseness about the atmosphere however charming individual people may seem on the surface. A word, a look, an action will sometimes indicate lack of empathy between people—beween manager and subordinate, between two secretaries, between two people working side by side.

Negative conflict is dangerous because it is destructive. It is the result of an "each for himself" attitude by which effective group results can never be achieved. In this situation people are usually on the defensive. There are managers who will never accept, or give credit for other people's ideas, subordinates who will not accept criticism, however justified, well-intentioned or constructive.

Positive conflict on the other hand can generate a competitive spirit and enthusiasm, and can bring out the best in people. There are many situations at work where people need conflict to stimulate them to greater efforts, both physical and mental. Provided conflict is recognised as a means of stimulation it can generate creativity, ideas for solving problems, analysis of the pros and cons of decisions and suggested courses of action, the setting of objectives and can ultimately ensure effective communication in the widest sense of that term.

Relationships

What do we mean by "establishing relationships"? There are various levels of relationship. In any organisation people working together may well have to establish:

(*a*) a working relationship with people involved in the same job;
(*b*) a working relationship with people, both inside and outside the organisation, indirectly involved in their work;
(*c*) a social relationship with people in the location in which they work (with whom they may or may not be involved in the job);
(*d*) a social relationship with restaurant staff, maintenance and other service staff.

Almost inevitably a social relationship tends to be established with the people with whom one is working on the job. The extent of this social relationship will depend very much on the individual personalities of the people concerned. It is this social relationship which so often creates problems in the working relationship. Sally and Jane may work quite happily together on the job but Sally smokes and Jane does not. Normally Jane "puts up with" Sally's smoking but a day comes when Jane is tired, overwrought for some reason and suddenly Sally's smoking becomes unbearable. The ensuing row sours their social relationship and inevitably affects their working relationship.

People who do not "get on together" because of different personalities have to make a positive effort to subjugate their dislike of each other in the interests of the job. A positive attitude to the situation helps enormously. No one is all bad. We must ask ourselves "What are his good points?" If he is good at his job we can respect him for that. If he is a hard disciplinarian but invariably fair we can respect him and, indeed, admire his courage in carrying out his principles—even though we may not like him for it!

If there is a personality "problem" it is essential to identify the causes and then take positive action. If we bottle up a "grouse" it builds up into an antipathy out of all proportion to its importance. People often do not realise that they have irritating habits, that they are negative, or even that they are capable of achieving much more than they do. They may have formed an erroneous opinion of your attitude to them; they may feel insecure. Insecurity is a common feeling and can present serious difficulty in all sorts of circumstances but typically when an "outsider" is brought in to do a job they hoped would be theirs. When people are asked if they would like to attend a training course an initial reaction may be a negative "Why? I do my job properly don't I?" This highlights the need for the "right approach" in all circumstances and this means that the approach may have to be different to each person.

Difficulties with some people can be overcome in a "jokey" way. Others would regard this as insinuating and resent it, whereas they would respond favourably to a mature, carefully thought out approach. There are, of course, certain circumstances when "silence is golden" and it is better to let a person overcome a difficulty which is only temporary. Generally, however, it pays to bring problems into the open and discuss them in an adult manner. This is often better done sooner rather than later.

Working together

Earlier in the Chapter we discussed the needs of individuals as employees and suggested ways in which the employer, or manager (as the employer's representative), can help to provide the right "climate" for each person to do his job to the best of his ability. Many people find it difficult to identify with an impersonal organisation. They need to feel part of a group of people whom they can know. Experiments have been carried out in factories in which groups of people have been made responsible for a complete operation between them. Previously each person had been responsible for a particular part of an operation only. In a small group each person may perform several parts of the operation and sees the end result of his efforts. He also knows that if he does not give of his best his colleagues suffer for his failings. It is also in everyone's interests that people should help each other.

A relatively new approach to group working is the setting up of "Quality Circles". This technique was developed in Japan where it is used most successfully where work is often repetitive and monotonous. Similarly in Britain there have been amazing results in some organisations from individual people who previously would never have volunteered an idea or given thought to a problem. The idea of quality circles is that a group of people have certain objectives to meet. Any problems that arise, any decisions that have to be made in the course of meeting those objectives are the responsibility of the group. The creativity engendered by this sense of responsibility can be substantial. Perhaps one of the reasons is that a problem solved benefits the group as a whole and therefore respect, admiration and gratitude is forthcoming on a personal level from colleagues within the group.

Group dynamics

We have said that individuals can identify more easily with a small number of people than with large groups. Depending on what the group objectives are, the size of the group may be important. Too small a group can mean that difficult individuals create havoc because they can override other people. Similarly strongly dominant personalities can "take charge" to the extent that creativity and enthusiasm in the less dominant personalities is effectively eliminated. Too large a group can mean that there is such a mix of personalities, leaders, followers and troublemakers that cliques develop and negative conflict results.

Every group must have objectives which should "stretch" the group as a whole and the individuals within it, though the objectives must be attainable, of course. They must be analysed to determine the strengths which are required within the group and the people should be chosen, as far as possible, for these strengths. Where creativity and generation of ideas is required it may be useful to choose dominant personalities who will provide a challenge to each other. Where more routine work is the objective it would be important to build the group of people who have, or could build, good social relationships since the work itself may provide little challenge. In this situation it would be vitally important that there should be good working relationships throughout the group and these most easily result from good social relationships.

Where leadership in a group is needed—and it usually is—it is necessary to find a person with the appropriate personality and leadership skills. Good leaders encourage/allow other members of the group to develop their potential by making their contributions and assessing their merit. If this happens even the strongest personalities can be integrated into a team because there is a positive atmosphere within it.

It takes time, effort, patience, courage and tolerance on the part of every member of the group to mould the individuals into an effective working group. The success of the group depends on each individual—a weak link in the chain means that the whole chain is weak.

SUMMARY

1. Everyone has needs as an individual person, as a worker, as a member of a team.

2. Possibly the two most important needs of people at work are security and job satisfaction.

3. Motivation is an important factor in helping people to fulfil their own needs and this should be provided both at organisational level and at individual level.

4. Company policies play a major role in fulfilling the needs of the people who make up the work force.

5. Employment legislation is intended primarily to give employers and employees statutory rights which ensure fair practices.

6. Everyone working in an organisation has moral rights and obligations towards each other and the organisation.

7. It is necessary to understand that many people have fears or anxieties. These cannot be ignored.

8. It is the responsibility of the employer and management to generate the "right" attitudes.

9. The attitude to changes of any sort must be handled with understanding and consideration. Fears must be understood and taken into account so that the right approach is used.

10. It is very important to encourage each individual to achieve self-development.

11. Teamwork is achieved by hard work on the part of the team leader who must understand the process of team building and be a member of the team himself.

12. The decision-making process, the methods of making decisions and the method to be used in particular situations must be understood by everyone in a team.

13. Conflict can be used constructively to the benefit of individuals and of the group provided it is recognised as a force for stimulation of positive attitudes and actions.

14. Negative conflict is destructive, resulting in defensive attitudes and ruthless application to achievement of personal aims.

15. Good working relationships depend to a large extent on good social relationships, especially where routine work is involved. Dislike of an individual can be overcome by positive thinking which can create respect for that person's strengths.

16. People identify with a group rather than an organisation. By creating group working situations individuals are better able to develop their innate abilities.

17. The success of a group depends upon it having realisable but challenging objectives.

SELF-ASSESSMENT QUESTIONS

Answer all questions as quickly as possible. Do not turn back to the Chapter until you have completed this test.

1. What is meant by "the need to be needed" in terms of human needs?

2. People work for many reasons. What are the two major reasons for the majority of the working population?

3. Most people need a minimum of "security" in their working life. Give five aspects of work and/or working life which provide this feeling of security.

4. What is meant by the term "motivation".

5. There are 25 Acts of Parliament which contain at least one clause relating to employment in some way. State twenty points about employment covered by employment legislation.

6. What is the difference between statutory rights and moral rights of the employee? Give three examples of each.

7. Give five examples of attitudes which could be described as "the right attitude" of an employee.

8. Why do people often resist change? What do you think is the best way for an employer to deal with this problem?

9. What do you consider the right attitude of an employee to be?

10. State at least five ways in which the "right" attitude can be encouraged in employees.

11. What is the main purpose of team-building in the work situation?

12. If you were a manager what methods could you use to mould your subordinates into an effective team?

13. State five ways in which a manager can make decisions affecting his subordinates.

14. What is the most important factor affecting the ability of a group of people to work together?

ASSIGNMENTS

Assignment 1

Divide into groups of four people. Discuss the following questions.

(*a*) What is job satisfaction? Provide a definition.

(*b*) How can a manager help a subordinate to achieve job satisfaction?

(*c*) In what ways can an employer, i.e. the company/organisation, ensure that there is a maximum opportunity for employees to have job satisfaction?

Note: This assignment could be used individually to give written answers to the questions.

Assignment 2

(*a*) Prepare a list of ten factors which motivate people at work. Make twelve copies of your list.

(*b*) Interview twelve people who work in four different types of job in three different organisations if possible. (For example, in each of three organisations interview a typist, an accounts clerk, a computer operator, a salesman.) Give each person a copy of the list of motivation factors and ask him/her to indicate the order of importance of the factors to him/her.

(*c*) When the twelve lists have been completed use the original list (your copy) to analyse the answers. A suggested method is shown below.

Motivation Factor	1	2	3	4	--------------------	12
Salary						
Social Club						
etc.						

(*d*) Compare the "average" order of factors with each of the completed sheets. Discuss any major differences with colleagues.

Assignment 3

Divide into groups of six to eight to discuss the following questions.

(*a*) Prepare a list of at least twenty points which can cause irritation between individuals working together in an office. For example, some people like a lot of fresh air and want the windows open even in the coldest weather, while others cannot bear draughts.

Each person in the group must contribute at least two points which may be from personal experience or from observation in his/her place of work or at college.

When the list has been compiled decide whether any action can be taken in each case and if so, what action would be appropriate. If action is not appropriate how can the person who suffers the irritation be helped to "live with it"?

(*b*) Imagine that your group is given a major project to work on as a team and that you have not worked together before in this way.

You may know each other quite well or only slightly. Whichever is the case, discuss the problems which are likely to arise

(*i*) for each of you as individuals; and

(*ii*) for any leader who has to take charge of the group.

Index